# GOTHIC ROMANTICISM

# Nineteenth-Century Major Lives and Letters

*Series Editor: Marilyn Gaull*

The nineteenth century invented major figures: gifted, productive, and influential writers and artists in English, European, and American public life who captured and expressed what Hazlitt called "The Spirit of the Age." Their achievements summarize, reflect, and shape the cultural traditions they inherited and influence the quality of life that followed. Before radio, film, and journalism deflected the energies of authors and audiences alike, literary forms such as popular verse, song lyrics, biographies, memoirs, letters, novels, reviews, essays, children's books, and drama generated a golden age of letters incomparable in Western history. *Nineteenth-Century Major Lives and Letters* presents a series of original biographical, critical, and scholarly studies of major figures evoking their energies, achievements, and their impact on the character of this age. Projects to be included range from works on Blake to Hardy, Erasmus Darwin to Charles Darwin, Wordsworth to Yeats, Coleridge and J. S. Mill, Joanna Baillie, Jane Austen, Sir Walter Scott, Byron, Shelley, Keats to Dickens, Tennyson, George Eliot, Browning, Hopkins, Lewis Carroll, Rudyard Kipling, and their contemporaries. The series editor is Marilyn Gaull, PhD from Indiana University. She has served on the faculty at Temple University, New York University, and is now Research Professor at the Editorial Institute at Boston University. She brings to the series decades of experience as editor of books on nineteenth century literature and culture. She is the founder and editor of *The Wordsworth Circle*, author of *English Romanticism: The Human Context*, publishes editions, essays, and reviews in numerous journals and lectures internationally on British Romanticism, folklore, and narrative theory.

PUBLISHED BY PALGRAVE:

*Shelley's German Afterlives*, by Susanne Schmid
*Romantic Literature, Race, and Colonial Encounter*, by Peter J. Kitson
*Coleridge, the Bible, and Religion*, by Jeffrey W. Barbeau
*Byron: Heritage and Legacy*, edited by Cheryl A. Wilson
*The Long and Winding Road from Blake to the Beatles*, by Matthew Schneider
*British Periodicals and Romantic Identity*, by Mark Schoenfield
*Women Writers and Nineteenth-Century Medievalism*, by Clare Broome Saunders
*British Victorian Women's Periodicals*, by Kathryn Ledbetter
*Romantic Diasporas*, by Toby R. Benis
*Romantic Literary Families*, by Scott Krawczyk
*Victorian Christmas in Print*, by Tara Moore
*Culinary Aesthetics and Practices in Nineteenth-Century American Literature*,
    Edited by Monika Elbert and Marie Drews
*Poetics en passant*, by Anne Jamison
*Reading Popular Culture in Victorian Periodicals*, by Alberto Gabriele
*Romanticism and the Object*, Edited by Larry H. Peer
*From Song to Print*, by Terence Hoagwood
*Populism, Gender, and Sympathy in the Romantic Novel*, by James P. Carson
*Victorian Medicine and Social Reform*, by Louise Penner
*Byron and the Rhetoric of Italian Nationalism*, by Arnold A. Schmidt
*Gothic Romanticism*, by Tom Duggett

FORTHCOMING TITLES:

*Royal Romances*, by Kristin Samuelian
*The Poetry of Mary Robinson*, by Daniel Robinson

# Gothic Romanticism

## Architecture, Politics, and Literary Form

*Tom Duggett*

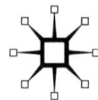

GOTHIC ROMANTICISM
Copyright © Tom Duggett, 2010.
All rights reserved.

First published in hardcover in 2010 by PALGRAVE MACMILLAN® in the United States—a division of St. Martin's Press LLC, 175 Fifth Avenue, New York, NY 10010.

Where this book is distributed in the UK, Europe and the rest of the world, this is by Palgrave Macmillan, a division of Macmillan Publishers Limited, registered in England, company number 785998, of Houndmills, Basingstoke, Hampshire RG21 6XS.

Palgrave Macmillan is the global academic imprint of the above companies and has companies and representatives throughout the world.

Palgrave® and Macmillan® are registered trademarks in the United States, the United Kingdom, Europe and other countries.

ISBN: 978–1–137–29812–6

Library of Congress Cataloging-in-Publication Data

Duggett, Tom.
    Gothic romanticism : architecture, politics, and literary form / Tom Duggett.
        p. cm.—(Nineteenth-century major lives and letters)
    ISBN 978–0–230–61532–8 (hardback)
    1. Lake poets. 2. English poetry—19th century—History and criticism. 3. Gothic literature—Great Britain—History and criticism. 4. Literary form—History—19th century. 5. Romanticism—Great Britain. 6. Architecture in literature. 7. Gothic revival (Literature)—Great Britain. 8. National characteristics, American, in literature. I. Title.

PR590.D84 2010
821.709—dc22                                                2009040669

A catalogue record of the book is available from the British Library.

Design by Newgen Imaging Systems (P) Ltd., Chennai, India.

First PALGRAVE MACMILLAN paperback edition: December 2012

10  9  8  7  6  5  4  3  2  1

*For Qian—and Benjamin*

*It may be proper to state whence the Poem, of which* The Excursion *is a part, derives its Title of* The Recluse.—*Several years ago, when the Author retired to his native Mountains, with the hope of being enabled to construct a literary Work that might live, it was a reasonable thing that he should take a review of his own Mind, and examine how far Nature and Education had qualified him for such employment. As subsidiary to this preparation, he undertook to record, in Verse, the origin and progress of his own powers, as far as he was acquainted with them…—The preparatory poem is biographical, and conducts the history of the Author's mind to the point when he was emboldened to hope that his faculties were sufficiently matured for entering upon the arduous labour which he had proposed to himself; and the two Works have the same kind of relation to each other, if he may so express himself, as the Anti-chapel has to the body of a gothic Church. Continuing this allusion, he may be permitted to add, that his minor Pieces, which have been long before the Public, when they shall be properly arranged, will be found by the attentive Reader to have such connection with the main Work as may give them claim to be likened to the little Cells, Oratories, and sepulchral Recesses ordinarily included in those Edifices…It is not the Author's intention formally to announce a system: it was more animating to him to proceed in a different course; and if he shall succeed in conveying to the mind clear thoughts, lively images, and strong feelings, the Reader will have no difficulty in extracting the system for himself.*

—William Wordsworth, *Preface to* The Excursion *(1814)*

*[*The Excursion*] affects a system without having any intelligible clue to one.*

—William Hazlitt, The Spirit of the Age *(1825)*

# Contents

*Preface to the Second Edition* ix
*Acknowledgments* xiii
*Abbreviations* xv

Introduction 1

1 Romantic Poets and Gothic Culture 25

2 Radical Gothic: Politics and Antiquarianism in *Salisbury Plain* (1794) 67

3 "By Gothic Virtue Won": Romantic Poets Fighting the Peninsular War 97

4 Wordsworth's Gothic Education 143

Conclusion   The Staring Nation 169

*Notes* 185
*Bibliography* 193
*Index* 209

# Preface to the Second Edition

This is a lucky book. Since it first appeared in 2010, *Gothic Romanticism* has had the fortune of being mapped into the fields of Romanticism and Gothicism by a number of leading scholars.[1] The generous reviews the book has received have expanded its significance in ways that I scarcely imagined while researching and writing it, and have led to this second edition. This preface is my attempt to register and respond to such readings. Perhaps most significantly, and luckiest of all, the Modern Language Association of America has recognized *Gothic Romanticism* as a book with a wider appeal by awarding it the 2010/11 MLA Prize for Independent Scholars. Because this second edition is a direct result of the MLA prize, and because the prize citation provides a stimulating summary of the book's arguments and effects, I would like to quote it in full here:

> *Gothic Romanticism* is a compellingly ambitious study of the pursuit of a purer and better gothic in late-eighteenth and early-nineteenth-century England. Focusing on Wordsworth and the Lake Poets' attempt to refine a coarser, more sensational gothic as set forth in the novels of Radcliffe and Scott and in antiquarian curiosities, Duggett weaves sustained analysis of their poetry with thoughtful commentary on medieval architectural imagery and history, the turn to conservative politics, and educational reform. This multileveled investigation demonstrates in engaging prose the centrality of a cultivated rhetoric of a gothic aesthetic in this period while provocatively suggesting its relevance to a post-9/11 era where architecture "has assumed an importance that seemed without precedent." *Gothic Romanticism* goes far in detailing such a poetic, cultural, and historical precedent.

Ambitious, multileveled, provocative. This triad of evaluative adjectives fits the book well, poised on the knife-edge between praise and blame—where, perhaps, originality lies.

"Ambitious" is certainly right. *Gothic Romanticism* is a book of progressively widening perspectives. It begins with a question about Wordsworth's analogy between his works and a "gothic Church" in the Preface to the now-neglected *Excursion* (1814), and ends with an account of the "Gothic" scene of British culture between the 1790s and 1830s that devolves upon the present. If the book is, as the MLA panel put it, "*compellingly* ambitious," I suspect it is for this reason. It is itself a piece of imperfect architecture, its design not distinct from its execution. "[T]he absurdity...of attempting to support [such] bold and massive entablatures...upon [such] slender and grotesque columns...must be evident." So said the *Augustan Review*—in a review quoted in these pages—of Coleridge's *Christabel* and the originality of the Lake Poets versus Byron and Scott. But this book itself is in a like case. I can only hope that its slender evidentiary supports hold their weight as well as the "columns" of those "Architects of the Lakes" in fact held theirs. And as the building continues to settle and spread its weight, I have chosen not to attempt to improve the original construction, argument, and evidence of the first edition. Besides a couple of typos corrected, a new cover image, and a new note or two added, the book stands as it was. A deposit of additional supporting material is located instead on the book's website, http://gothicromanticism.weebly.com, to which all readers of the book itself have full access.

"Multileveled." The MLA's second adjective is also, I think, accurate. There is a connection to the "ambitious" unfolding perspectives. But the book is also trying quite deliberately to do several things at the same time. The attempt at what Nick Groom calls "a significant recasting of William Wordsworth as the chief architect of emergent Gothic culture" is routed through what Gregory Leadbetter refers to as an exposition of "the dynamic fusion of the poetic and the constitutional imagination...so fundamental to the common law cultures of the world." Read this way, *Gothic Romanticism* provides a suspended gloss on the social and historical presence intuited as "something far more deeply interfused" in Wordsworth's "Tintern Abbey." Elizabeth Massa Hoiem's review puts the point evocatively. The book's tracing of "the easy transposition of Gothic imagery between politics, architecture, and literature...allows for a richly layered, oddly cyclical national historical narrative, where the past is disjointedly present in landscapes, and this history is inscribed within literary works...which use Gothic buildings as organizing structures." Change "easy" to "uneasy"—because the Gothic suffusion of British culture through its architecture, politics, and literature was, as the book shows, gradual, "disjointed," and contested—and I think this gets it exactly right.

And "provocative"? Well, the post-9/11 perspective on Romanticism—or the Romantic "precedent" for Anglo-American culture after 9/11—is designed to provoke a response. Some readers have rejected the proposed "precedent" in Keatsian terms as a "palpable design." Others have seen it as, in Jeffrey C. Johnson's phrase in his review, heightening the stakes of the argument. It is not for me to judge which response is right. But I can say that the parallel is proposed in all seriousness, and with all humility, and that the book defers its application to the reader's own sense. I might further add that 9/11 was almost unavoidable in a book so preoccupied with historicity and its architectural signs, and with attempts (its own included) to emerge into historical self-awareness. This is a biographical truth, too. I wrote the doctoral thesis that underlies this book between 2004 and 2007, largely in St Andrews. In 2008, a year's intensive teaching at Bristol gave me distance and perspective on that thesis. By 2009, newly removed to China, I saw through their sudden absence how my own place and time had directed and informed my work. "And yet the building stood, as if sustained / By its own spirit" (*1805* II, 295–296). Open to such influxes, and writing in self-defence, I proposed my "suspended reading" of recent Anglo-American culture through Romantic-period Gothicism. It was already, in 2010, another era. And now, in the last months of 2012, as the decade of war in Iraq and Afghanistan recedes into the twilit region of unremembrance between current affairs and history, the "provocative" power of the analogy may be fading too. The great recession of 2008 has, as I write, largely displaced September 2001 as historical event horizon. But as economic and historical crisis continues to wrack Europe and America, the resonance of the earlier catastrophe has if anything only deepened and spread. If the twin towers inscribed the bar-charts of modern commerce into the city skyline, the way the "tridents," the Gothic arches at the base, survived the fall of those towers now seems fraught with new meaning. Now installed behind glass at the 9/11 memorial, those "trees," those architectural echoes of the wild woods, relapsed to silence and slow time, point mutely to the irreducible cultural residue upon which our commercial modernity is founded—and which endures the wreck of its decay.

So the MLA's triple label, "ambitious, multileveled, and provocative," is one that *Gothic Romanticism* is proud to wear. And these qualities, I hope, will help this second edition of the book to engage the wider audience that the MLA prize points toward. As its title suggests, *Gothic Romanticism* offers a bridge between modern Gothic and Romantic studies. It does different things for each discipline: providing deepened historical perspective for students of the Gothic, and widened cultural context for readers of Romanticism. As mentioned above, the book has a companion website and online forum/archive, at http://gothicromanticism.weebly.com, which should be of use to all readers. The website features copies of (or links to) the images discussed in the book, a readers' forum for questions and discussion, and a readers' resources section that is continually updated. There are further "practical implications" for university teachers and students. As Elizabeth Massa Hoiem suggests in her review of the book, one prospect that it raises is for "a course on literature of the Romantic period [taught] entirely as a Gothic topics course, without striking canonical poets from the syllabus." *Gothic Romanticism* has a long argument about Wordsworth, early Romanticism, and Gothic culture, which would suit such courses perfectly. But it is also adaptable to other course types, with the individual chapters standing by themselves, and providing accessible case studies of important cultural episodes: chapter two on the French Revolution and British responses, chapter three on the Napoleonic and Peninsular wars, chapter four on debates over religion and national education, and a concluding chapter on Gothicism and new visual technologies.

*Gothic Romanticism* remains what it always was: an academic monograph that asks its readers to work. But it does, I hope, make good on the promise that this affordable paperback edition implies. Every detailed argument and every apparent digression is a path to a clear point; each chapter's beginning as deliberately open and evocative as its ending aims to be memorable, multileveled—and provocative, too.

TOM DUGGETT<br>
August 2012

# Acknowledgments

This book started life as a doctoral thesis at the University of St Andrews. The project would never have got started had it not been for the moral support of Douglas Dunn, and it would not have been feasible without the financial support of the Carnegie Trust for the Universities of Scotland. I am more indebted that I can fully express to my PhD supervisors, Nicholas Roe and Susan Manly. They stuck with my project through all its windings through four long years, and never failed to point me in the right direction. My PhD examiners, Jane Stabler and Tim Fulford, gave me invaluable advice on how to go about bookifying the thesis, and Marilyn Gaull's breadth of knowledge and experience were vital in helping me discover where to pitch the argument of the book. Parts of the book were written during a teaching fellowship at the University of Bristol in 2007–8, during which time I benefited greatly from the conversation and advice of Tim Webb, David Punter, Ralph Pite, Stephen Cheeke, John Lyon, and Andrew Bennett.

Some sections of the book have previously appeared in journal publications. Chapter one incorporates materials previously published in *The Wordsworth Circle*, 38:4 (2007) and in *Romanticism* 15:3 (2009). Parts of chapter two were published in *Romanticism*, 13:2 (2007). Chapter three extends and expands upon an essay previously published in *The Review of English Studies*, 58 (2007), and some sections from the conclusion were included in a review essay for *European Romantic Review* 20:5 (2009). I am grateful to the publishers of these journals for permission to reuse these materials here. I would also like to thank everyone at Palgrave Macmillan who worked on this book, and helped make publishing it such a pleasure.

The book was completed in Shanghai, where I was able to see more clearly what I had been arguing all along about British culture in the eighteenth and nineteenth centuries, and where new family and friends gave me much needed encouragement to get it finished. My deepest thanks go to my mother and father, Gail and Michael, who made many sacrifices for many years to give me every opportunity to seek prowess in my chosen field, and to my brother, Joe, who has also been my greatest friend, an unfailing support in times of need. But not a word would have been written without the love and belief of my wife, Qian, who carried me even when she was weary, and comforted me even when she needed comfort most. To her, and to our little Wilma, this book, and every moment's time and effort that it represents, is dedicated.

# Abbreviations

*BL*—Coleridge, *Biographia Literaria*, ed. James Engell and W. Jackson Bate, 2 vols. (London: Princeton University Press, 1983)

*CLSTC*—*Collected Letters of Samuel Taylor Coleridge*, ed. E. L. Griggs, 6 vols. (Oxford: Clarendon Press, 1956–71)

*EY*—*The Letters of William and Dorothy Wordsworth: The Early Years, 1787-1805*, ed. Ernest De Selincourt, 2nd edition, rev. Chester L. Shaver (Oxford: Clarendon Press, 1967)

*FN*—*The Fenwick Notes of William Wordsworth*, ed. Jared Curtis (London: Bristol Classical Press, 1993)

*GM*—*Gentleman's Magazine*

*LY*—*The Letters of William and Dorothy Wordsworth: The Later Years*, ed. Ernest De Selincourt, 2nd edition, rev. Alan G. Hill, 4 vols. (Oxford: Clarendon Press, 1978–88)

*MW*—*William Wordsworth: The Major Works*, ed. Stephen Gill (Oxford: Oxford University Press, 1984)

*MY*—*The Letters of William and Dorothy Wordsworth: The Middle Years*, ed. Ernest De Selincourt, 2nd edition, rev. Mary Moorman and Alan G. Hill, 2 vols. (Oxford: Clarendon Press, 1969–70)

*Prose Works*—*The Prose Works of William Wordsworth*, ed. W. J. B. Owen and Jane Worthington Smyser, 3 vols. (Oxford: Oxford University Press, 1974)

*QR*—*Quarterly Review*

*SPP*—*The Salisbury Plain Poems of William Wordsworth*, ed. Stephen Gill (Ithaca: Cornell University Press, 1975)

*WDR*—*The White Doe of Rylstone; or, The Fate of the Nortons*, ed. Kristine Dugas (Ithaca: Cornell University Press, 1988)

*1799*; *1805*; *1850*—*Prelude* texts from Jonathan Wordsworth, ed. *The Prelude: The Four Texts*. London: Penguin Books, 1995.

# Introduction

Amid the wreckage of the towers, the pointed arches stood. Ground zero looked strangely like a Gothic ruin. And in the aftermath, as the airborne dust of the pulverized buildings settled in silence across America, architecture assumed a cultural importance that seemed without precedent. Endlessly replicated in the photography, the film, and the television of the years before 2001, the twin towers of New York's World Trade Center continue to haunt us in their simultaneous presence and absence—like a twenty-first-century version of the ghost in *Hamlet*. After President Bush misspoke of a "crusade" against Islamic terrorism, and cultural figures such as Don DeLillo wrote of the terrorist attacks as an attempt "to bring back the past," to make the American dream of the future yield "to medieval expedience, to the old slow furies of cut-throat religion" (2001, 37), we found ourselves living in a sort of new middle ages. The recrudescence of a faith-based politics gave an obvious contemporary relevance to the historical events and cultural formations of the medieval period. And the clock-and-calendar-time, the "homogeneous empty time" of western modernity, seemed suddenly shot through by an apocalyptic consciousness of a sort disowned by cultural memory. As the political scientist Jenny Edkins puts it, the events of September 11, 2001 saw "trauma time collid[e] with the time of the state, the time of capitalism, the time of routine," producing a "curious unknown time, a time with no end in sight" (qtd. in Simpson 2006, 4). The events of that day were, as David Simpson notes, "widely interpreted" as a hiatus in "the deep rhythms of cultural time, a cataclysm simply erasing what was there rather than evolving from anything already in place...an unforeseen eruption" of regressive elements into the "steady-state progressivism" of post–cold war America (Simpson 2006, 4). The strange absence (and hallucinated presence) in the Manhattan skyline was the (in)visible symbol of the traumatized feeling that the time was out of joint; that America had, impossibly, fallen into history. Indeed, part of the uniqueness of the phenomenon was the way the fall of the towers entered instantly into the consciousness not only of New Yorkers or Americans, but of anyone in the world with access to a television, a computer, or a newspaper—and emerged almost instantly as mythic, rubbed smooth overnight into the uncannily resonant cultural coin, 9/11.

But we don't have to go far in the study of British Romanticism to find a cultural obsession with architecture—and particularly Gothic architecture—that is equally pervasive, equally politically charged, and, this book argues, equally definitive of a cultural moment. When, in the wake of the fall of the Bastille, Edmund Burke meditated upon the "fresh ruins," the "chasm that once was France," and urged the French nation to rebuild the edifice of its old "Gothic" constitution, Tom Paine painted him as immured "in the Bastille of a word" (Burke 1987, 31–34 and 1790, 5; Paine 1995, 188, 132). When, in 1792, Hannah More sought to show the resistance of the English commons to French rationalist philosophy, she used the allegory of a virtuous blacksmith refusing to destroy a "fine old castle" merely on account of "a dark closet, or an awkward passage, or an inconvenient room or two" (qtd. in Gilmartin 2007, 94). When, in 1794, the Pitt ministry prosecuted radicals for treason, it accused them of imagining and seeking to contrive the "horrible ruin and devastation" of the British constitution, with the king buried under the rubble of a "glorious fabric...cemented with the best blood of our ancestors" (qtd. in Pfau 2005, 163). When, in 1807, the Ministry of All the Talents initiated a program of constitutional reform, its conservative opponents pictured its policies as a new Gunpowder Plot, as a mine laid underground to blow up the Gothic edifice of government. And when in 1814 William Wordsworth likened his poetic oeuvre to a "gothic Church," William Hazlitt figured him as one of the hirelings of old corruption supporting the restoration of the old Gothic order of Europe—complete with a revival of Jesuitism and the Spanish Inquisition—with the "chaunting of *Te Deums* in all the churches of Christendom" (*The Examiner*, August 28, 1814, 558).

If the recent prevalence of architectural imagery is thus not without precedent in the Romantic period, nor is its affiliation with the sense of history. The cultural phenomenon by which the multifarious and complex events of 11 September, 2001 were abbreviated by common consent into the calendrical cipher "9/11" was, indeed, newly theorized in the Romantic period. John Horne Tooke, one of the men accused by the Pitt ministry in 1794 of designing the ruin of the constitution, argued in his seminal treatise on "Winged Words" that the fundamental process of language was the communal, cumulative, and anonymous activity of abbreviation. Words were generated and refined by the compressive activities of innumerable minds upon the common materials of historical existence (Manly 2007, 52). Language was not abstract, arbitrary and elite, but concrete, historical and popular in character. The way the cataclysmic events of the French Revolution were, by common convention, compressed into a catalogue of resonant "days," was a proof of the popular ownership of language; a proof that conservative thinkers such as Burke acknowledged even as they mocked the cant language of "the emancipating year of 1789" (Burke 1987, 32). Indeed, if the decade since 9/11 has sometimes been imagined as a compressed recapitulation of the middle ages, with a revival of the ideas of sacrifice and duty in America and in Britain, then the Romantic period, haunted everywhere by a sense of historical recurrence, and marked by all-out ideological warfare between the past and the future, between religiosity and atheism, was still more conscious of itself as a "Gothic" period. It was, as the hero of Walter Scott's novel, *The Antiquary* (1816), put it, a "Gothic generation" (Watson, ed. 2002, 150). Wordsworth wrote of France during the Revolution as possessing "the attraction of a country in Romance" (*1805* X, 697), and nowhere was the Gothic self-imagination of the period more pronounced than in poetry.

Long before there was any such thing as "Romanticism," there was a critical view of the gathering shift away from neo-classicism as the return of a "Gothic poetry." Richard Hurd's *Letters on Chivalry and Romance* (1762) helped lay the groundwork for this idea by developing a historicist account of poetic appreciation, according to which the poetry of the middle ages was to be read and appreciated by reference not to classical rules, but by reference to its circumambient social context. In anticipation of the modern discipline of "cultural poetics," Hurd suggested a reading of such poetry as a culturally legible encryption of historical conditions. In Hurd's words:

> When an architect examines a Gothic structure by Grecian rules, he finds nothing but deformity. But the Gothic architecture has its own rules, by which, when it comes to be examined, it is seen to have its merit, as well as the Grecian…The same observation holds of the two sorts of poetry. Judge of [Spenser's] Faerie Queene by the classic models, and you are shocked with its disorder: consider it with an eye to its Gothic original, and you find it regular. The unity and simplicity of the former are more complete: but the latter has that sort of unity and simplicity, which results from its nature…The Faerie Queene…as a Gothic poem derives its *method*, as well as the other characters of its composition, from the established modes and ideas of chivalry. (Hurd 1811, IV, 296–97)

As Alex Davis notes, Hurd's positioning of Spenser as the last of the Goths generates a historiographically crucial double view of the age of chivalry as irretrievably lost, and as preserved for future restoration in the literature of the Elizabethan age (Davis 2003, 233). Thomas Percy took on these ideas in his massively influential collection of *Reliques of Ancient English Poetry* (1765). The *Reliques* developed a view of England as a Gothic nation, and of English poetry as properly called "Gothic." Percy saw chivalry "as in embrio" among the ancient Goths, and traced the forms of the ballad and the Romance back "in a lineal descent from the ancient historical songs of the Gothic Bards and Scalds," and forward to the history plays of Shakespeare (Percy 1775, III, vi–viii). Percy's creative reconstruction of a Gothic tradition in English poetry is clearly visible in his choice of epigraph from one of the early editors of Shakespeare, Nicholas Rowe. As Christine Baatz has suggested, Rowe's prologue to the *Tragedy of Jane Shore* (1714), inaugurates an important shift in literary perspective by grouping medieval writers with the "ancients" rather than (as was then conventional) with the "moderns" (Korte, Schneider, and Lethbridge, eds. 2000, 121). By imagining a division between "ancient" and "modern" English poetry, Rowe opened up the apparently paradoxical possibility of a renaissance from within the domestic vernacular tradition. The dawning possibility of a vernacular classic is poignantly articulated in the prologue's Augustan couplets on the "good old taste" of the medieval ballad:

> Those venerable ancient song-enditers
> Soar'd many a pitch above our modern writers…
> In such an age, immortal Shakespeare wrote,
> By no quaint rules, nor hampering critics taught;
> With rough majestic force he mov'd the heart,
> And strength and nature made amends for art.
> (Rowe 1791, x)

Percy, writing in the wake of Hurd's thoroughgoing account of "Gothic" poetry, adapted these lines for his own collection of ballads. Altering "Those" to "These" so as to identify his collection with the whole body of ancient English song, Percy also elided the lines referring directly to Shakespeare, and amended "he mov'd" to "they mov'd." With these small but significant changes to Rowe's lines, Percy assimilated Shakespeare to a larger English Gothic tradition. By a further historical paradox, Percy contrived to give his anonymous medieval minstrels poetic priority over Shakespeare precisely by extending to the corpus of old English poetry the kind of editorial procedures that Rowe and other eighteenth-century editors had previously developed in "constructing a literary monument" to "Gothic genius" out of the "shabby ruin" of Shakespeare (Groom 1999, 11).

Percy's creative antiquarianism was massively influential. It ramified throughout the myriad works of what James Chandler calls "novel antiquities" published around the turn of the century (Chandler 1998, 277), including John Brand's *Observations on Popular Antiquities* (1813). As Susan Manly notes, antiquarians such as Brand identified the Reformation as the watershed moment in English literary history. The Reformation had seen "popular customs and rituals...expressive of national character" almost "obliterated" by "the weight of...book-centred authority." "[C]onsecrated to the fancies of the multitude, by an usage from time immemorial," in Brand's phrase, these rituals were thus forced underground, "committed as a venerable deposit to the keeping of *Oral Tradition*" at the very moment that they were "erased by public authority from the *written Word*." Catholic ritual was thus inscribed (or literally encrypted) in the rhythms of the common language with a permanency directly proportional to the virulence with which it was expunged from the historical record (Manly 2007, 70–71). With language thus conceived as an encryption of historical consciousness, the antiquarian cataloguing of popular song by figures such as Brand, Percy, and Joseph Ritson was a way of healing the historical breach, and reuniting the written and the spoken language. The ballad collection was a direct portal to what Sue Chaplin calls an "almost mystical" articulation of "the spirit of the English people" (Chaplin 2007, 43).

These ideas devolved upon James Mackintosh's stadial theory of English poetry in his 1813 review of Madame de Staël's *D'Allemagne* (1810) for the *Edinburgh Review*. Mackintosh called England "the most illustrious of German nations," distinguished by its "romantic and chivalrous" poetry, and continued:

> Nature produced a chivalrous poetry in the sixteenth century; learning in the eighteenth. Perhaps the history of English poetry reflects the revolution of European taste more distinctly than that of any other nation. We have successively cultivated a Gothic poetry from nature, a classical poetry from imitation, and a second Gothic from the study of our own ancient poets. (*Edinburgh Review*, October 1813, 207)

As Robert Miles notes, "Gothic poetry from nature" here denotes the poetry of the Elizabethan age, while "second Gothic" signifies the Lake Poets, William Wordsworth, Samuel Taylor Coleridge, and Robert Southey, who drew inspiration from Shakespeare and the other "ancient poets" (Spooner and McEvoy, eds. 2007, 16). According to Miles,

> [i]t was the Victorians who dubbed this "second Gothic poetry" "Romanticism," and the tale of terror "Gothic." Thus we may say that it is an accident of literary history that we do not refer to the poetry of the early nineteenth-century as "the Gothic revival," just as we do its architecture... [W]hile the poems and novels of the period shared the general taste of Gothicism, the later retrospective classifications of literary history dubbed the one Romantic, and good, the other Gothic, and bad. (Spooner and McEvoy, eds. 2007, 16)

While accepting Miles's broad claim that the poetry of the early nineteenth century needs to be understood in the context of the larger movement known as the Gothic Revival, this book also seeks to show that it was by no means simply "accident" or "retrospect" that led to the Gothic/Romantic split. Indeed, my argument throughout the book is that the first-generation Romantics were active participants in the creation of a wider "Gothic" culture—but that they were determined to create a distinctive, purer Gothic in literature, and thus to some extent put in place the distinction in taste that was, by a further irony of literary history, subsequently reified as Romantic/Gothic. The aim of much of my literary archaeology is to restore the fluidity of the distinction as it was in the period itself, and to show how the Romantics aimed to create a "second Gothic poetry" in order to bring into being a second Gothic culture, in the manner intimated by Hurd, and realized in Victorian culture through the work of revivalists such as Augustus Pugin and Kenelm Digby (Fay 2002, 87).

In this argument for the Lake Poets as initiating a schism within the "general taste" for the Gothic, my argument comes close to that of Michael Gamer's recent study, *Romanticism and the Gothic* (2000). But in fact this superficial similarity helps to bring out the distinctive concerns of this book. Where Gamer seeks to show the process of generic differentiation by which Romanticism emerged as a distinct literary discourse out of the larger cultural formation of the Gothic, and reflects this fact in his appositive title, this book seeks to trace the attempt of the Lake Poets to appropriate the designation of Gothic for their own cultural project, and argues that their literary creations became rather *more* than less self-consciously "Gothic"—an argument reflected in my adjectival noun of a title. Where Gamer is concerned to reify and to hold apart two distinct genres, in order to excavate their genetic commonality, I am concerned to study an identifiably "Gothic" phase or strand within Romantic writing; to claim and to *qualify* a part of canonical Romanticism as Gothic in a hitherto underappreciated sense. In short, whereas Gamer sees Romanticism refining itself out of the Gothic, I argue that the phenomenon known as Romanticism is a reform movement within the Gothic—less a break-away reformation movement than a program for a counter-reformation.

*Gothic Romanticism* explores the nexus of architecture, politics, and literary form in order to read afresh the works of the Lake Poets—William Wordsworth, Samuel Taylor Coleridge, and Robert Southey. These three writers, friends, and neighbors for thirty years, had abiding interests in the correlation of politics with literary and architectural form, and all of them sought to create "Gothic" works better and purer than Ann Radcliffe's novels or the poetry of the Della Cruscan school; a project that might be expressed in the conceptual shorthand of refining "Gothick" into "Gothic." Whatever their rivalries and disagreements, the Lake Poets were thus always in some sense co-partners in what Nick Groom has called a wider "Gothic cultural enterprise" (Groom 2006, 182). But they were frequently quite self-conscious about it too. Perhaps the largest example of a self-consciously "Gothic" project is the scheme of Wordsworth and Coleridge for a collaborative philosophical epic to be entitled *The Recluse*—for which Wordsworth used the figure of a "gothic Church," and which Coleridge envisaged as resembling a Gothic cathedral in growing organically, with a "plan not distinct from the execution" (Raysor, ed. 1936, 7). An equally self-conscious Gothicism informed Southey's series of publications—"a long series of labours," as he called it (Southey 1855, 226)—on the literature and culture of medieval Spain, and his writings on English literary history. As David Fairer has shown, Robert Southey, poet laureate, promulgated a "Gothic" narrative of English literary history in 1814 (Pratt, ed. 2006, 1–17). Writing in the October edition of the *Quarterly Review*, Southey gave an account of English poetry that adapted the long-standing view of the British Constitution as transmitted from time immemorial, and as resembling a venerable Gothic edifice in its "varied tenor of perpetual decay, fall, renovation, and progression" (Burke 1987, 30). He claimed that in England's poetry, "as in our laws and institutions, however it may have been occasionally modified by the effect of foreign models, a distinct national character has predominated" (*QR* 12:23 (1814), 60). And, developing the latent Gothicism of Wordsworth's Preface to *Lyrical Ballads*, with its account of the way that "language and the human mind act and re-act on each other" (*Prose Works* I, 140), Southey went on to suggest that "our national character and our language" had "acted upon each other" so as to "purchase condensation and strength" at the slight expense of Latinate "euphony" (*QR* 12:23 (1814), 66). After tracing the unique resources of the English language back to an Anglo-Saxon base, treating the revolutions in poetry as an index of the spirit of English history, and portraying the literary-historical enterprise of Thomas Percy as serving to return English poetry into its rightful course, Southey concluded that, "[t]o borrow a phrase from the Methodists, there has been a great revival in our days—a poetry out of the spirit" (90).

*Gothic Romanticism* aims to document these "Gothic" projects, to investigate the interrelationships between them, and, further, to correlate them with a series of notable episodes in the development of a Gothic national culture. The largest argument of this book is that, from the mid-1790s until at least the early 1830s, British culture was self-consciously "Gothic," and that Wordsworth, Coleridge, and Southey were instrumental in making it so. It is my contention that not only was there an identifiable cult of the Gothic—and that there is, hence, a sub-set of literary and social practice in the late-eighteenth and early-nineteenth centuries that might be called "Gothic culture"—but that the infiltration of Gothicism into the discourses of literature, architecture, and politics, and its osmotic passage between these discourses, makes it possible to speak of early nineteenth-century British culture at large as a "Gothic culture." In this, I seek to give form and body to Maurice Levy's general sense that "Gothic" was "the historically dated response of the English psyche to what was happening on the far side of the Channel" after 1789—a historically calibrated national-imaginary "regression" to the ethos of the period before the dawn of the Enlightenment (Smith and Sage eds. 1994, 2). Edmund Burke's *Reflections on the Revolution in France* (1790) made precisely this "Gothic" response, decrying the French Revolution as the death-knell of the "age of chivalry," and opposing the "cold sluggishness" of an English "national character" unchanged since the fourteenth century, to the quicksilver experimentalism of the over-enlightened French (Burke 1987, 66, 75–77). From this caricature of contrasting national characters and contrasting feelings for history flowed many of the subsequent ideological attempts to position Britain as the "Gothic" anti-type to post-revolutionary France.

Wordsworth—in part because his Gothicism is both more subterranean and more thoroughgoing than that of his contemporaries—provides my core case study in the formation of a national Gothic culture. In perhaps his best-known statement of literary mission, Wordsworth offered the second edition of the *Lyrical Ballads* (1800) as a corrective to the recent rash of "frantic novels, sickly and stupid German Tragedies, and deluges of idle and extravagant stories in verse" (*Prose Works* I, 128–30). Written at a time when the terms "German" and "Gothic" were effectively synonymous, and were both associated with an "alien" extremity in politics and in literature, the Preface to *Lyrical Ballads* can be seen as a declaration of war on the literary and political Gothic. Thus, for David Punter, Wordsworth cut himself off from a project—the development of Gothic literature—in which almost all of the other major figures of British Romanticism participated (Punter 1996, 87, 112). But even in his ostensible farewell to Gothic, Wordsworth's alignment of his own work with a defense of the "elder writers" Shakespeare and Milton represents a choice of literary inheritance that many of his readers would in fact have recognized as Gothic. Alexander Pope had famously likened Shakespeare's works to "an ancient majestick piece of Gothic Architecture" in their strength and solemnity, and, more recently, Edmund Burke had found in *Paradise Lost* the poetic equivalent of the Gothic cathedral's architectural sublime (Pope 1728, I, xxv; Burke 1757, 49–53). Wordsworth's attack on "sickly and stupid German" writing is thus legible as less a rejection than a selection of Gothic; as a manifesto for a Gothic mode better and purer than that represented by the Gothic novel or the Gothic stage, or what Elizabeth Fay calls the acceptance of a "knightly" quest or "crusade against the misuses of sensibility" (2002, 84).

Wordsworth's poetry of the 1800s and 1810s is filled with celebrations, of gradually diminishing hesitancy, of what a fragment-poem of 1808 calls "Gothic Virtue," culminating in the figure of *The Excursion* as a "gothic Church." In the liberty sonnets of 1802, Wordsworth envisages "halls" hung with "Armoury of the invincible Knights of old" sheltering England's "ancient...dower / Of inward happiness." In "To the Men of Kent" of 1803, he imagines the Norman Conquest—and by extension Napoleon's army for the conquest of England—foundering on Kentish "charters" of liberties that were habitually described by legal writers as "Gothic." In *The Prelude* of 1805, he figures Britain as a Gothic fortress, the "last spot of earth where freedom now / Stands single in her only sanctuary" (X, 981–82). In *The Convention of Cintra* (1808), he speaks of the constitutional "duty to restore the good which has fallen into disuse;" to "rear" a "new fortress...upon the ancient and living rock of justice" (*Prose Works* I, 342). And in book five of *The Excursion*, he pictures the staunchly patriotic Poet as rapt in "temperate awe / And natural reverence" (V, 139–49) before the Gothic church of St Oswald's, Grasmere. Put like this, the "Gothic" tenor of Wordsworth's poetic enterprise seems obvious, positive, and uncomplicated. But that is only half the story.

### GOTHS OF EVERY AGE

In "Winter," the concluding part of *The Seasons* (1726–30), James Thomson imagined the coming of the Goths: a "boisterous race" who, "with dreadful sweep/ Resistless rushing o'er the enfeebled" Roman empire, "relumed the flame" of liberty and gave "the vanquished world another form" (ll. 837–42). Expanding on this view in *Liberty* (1735–36), Thomson spoke of how the Gothic "people, fierce with freedom, rushed / From the rude iron regions of the north, / To Libyan deserts swarm protruding swarm, / And poured new spirit through a slavish world" (IV, 802–5). But the "Gothic states" thus produced had kings that "engrossed...power," and it was only in their successor, "Britain's matchless constitution," with its checks and balances, that liberty had become a lasting establishment (IV, 806–14). The Goths were now departed, but in the English nation their "tide" had "grown full," and the term "Gothic" remained behind to signify dignity and strength. Except, that is, when it came to architecture. "In Architecture too thy rank supreme," Thomson apostrophized Greece:

> Such thy sure rules, that Goths of every age,
> Who scorn'd their aid, have only loaded earth
> With labour'd heavy monuments of shame.
> (II, 373–76)

In stark contrast with the antiquary Richard Hurd, who thirty years later would argue both that "the Gothic architecture has its own rules," and that the "Gothic" culture upon which those rules were patterned was "never likely to subsist again" (Hurd 1811, IV, 296–97), Thomson saw the Gothic in art as both a barbarous and a recurrent phenomenon. Every age has its own Goths, Thomson suggests, who by scorning the aid of classical rules, only create "labour'd heavy monuments of shame."

Time transfigured both views into untruth. The position that neither Hurd nor Thomson could imagine—that Gothic could be revived *and* reduced to rule—had become a commonplace by the end of the first decade of the nineteenth century. It had been instantiated in architecture by works such as Batty Langley's *Ancient Architecture, Restored, and Improved* (1742), which sought to counteract the prevailing view of Gothic as a "coarse," "artless," and "devia[nt]" style derived from the "ravages of the *Visigoths*, in the 5$^{th}$ century" (Chambers 1728, I, 173, 129), by systematizing Gothic architecture into "orders" comparable with those developed by Palladio for the classical mode (Langley, 6–7). And as Simon Bainbridge has suggested, the wholesale reimagining of medieval "Gothic" culture in the modern ballads of Walter Scott worked to create a self-consciously Gothic culture in wartime Britain. In 1811, the *Eclectic Review* argued that in poems such as *The Lay of the Last Minstrel* (1805), *Marmion* (1808), and *The Lady of the Lake* (1810), Scott had taken on "the ancient function of a bard, to celebrate military prowess, and set off pride, ferocity, and revenge." His "exquisite delineations—of a fierce and licentious age" had made his readers into medievals, into Gothic subjects: "they reconcile us to the manners they illustrate, and assimilate us to the characters they describe" (qtd. in Bainbridge 2003, 138). In October 1810, Coleridge told Wordsworth that it was "time to write a Recipe for Poems of this sort":

> The first business must be a vast string of patronymics and names of Mountains, Rivers, &c.... Secondly, all the nomenclature of Gothic Architecture, of Heraldry, of Arms, of Hunting & Falconry—these possess the same power of reviving the caput mortuum & rust of old imagery—besides, they will stand by themselves...Some pathetic moralizing on old times, or any thing else, for the head & tail pieces—with a Bard (*that* is absolutely necessary) and Songs of course—For the rest, whatever suits Mrs. Radcliff, i.e. in the fable, and the Dramatis Personae, will do for the Poem—with this advantage, that however thread-bare in the Romance Shelves of the circulating Library it is to be taken as quite new so soon as told in Rhyme—it need not be half as interesting—& the Ghost may be a Ghost—or may be explained—or both may take place in the same poem—Item—the Poet not only may but must mix all dialects of *all ages*—and all styles, from Dr. Robertson's to the Babes in the wood. (Hayden, ed. 1996, 59–60)

"[I]t is to be taken as quite new so soon as it is told in Rhyme." Coleridge's humorous remarks are directed against the alleged vulgarity of Walter Scott's genre-crossing metrical romances. But they also capture something of what this book will argue Coleridge and his fellow Lakers were attempting in all seriousness to do in a series of works in the early nineteenth century: to move beyond the generic themes and paraphernalia of Gothic fiction, and beyond Scott's artificially animated antiquarianism, toward a purified Gothic *style* that would reconnect with the genuine resources of the language, and truly make English poetry new.

Antiquarianism was, as I shall argue at greater length in the coming chapters, a vital stage in the revivification of English Gothic. But for the Lake Poets it was only a stage, and one that they wanted (often rather defensively) to believe they had outgrown. This position emerges with luminous clarity in the case of Wordsworth's poem of "feudal times," *The White Doe of Rylstone*, written in 1807–8, but not published until 1815. Scott, having heard that Wordsworth was projecting a poem on the history of the Norton family and the Catholic uprising of 1569, wrote to Wordsworth in early 1808 with an offer to send on a range of antiquarian materials ("curious letters from a spy, sent in to Scotland at the time" [qtd. in Chandler 1984, 173]) that might assist with the composition. Wordsworth's response, written in the throes of his agonized decision to withhold the poem from immediate publication after its lukewarm and even "openly derisive" reception by Charles Lamb and William Hazlitt (*WDR* 11), affects to be offhanded, but is characteristic:

> Thank you for the interesting particulars about the Nortons; I shall like much to see them for their own sakes; but so far from being serviceable to my Poem they would stand in the way of it; as I have followed (as I was in duty bound to do) the traditionary and common historic records –. Therefore I shall say in this case, a plague upon your industrious Antiquarianism that has put my fine story to confusion. (*MY* I, 237)

As James Chandler notes, there is a kind of "nervous laughter" detectible in this "playful but self-conscious curse" on "industrious Antiquarianism" (1984, 174); a nervousness that derives, I would argue, from Wordsworth's recognition that Scott was effectively proposing an artistic takeover, a recruitment of Wordsworth to what Jonathan Farina calls his "nationalist, metonymic, realist aesthetic" of "local density and self-conscious humour" (Farina 2007, 177). As Wordsworth would have been well aware, Scott's influence already loomed large over *The White Doe*, since Wordsworth's source for his story appeared in Thomas Whitaker's *History and Antiquities of the Deanery of Craven* (1805), with a note suggesting that had the events taken place in the purlieus of the "Ettrick Forest [or] the precincts of

Dryburgh or Melrose, the elegant and ingenious editor of the Border Minstrelsy would have wrought it into a beautiful story" (Whitaker 1805, 382–83; *WDR* 5). In offering up historical "particulars," which contained information that revealed the "popular tradition" in Whitaker to be "totally groundless" (qtd. in *WDR* 7), Scott could have been seen as renewing his prior claim to this artistic ground. Wordsworth thus found himself in an awkward posture of mingled complicity and competition with Scott: pre-empting Whitaker's imagined Scottish invasion of Wordsworth's poetic grounds in the north of England, whilst himself trespassing upon Scott's artistic propriety in the modern ballad of "feudal times." His "playful" response to Scott's advances in the May letter is thus actuated by the need to resist assimilation and to articulate a countervailing aesthetic. "[P]ut...to confusion" by the onslaught of (Scott-ish) history, Wordsworth is driven into the refuge of his own earlier argument in the Preface to *Lyrical Ballads* of 1800 that the poet is a traditionalist, "an upholder and preserver," one who "binds together" common materials, and a human type that is especially to be contradistinguished from the man of (historical) science (*Prose Works* I, 167). Antiquarian materials are, for Wordsworth, only that—curiosities that one looks at "for their own sakes." They are, indeed, antithetical to "Poem" and "story," and Wordsworth thus positions himself as a historical Poet rather than a historical scholar—an agent of "confusion" in its positive sense of opposition to the dryasdust mentality of those who are able, as he put it in *The Prelude* of 1805, "to class the cabinet / Of their sensations" (II, 228–29). In August 1808, still hard at work on the revisions to *The White Doe*, Wordsworth again articulated his distance from Scott. Scott's *Marmion, A Tale of Flodden Field* (1808) had, Wordsworth told Scott, gained its end, but it was "not in every respect the end which I should wish you to propose to yourself...both as to matter and manner" (*MY* I, 264). Turning the rhetorical tables upon the industrious antiquary, Wordsworth was now the one proposing the right way to do Gothic poetry. This process of self-differentiation from Scott continued in Wordsworth's 1814 figure of his whole oeuvre as a "gothic Church," a structure whose communal and spiritual nature presents a pointed antithesis to what (according to Henry Crabb Robinson) Wordsworth saw as Scott's "trad[e] in poetry," with "the size of his poem being adapted to that of the building it was written to pay for" (Morley, ed. 1938, II, 534). And since *The White Doe* as published in 1815 was a poem in which Wordsworth endeavored, as he later told Isabella Fenwick, to replace the sort of focus on "the surfaces of things" found in Scott's poetry with attention to their "moral & spiritual" dimensions (*FN* 32–33), it seems clear that he was throughout this period consciously striving for a purer Gothic, conceived in explicit distinction with Scott's creative antiquarianism.

But as I have been suggesting, and as Wordsworth's withholding of his "feudal" poem until 1815 illustrates, the project for a better Gothic was fraught with difficulties and anxieties. Gothic culture as the Lake Poets conceived it was, to borrow a phrase from Matthew Arnold, powerless to be born. It had to wait, in a sense, for the public development of the antiquarian, museum-going, origins-hunting taste by which it could be appreciated—which development was, however, according to the Romantic theory of the autonomous domain of art, peculiarly the responsibility of the original writer. The dilemma was that the better Gothic was likely to be fatally wounded by exposure to what in 1815 Wordsworth, still smarting from the crushing reviews of *The Excursion*, called the present "benighted age" (*MY* II, 187), but that, as Coleridge first proposed, and as Wordsworth put it in the "Essay, Supplementary" of 1815, "every Author, as far as he is great and at the same time *original*, has...the task of *creating* the taste by which he is to be enjoyed" (*Prose Works* III, 80). The purer Gothic taste had to be created in the here and now if it was to fructify in posterity, and here again the source of anxiety and of enablement was the creative antiquarianism of Scott. This perplexity is vividly illustrated by Coleridge's belated publication of *Christabel* in 1816 (following the appearance of the travesty, "Christobell, a Gothic Tale," in the *European Magazine* (67 [1815], 345–46)), under a disclaimer that the poem had been written in 1797 and 1800, and that the "celebrated poets" whose works *Christabel* with its innovative syllabic meter now seemed to imitate, "would be among the first to vindicate me from the charge" of plagiarism (Coleridge 1816, vi–vii). If Coleridge thus reclaimed from Scott and Byron his own priority in the "Gothic cultural enterprise," it was at the cost of admitting that the original writer was in fact uniquely *unfitted* for the task of creating the taste by which he was to be appreciated; that, scandalously and potentially fatally for the whole project of a nationally regenerative return to literary origins, the popular priority of the simulacrum was the necessary condition of the posterior survival of the real thing. And since the belatedness of *Christabel* was due to Coleridge's acquiescence in Wordsworth's judgment that further Gothic pieces would harm the second edition of *Lyrical Ballads* as the *Rime of the Ancient Mariner* had harmed the first, Coleridge's offering of the poem in 1816 was also fraught with a tacit admission that the Lake School had failed at a corporate level in the national-historical task of leading the revival of Gothic culture. The *Augustan Review*'s dismissive review of *Christabel* put the point pithily. *Christabel* was indeed a poem "in the *manner* of Walter Scott and Lord Byron; that is to say, it resembles the productions of these authors in its general structure." But "the foundation and embellishments are decidedly in the Lakish taste," and "the absurdity... of attempting to support the bold and massive entablatures of the former artists, upon the slender and grotesque columns of the architects of the Lakes, must be evident" (*Augustan Review* 3 [1816], 16).

Coleridge had, nevertheless, been set on leading the revival of Gothic poetry since at least 1798, when he had charged Wordsworth with the task of writing the super-systematic and trans-historical "philosophical" poem on "Man, Nature, and Society," *The Recluse*. He told Wordsworth in 1799 that "of nothing but 'The Recluse' can I hear patiently," and he envisaged even the groundbreaking autobiographical poetry that would become *The Prelude* as a "tail-piece" for *The Recluse* (*CLSTC* I, 538). Throughout the early 1800s, Coleridge would "grieve" whenever it seemed—despite Wordsworth's completion of *The Prelude* in 1805 and of a "Prospectus" and putative "Book First" by 1806—that "'The Recluse' sleeps" (*CLSTC* I, 575). And he would resume the task himself in what Theresa Kelly calls the "gothic horror picture show" (qtd. in Thomas 2008, 172–73) of the *Biographia Literaria* (1817), when the publication of *The Excursion*, despite its prophylactic use of the figure of a "gothic Church," made him realize that Wordsworth was deviating from a truly "Gothic" model of organic interfusion. In a letter of May 30, 1815, Coleridge wrote to Wordsworth, justifying and dilating upon the "comparative censure" of *The Excursion* that he had expressed to Lady Beaumont, and which had thence made its way to Wordsworth. Wordsworth's architectural metaphor is here pointedly supplanted by an alternative figure of organic growth, according to which, for Coleridge, "the Poem on the growth of your own mind was as the ground-plat and the Roots, out of which the Recluse was to have sprung up as the Tree" (*CLSTC* IV, 573). Then, speaking of the poem now known to us as *The Prelude*, Coleridge makes a rather surprising claim:

> *This* I considered as "the Excursion;" and the second as "The Recluse" I had (from what I had at different times gathered from your conversation on the Plan) anticipated as commencing with you set down and settled in an abiding Home, and that with the Description of that

Home you were to begin a *Philosophical Poem*, the result and fruits of a Spirit so fram'd & so disciplin'd, as had been told in the former. (*CLSTC* IV, 574)

Coleridge's remarks—which have to be taken in the context of the estrangement between the two poets after 1810, and of his protracted failure to provide the "notes" that were to underpin the poem's philosophy—refer the *Recluse* scheme back to the dyadic structure of 1799. As such they represent a criticism of what Wordsworth himself called his prodigality ("circumspection, infinite delay" (*1805*, I, 244)) in returning the investment Coleridge had placed in his capacity to write the "First Genuine Philosophic Poem" (*BL* II, 156). Coleridge's expectation that *The Prelude* and *The Recluse* would form a "compleat Whole" (*CLSTC* IV, 573), while remaining distinct works, is both a rebuke to Wordsworth's tendency to introduce subdivisions into the project, and a rejection of the notion that *The Excursion* could form any part of *The Recluse*. It was instead precisely an excursion or holiday from the work that should have proceeded directly from the description of "an abiding Home" in "Home at Grasmere"—which had indeed been hastily finished and joined to the "Prospectus" in time to be presented to Coleridge, along with the completed *Prelude*, upon his return to England and the Lake District in October 1806 (Darlington, ed. 1977, 16–22). The retrospective rationalization of the scheme provided in the Preface to *The Excursion* was not, in short, to be trusted. The view is a fair one, and it also informs the work of scholars such as John Alban Finch and Kenneth Johnston in reconstructing the actual progress of *The Recluse* through close study of its "welter of textual instability" (Johnston 1984, xix).

But far from disqualifying the "Gothic" figure, a recognition of its retrospective nature only makes it the more clearly visible as a key point of intersection between Wordsworth's vision of his own career and the wider "Gothic cultural enterprise." If there is a clear reminiscence of Richard Hurd's recuperative account of "Gothic" poetry in the 1814 Preface's avoidance of formal "system" and preference for the "more animating…course" of alluding to the structure of a "gothic Church," then there is an equally clear echo of Hurd on the Gothic art-work observing only those rules that "resul[t] from its nature" in the claim of the Preface to *Lyrical Ballads* (1800) that the true artist was one who had so internalized the principles of his art as to be able to proceed "blindly and mechanically" with no other guide than the organic connectedness of his thoughts (*Prose Works* I, 126). But the new Gothic mode remained haunted, for all that, by

Thomson's prophecy of its abortiveness. There is, for example, a clear echo of Thomson's "Goths of every age" making "labour'd heavy monuments of shame" in Wordsworth's letter to George Beaumont of June 3, 1805, describing the depression he felt upon the completion of *The Prelude*:

> [W]hen I looked back upon the performance it seemed to have a dead weight about it, the reality so far short of the expectation; it was the first long labour that I had finished, and the doubt whether I should ever live to write the Recluse and the sense which I had of this Poem being so far below what I seemed capable of executing, depressed me much. (*EY* 594)

In writing *The Prelude*, Wordsworth had certainly "scorn'd the aid" of classical rules. In May he had told Beaumont that it was "a thing unprecedented in literary history that a man should talk so much about himself," and that any "redundancies" in the poem would likely prove "incurable." "The fault," Wordsworth wrote, "lies too deep, and is in the first conception" (*EY* 586–87). This "fault" in "conception" seems to recur in the June letter, in which *The Prelude* is figured as "a sort of portico to the Recluse, part of the same building"—with its inadvertent implication of a lack of structural or stylistic continuity between the "portico" and the "building;" as though a portico might *not* be part of the building of which it forms a part. Since this architectural figure of 1805 is clearly a prototype for the 1814 image of *The Recluse* as a "gothic Church," the possibility emerges that *The Recluse*—composed of parts written and conceived under widely varying historical conditions between the revolutionary 1790s and the wartime 1800s—might resemble less a typical "gothic Church" than London's Old St. Paul's Cathedral, famously pictured by Wenceslaus Hollar with Inigo Jones's seventeenth-century Palladian portico grafted incongruously onto the west front of the ancient Gothic fabric (Dugdale 1716, 150–151; no. 164).

Like Jones's architectural hybrid, the evolving design of *The Recluse* crystallizes the cultural and aesthetic sea-change theorized by James Mackintosh in 1813. Standing at either end of the Enlightenment, the two "churches," built respectively from bricks and books, provide a fitting emblem for Mackintosh's print-driven model of cultural progression from the Gothic to the neo-classical to the "second Gothic." Mark Schoenfield has perceived just such cultural and historical implications in the Gothic analogy. Wordsworth is, for Schoenfield, recruiting to his poetic project the role of social interfusion and cultural coherency that belonged to the church in the medieval period. The Gothic church is a communal structure, "the social functions of which overspill its confines into the courts, the shops, the farms, the day-to-day life of the town, and which, because its construction takes centuries, is used before completion and requires its occupants to complete it imaginatively" (Schoenfield 1996, 195). Schoenfield does not develop the point. But several facts suggest that there are buried referents behind Wordsworth's architectural analogies, and that one of those referents may indeed be old, Catholic, St Paul's. St. Paul's Churchyard had been the traditional home of the London print industry since the late fifteenth century, and Wordsworth's publisher, Thomas Longman, was based in nearby Paternoster Row. The association between Longman and St. Paul's was, in a certain sense, the occasion of part of *The Recluse*. It was during his visit to London in the spring of 1808 to arrange for Longman to publish *The White Doe* that Wordsworth had the vision of "The huge majestic Temple… / In awful sequestration" that would become the *Recluse* fragment, "St. Paul's" (Reed 1975, 377–81; Kishel, ed. 3–7, 59). Wordsworth's publishing career had, moreover, been tied to St. Paul's from the first: Joseph Johnson, who published Wordsworth's *Descriptive Sketches* and *An Evening Walk* in 1793, had his premises in the Churchyard (Johnston 1998, 248).

The cathedral Wordsworth knew and composed poetry upon was, of course, the firmly non-Gothic, neoclassical building of Christopher Wren. But the survival of the book trade in the vicinity, and the fact that Johnson's premises stood, as Leigh Hunt noted in *The Town* (1848), on "the site of the old episcopal mansion" (I, 69), might well have provided Wordsworth with an imaginative link back to a time when the old Gothic edifice had indeed "overspilled" with "social function." According to James P. Malcolm's *Londinium Redivivum*, published in 1802, the reign of Elizabeth had seen the Gothic cathedral's cloisters, chapels, and vaults turned variously into storehouses for wines, stones, and lumber, into premises for glaziers, carpenters, trunk-makers, players and bakers, and, occasionally, into schools (Malcolm 1802, III, 71–73). The possibility that old St. Paul's provides Wordsworth's model for his epic poem in both 1805 and 1814 is strengthened by the fact that he would have found good precedent for this model in the example of the poet he called his "great Predecessor," John Milton (*MY* II, 146).

In his 1785 edition of Milton's occasional poetry, which Wordsworth seems to have known by September 1808 (*MY* I, 266), Thomas Warton suggested that old St. Paul's was the "pattern of the Gothic style" behind the lines in *Il Penseroso* on "studious cloysters," "embowed" roofs, massy "antic pillars," and "storied windows richly dight, / Casting a dim religious light" (Warton, ed. 1785, 90–91). Since it seems clear that Wordsworth used Warton's edition of Milton in preparing the "Essay, Supplementary to the Preface" for *Poems* in January 1815 (*Prose Works*, III, 91, 55), and since the actual Gothic church that appears in the pages of *The Excursion* is described as "massy," and (in the edition of 1845) as possessing an "altar-window," "Varying its tincture with the changeful light" (V, 161–62; Bushell, Butler, and Jaye eds. 2007, 171n), it seems possible that the archetypal "gothic Church" of 1814 derives from Warton's argument for the patterning of Milton's lines upon old St. Paul's. Echoes of Warton's description of old St. Paul's "vaults, shrines, iles, pillars, and painted glass" (1785, 90) can be clearly heard in Wordsworth's description of his own "little Cells, Oratories, and sepulchral Recesses." And this in turn suggests the possibility that Wordsworth's emphasis upon the Gothic style of the "Church" is patterned upon Warton's statement that "Grecian proportions" like those of Wren's cathedral "gratify the judgment," but it is only Gothic architecture that can "affect the imagination" (1785, 90–91). It is admittedly not certain that Wordsworth had seen Warton's book by 1805. But if we now read this Gothic/Grecian distinction back into the 1805 image of *The Recluse* as a "building" with an incongruous "portico," it can be seen to imply the image of old St Paul's, and to hint at the possible incongruity of Wordsworth's "Gothic" art and the "classical" rigor required to write an epic.

However, *The Prelude* was self-consciously Gothic long before June 1805, and both before and after its completion its Gothic quality meant something quite different to Wordsworth. In the two-part *Prelude* of 1799, Wordsworth's description of how he and his school friends "ran a boisterous race," testing the limits of their liberty with "excursions far away" to the Gothic ruin of Furness Abbey, constitutes a clear (and clearly positive) allusion to Thomson's account of the "boisterous race" of Goths extending the bounds of liberty by conquering Rome (*1799*, II, 46, 92, 103–39). Here too, Wordsworth was actively boastful of his inability to reduce his poetic autobiography to classical rule—to "class the cabinet / Of [his] sensations, and in voluble phrase / Run through the history and birth of each / As of a single independent thing" (II, 258–61). He was unable to do this precisely because of the "Gothic" complexity and self-interfusion of a

>    soul, in which
> Not only general habits and desires,
> But each most obvious and particular thought—

> Not in a mystical and idle sense
> But in the words of reason deeply weighed—
> Has no beginning.
>
> (II, 262–67)

Echoing Edward Coke's well-known description of the English common-law as the "perfection of reason," deeply weighed in the experience of generations (Barrell 1992, 121), Wordsworth here valorizes the unclassical architecture of his poem by analogy with the unsystematic system of Gothic churches and of the fundamentally immemorial, uncodifiable, Constitution. By the time of his letter to the military theorist C. W. Pasley of March 1811, Wordsworth's perception of himself as a modern Goth had once again become positively enabling. In "determining the proportions and march of a Poem," he wrote, "[m]uch is to be done by rule; the great outline is previously to be conceived in distinctness, but the consummation of the work must be trusted to resources that are not tangible, though known to exist" (*MY* I, 146).

This book argues that Wordsworth's *Recluse* and the various cultural enterprises of his fellow Lakers need to be seen in the context of a larger literary culture that was—as many recent commentators have suggested—appreciably "Gothic." Susan Manly suggests that the 1790s radicalism that was the intellectual milieu of early Romanticism created a "composite culture which used received protocols in unusual ways," deploying antiquarian materials ("rites, sayings, ballads and superstitions") as a coded "challenge to the culture of politeness that was in the process of defining itself" (Manly 2007, 68). This "radical Gothic" is, as I will argue at greater length in chapter two, an important stream within the larger Gothic culture of the early nineteenth century, which is imaginable as the confluence of radical antiquarianism with the (broadly conservative) elaboration of the institutions of British nationalism.

According to James Chandler, British culture in the first two decades of the nineteenth century was dominated by the vogue for creating "storehouse[s] of the past" in such works of "novel antiquity" as John Brand's *Observations on Popular Antiquities* (1813) and William Hone's interactive *Every-day Book* of "Pastimes, Ceremonies, Manners, Customs" (1825–27). For Chandler, the "distinctive frisson" of this phenomenon was that it was only the ultra-modernity of the popular press and postal service that made the past thus accessible (1998, 277); the tools of historical and technological change that opened up the past for excavation also working to seal it off the more completely from the present. *The Excursion*, which uses "something of a dramatic form" to synthesize a mass of anecdotes, stories and local traditions, and which offers itself as part of a brand new "gothic Church" of words, is a striking instance of this cultural formation. Indeed, for James Garrett, what the *British Review* for September 1820 called Wordsworth's "new style of local poetry" was a product of the deep-cultural influence of national institutions like the museum on "Romantic era writers," who "created works that were already fragments" in emulation of the fragment-gathering and history-making procedures of "archaeologists, antiquarians, historians, and…museum curators" (Garrett 2008, 127, 150). The investment of the *Recluse* project in the cultural-nationalism of the Gothic was only deepened by Wordsworth's 1815 publication of his collected *Poems* complete with a complex taxonomical scheme that attempted to make these "small pieces" (the "cells, oratories, and sepulchral recesses" of the 1814 Preface) visible "under a two-fold view; as composing an entire work within themselves, and as adjuncts to the philosophical Poem, 'The Recluse'" (*Prose Works* III, 28). The scheme of *The Recluse* thus presents a striking aesthetic parallel to what Garrett calls Romantic museum culture's imagination of the nation as both "a particularized abstraction and a generalizable specific" (Garrett, 7): the poem imaginable as both a series of abstract tables of data on physical pages, and a set of articulated structures in a virtual church.

My arguments engage throughout with such ideas about the national and cultural orientation of the "Gothic cultural enterprise," and with a large body of existing scholarship on Romantic medievalism. The book also derives from my long-standing interest in the question of the "apostasy" by which, as William Hazlitt famously charged, the Lake Poets resiled from their youthful support for the democratic ideals of the French Revolution, and compromised their integrity by embracing the unreformed "Gothic" order. The rich complexity of this great reckoning between Hazlitt and the Lake Poets is perhaps best broached within the little room of this introduction by way of two quotations on the question of "turning" from Southey's self-exculpatory *Letter to William Smith* (1817), and Hazlitt's response in *The Examiner*. Southey figures liberty as the sun and himself as a watcher of the skies who has consistently followed its progress, and so "altered my position as the world went round." Hazlitt picks up this image, and has Southey "still looking in the West" for the sun that has newly risen in the east, not realizing that "the world has gone round a second time" (qtd. in Craig 2007, 1). Part of the interest of the comparison is that it foregrounds the way that ideas of fidelity and apostasy are constructed out of figurative language. Hazlitt and Southey actually agree in the figure, and both uses of it work in their own terms. But what is really interesting is that Hazlitt's recycling of Southey's figure convicts him of apostasy but humanizes him too. Hazlitt's introduction of the new day shows up Southey's self-absorption, his failure to imagine alternative views, and it is this unconscious selfishness that definitively marks him as a reactionary. But when re-read in the light of Hazlitt's remarks, Southey's image of a lifetime's effort seems to contain the tragic knowledge that the individual cannot, like the world, "go round a second time"—and what he loses in debating points he gains in elegiac power. In this sort of perplexity lies much of the real matter of apostasy, and one of the core arguments worked out across this book is that the supposed apostasy of the Lake School is better thought of as the development of a richly paradoxical "progressive Gothic politics"—a variety of Romantic conservatism inflected by the radical "Gothic" tradition within English republicanism.

The chapters of this book constitute a series of closely historicized readings of major works and their assorted paratexts. My first chapter focuses upon "Gothic" as a term in the literary-historical and political discourses of the eighteenth century, routing its discussion through the Preface to *The Excursion* so as to begin sketching out the "pregnant moment" of Gothic culture in 1814. Chapter two then seeks to situate Wordsworth in these discourses, and to confirm his paternity in the developing culture of the Gothic, by reading a prototypical "Gothic" text, *Salisbury Plain* (1794). Chapter three explores the engagement of the Lake Poets with the Peninsular War, reading Wordsworth's prose tract, *The Convention of Cintra* (1809), Coleridge's *Letters on the Spaniards* (1809), and Southey's *Chronicle of the Cid* (1808) and *Roderick, the Last of the Goths* (1814). My argument here is that not only was the Peninsular campaign the key episode in the Lake Poets' thinking about the nation, and in their transition from dissent to loyalism, but that their development in these works of a "progressive Gothic politics" was part of a wider British and European romantic-conservative movement sparked by the Spanish uprising against Napoleon. Chapter four turns from this "Gothic" issue to another in the shape of the British and European debate on national education, particularly as represented in Wordsworth's *Excursion*. It argues that the Lake Poets' advocacy of Andrew Bell's "Madras" system of pupil-tuition shows their Gothic politics in action. The concluding chapter then explores the contribution of the Romantic culture of the Gothic to the gathering pictorial and Arthurian turn in English verse, with a particular focus on *The White Doe of Rylstone* (1815).

This book is, then, a work of cultural history as much as of literary criticism, and it makes no apology for often keeping a tight focus on short historical periods. But the chapters of this book can also be read under something like Wordsworth's "two-fold view," as both composing within themselves a close study of a formation within the literary culture of the years 1789 to 1815, and as constituting a continuous background commentary upon Anglo-American culture in the decade after 9/11. The various parts of the book study cultural formations that are uncannily parallel to those of its own cultural and historical moment, with chapter two centered upon a haunting architectural absence, chapter three focused upon a conflict between a religiously inspired guerrilla insurgency and an overwhelmingly superior modern army, chapter four exploring debates over the desirability of religiously informed and openly sectarian methods of education, and the conclusion discussing the implications of new visually oriented technologies of information for the sense of culture and of history. This book thus hopes to provide an oblique approach to understanding the dynamics, if not the particulars, of its own (fast receding) cultural moment. My reading of the "Gothic culture" of early nineteenth-century Britain is also, I hope, legible—to borrow a term from Stephen Greenblatt on *Hamlet* (2002, 5)—as a "suspended reading" of post-9/11 culture; a reading "distributed in tiny, almost invisible particles throughout" the book.

CHAPTER 1

ROMANTIC POETS AND
GOTHIC CULTURE

On November 26, 1814, William Wordsworth wrote to his younger brother Christopher to express his relief on hearing that his "intentions" in sending him a copy of *The Excursion* had been "fulfilled" (*MY* II, 170–171). The poem was the only section of *The Recluse*—the "philosophical poem" against postrevolutionary despair planned with Samuel Taylor Coleridge back in 1798 (*CLSTC* I, 527)—that Wordsworth had been able both to complete and to publish. But like its long-suppressed autobiographical precursor, *The Prelude*, described by the *Eclectic Review* as a "large fossil relic...newly dug up" in November 1850 (551), *The Excursion* had in some ways already missed its moment when it appeared in July 1814. The poem's tone of stoic optimism was perhaps better suited to the earlier, darker days of the war against Napoleon, and its materials were—as with the first book's story of "The Ruined Cottage"—in some places almost two decades old. In the event *The Excursion* fell, as William Hazlitt put it, "still-born from the press" (Cook ed. 1999, 353). The expensive first edition (in quarto, priced at £2 2s) still loaded the shelves at Longman's into the 1830s (St Clair 2004, 201; Gill 1998, 17). But with the abdication of Napoleon and the restoration in France and across Europe of what Edmund Burke had called the old Gothic order (Burke 1796, 110), Wordsworth clearly cherished high hopes of the poem, likened in its preface to the "body" of a "gothic Church" (1814, ix), catching the zeitgeist. "I should," he wrote to Christopher,

> have been sorry had you not been pleased with it; sorry both as a poet and an Englishman. I hear from many quarters high commendations

and not a few from members of your Profession. Yesterday I had a letter from Sir George Beaumont in which he says the Bishop of London is enchanted with The Excursion, and indeed I hear but one opinion on the subject! (*MY* II, 171)

If Christopher Wordsworth, Doctor of Divinity, Dean of Bocking, and founding member of the National Society for Church education, had failed to appreciate this "gothic Church" of a poem, then Wordsworth's "intentions" must have miscarried seriously indeed. It would have been a double failure of communication. "As a poet," it would have meant for Wordsworth a breakdown of his desired sympathy with his audience. And "as an Englishman," it would have meant a dysfunction in the "Constitutional Sort of Reverence" that such Whig periodicals as the *Gentleman's Magazine* had for decades consistently depicted as unfailingly communicated by England's Gothic architecture (*GM* 9 [1739], 641).

I suggested in the introduction that Wordsworth's allusion to Gothic architecture was bound up with the wider movement known as the Gothic Revival, and in this chapter I want to begin fleshing out this argument by paying closer attention to the social and discursive contexts within which it appeared—with particular attention to its inflexion by periodical culture. Indeed, periodicals like the *Gentleman's* fostered a "Gothic" aesthetic not only through their thematic content—each number containing a welter of loosely assorted textual and pictorial details on churches and other antiquities—but also through their serial nature. For theorists of periodical culture like Paul Keen, the "disconnected form" of the miscellaneous periodical operated in dialectical relationship with the fragmentation of knowledge in modern commercial society to generate a connective mentality peculiarly suited to the new culture of reading and writing (Keen 2008, 204). The miscellany's enjambment of topically and stylistically disjunctive material constituted a new form of cultural poetics, with what Keen calls "a strategic enactment of proliferation which challenged readers to locate their critical strategies in the discontinuities of modern knowledge" (205). Periodicals like the *Gentleman's* thus provided Wordsworth and his peers with a model of what the antiquarian miscellanist Isaac D'Israeli theorized in his *Essay on the Manners and Genius of the Literary Character* (1795) as "subterraneous" reading, in which a coherent deep-cultural scheme is inferred or intuited from a thick reading of randomly scattered— and *therefore* metonymic—pieces and parts (Ferris 2006, 524–30). Wordsworth acknowledged the claims of this aesthetic of inductive and associative reading in the Preface to *Poems* (1815). Presenting his "poems, apparently miscellaneous" in a complex taxonomical scheme of interlocking genres and biographical periods whose principal function was, as James Garrett has suggested, to materialize the spectral body of the author (2008, 45–48), Wordsworth nevertheless claimed that he "should have preferred to scatter the contents of these volumes at random, if I had been persuaded that, by the plan adopted, any thing material would be taken from the natural effect of the pieces, individually" (*Prose Works* III, 28). And composing the Preface to *The Excursion* some time between late April and early August 1814 (*Prose Works* III, 3, 10), Wordsworth had relied still more heavily upon the receptive and reverential attitude of his audience. The Preface's "allusion" to the structural principles of Gothic architecture was pointedly aimed at "the attentive Reader," and Wordsworth equally pointedly refused (perhaps stung by the repeated barbs against his "new system" of poetry and the poetical "sect" of the Lake Poets from Jeffrey of the *Edinburgh Review*) "formally to announce a system" (1814, ix–x). He found it "more animating," he said, "to proceed in a different course, and if he shall succeed in conveying to the mind clear thoughts, lively images, and strong feelings, the Reader will have no difficulty in extracting the system for himself" (1814, x).

But "extracting the system" of this "gothic Church" in fact required considerable ingenuity of the "Reader." For where the definite function of "Anti-chapel" ("the outer part at the west end of a [college] chapel" [*OED*]) was assigned to the unpublished *Prelude*, the published *Excursion* was given only the vague and disjointed designation of "the second part" of the "body," and the frequently republished *Lyrical Ballads*, downgraded to "minor Pieces," were jumbled together as "little Cells, Oratories, and sepulchral Recesses" (1814, vii–ix). Professing himself, as in the unknown *Prelude*, no "slave" of the "false secondary power," and unskilled "to class the cabinet / Of [his] sensations" (*1805* II, 220–229), Wordsworth thus referred the intelligibility of the whole *Recluse* scheme to the "attentive Reader"—who might intuit the contours of the absent edifice from an archaeological reading of its extant peripherals, according to his own notions of architecture. The proper reader of *The Recluse* was thus implicitly posited as one of the "One only in ten thousand" described in *The Prelude* as possessed of the imaginative ability to "build up greatest things / From least suggestions," "willing to work and to be wrought upon" (*1805* XII, 91; XIII, 90–100). This was a drastic circumscription of the potential audience of *The Recluse*. And while such passages in *The Prelude* gave substance to the 1814 Preface's claim for the subterraneous mode of *The Recluse*, the unpublished status of that poem meant that Wordsworth's drift was bound to be far from obvious even to those higher minded contemporaries whom he intended to address. In his sketch of Wordsworth in *The Spirit of the Age* (1825), William Hazlitt summed up the problem: *The Excursion*, he wrote, "affects a system without having any intelligible clue to one" (Cook ed. 1999, 353).

By the time of his letter to Christopher in November 1814, Wordsworth had begun to feel rather anxious regarding his readers' imaginative sympathy. In mid-August the first installment of Hazlitt's three-part review for *The Examiner* mixed its high praise for the poem with a deeply negative reading of the "Gothic" plan for *The Recluse*. "[T]his very original and powerful performance," Hazlitt speculated, might nevertheless "remain like one of those stupendous but half-finished structures which have been suffered to moulder into decay, because the cost and labour attending them exceeded their use or beauty" (*The Examiner*, August 21, 1814, 541). The "crushing" review of *The Excursion* by Francis Jeffrey in the November edition of the *Edinburgh Review* dismissed the Preface's careful "allusion" to Gothic architecture as an "attempt...rather unsuccessfully made to explain the whole design" (Robert Woof, ed. 2001, 382).[1] And even Wordsworth's friend Charles Lamb's review for the *Quarterly* (published January 8, 1815 after substantial alterations by the editor William Gifford [Wu 1995, 128]) passed over the *Recluse* plan in silence, calling *The Excursion* "in itself, a complete and legitimate production" (Robert Woof, ed., 407). If the *Quarterly*'s application of the language of completeness and legitimacy to the published poem implies the illegitimacy of Wordsworth's attempt to define *The Recluse* in terms of parts withheld or unwritten, the *Augustan Review* interpreted the plan as a hackneyed recourse to the inexpressibility motif belabored by authors of "sensibility" like Laurence Sterne:

> The *first* not having been completed to the author's satisfaction, the second division has been published (as usual), at the *earnest entreaties* of some valued friends—'its interest not depending, in any great degree, on the preceding part.' The want of connection is therefore candidly acknowledged; and as a kind of *prospectus* of the *whole* poem, a passage is given in the preface, from the conclusion of the first book of the 'Recluse,' *not yet published*. (*Augustan Review* 1 [1815], 347)

The Shandean absurdity of founding *The Excursion* in unpublished and unwritten works—of tracing its lineage in absence and in futurity—leads the *Augustan* to assume that *The Recluse* might never be completed because it had never seriously been contemplated. Thus was set the pattern of ruining readings of the plan that would later culminate in Byron's jibe in the "Dedication" to *Don Juan* at Wordsworth's "rather long 'Excursion,'" whose comprehensive reader "would be able / To add a story to the Tower of Babel" (Steffan and Pratt, eds. 1957, II, 11), and in Blake's telling Henry Crabb Robinson that "the preface to the Excursion" had "caused him a bowel complaint which nearly killed him" (Bentley, ed. 1969, 323–26). Clearly, neither "coxcomb" Jeffrey nor "cockney" Hazlitt was Wordsworth's ideal "attentive Reader." Hazlitt had indeed been attacked in the *British Critic* for November 1806 for attempting "to undermine the Christian Religion" by none other than Christopher Wordsworth (Robert Woof, ed., 368). And though Wordsworth had certainly read Hazlitt's review by the end of October, it is unclear whether he ever knew either Jeffrey's or Lamb's reviews other than by report (Wu 1995, 104, 118–19, 128–29). Nevertheless, the rest of his letter to Christopher reveals his misgivings: "I have not yet heard anything of the Sale of the Excursion; which I should have done had it been such as was likely to lead the way to the steady demand of a second Edition" (*MY* II, 171).

Wordsworth would have known the potential dangers of playing on the fragmentary connotations of the Gothic. They had been amply demonstrated a few years earlier in the hostile reception (to which Wordsworth was alerted by Southey [Wu 1995, 11]) of Anna Barbauld's poem prophesying British decline and the transfer of world-empire to America, *Eighteen Hundred and Eleven*. Barbauld's poem generated a proleptic imagination of the nation as a Gothic ruin:

> Night, Gothic night, again may shade the plains
> Where Power is seated, and where Science reigns;
> England, the seat of arts, be only known
> By the grey ruin and the mouldering stone...
> (Barbauld 1825, I, 238–39, ll. 121–24)

James Chandler has suggested that the critical savaging Barbauld received from John Wilson Croker of the Tory *Quarterly Review* was occasioned by *Eighteen Hundred and Eleven*'s development of a subversive historicist sensibility that took Britain as the entropic "meter" of the state of the world (Chandler 1998, 110–120). But beyond this, Croker's particular indignation at the poem's fantasy of Britain as a

Gothic ruin (*QR* 7:14 [1812], 310–312) suggests that Gothic architecture was, at this historical moment, intimately associated with the British national imaginary. Images of Gothic ruination tapped into deep reserves of anxiety about Britain's long-term imperial standing.

With this case in recent memory, whose issue had been Barbauld's retirement from the literary scene, it would not have been lost on Wordsworth that the reviews of *The Excursion* made his "gothic Church" look uncomfortably similar to Barbauld's English ruins. After all, the Gothic architecture of the Preface clearly alluded at some level to the earlier place-and-date-poem, "Lines, Written a few miles above Tintern Abbey, On revisiting the banks of the Wye during a tour, July 13, 1798;" a poem whose dominant tropes of litotes and repetition activate the allusion in the title date to the eve of the seismic historical and geopolitical shifts of the French Revolution. Wordsworth's fervent vision of a declining nation of selfish men in "dreary" cities, articulated during a "tour" of national ruins, indeed anticipates much of Barbauld imagination of the nation as a shadow of its former self, firmly relegated to the domain of past-ness by American tourists, filled with "duteous zeal," making "pilgrimage" to its ruins to "press the sod" formerly "By statesmen, sages, poets, heroes, trod" (Barbauld 1825, I, 239, ll. 129–31; *MW* 131–35).

James Garrett suggests that both Barbauld's poem and "Tintern Abbey" envisage the transformation of the nation into a "national museum that has come to encompass virtually every part of the nation itself" (2008, 12). Since, for Garrett, the museum impulse is intimately associated with nationalism, the politics of Wordsworth's poem are relatively straightforward. If "the poet [is] a guide pointing to the noticeable features of the landscape" (158), and if the reader's "responsiveness" to his "cues" is necessary to prove a "right to citizenship" (160), then the poet is also the guardian and gatekeeper of the nation as currently constituted. But this is to reckon without the contemporary view of date-poems like Barbauld's and Wordsworth's as highly political, and as subversive of the existing order. To place something in a museum is, by the same token, to confirm its real-world impotency—the artifact's accumulation of cultural resonance occurring, according to Stephen Greenblatt (1990, 89–90), simultaneously with its amputation from its enabling social and material context. And since it seems to have been the museum-treatment given to the nation in Barbauld's poem that angered Croker, Wordsworth might well have feared that his architectural figure of 1814 lent itself too readily to a similarly hostile reading.

Wordsworth had certainly tacked dangerously close to the same historicist wind in his earlier publications. "London, 1802," for example, places and dates very specifically the description of England as "a fen / Of stagnant waters," with her "dower" of happiness, Gothic "hall and bower," now "forfei[t]" (*MW* 286; ll. 2–6; see also Chandler 1998, 121n). And in this connection it is intriguing to note that whereas in Wordsworth's 1807 publication, *Poems, in Two Volumes*, this sonnet is the first in a series of nine of the "Sonnets Dedicated to Liberty" indexed anonymously under the "historicist" rubric of sonnet thirteen, "Written in London, September, 1802," it appears in the 1815 publication *Poems* (like the other sonnets) indexed instead by its own time-and-place non-specific opening phrase, "Milton!—" (1807, I, iv; 1815, I, xlix). This difference in titling in publications on either side of *Eighteen Hundred and Eleven* is registered only in their tables of contents, and not in their actual texts, which both have the same time and place specifications. But since Wordsworth told Lady Beaumont that the sonnets of the 1807 edition "collectively make a Poem on the subject of civil Liberty and national independence" (*MY* I, 147), we should be slow to dismiss a change of emphasis even within such paratextual matter. In fact, a closer look at the two tables of contents reveals a clear shift away from an historical presentation of the sonnets. The table of 1807 mirrors the argumentative form used in many of the sonnets themselves, with ten lines stating the problem "London, September, 1802," a turn at the eleventh line with "To the Men of Kent. October, 1803," and a final couplet headed "Anticipation. October, 1803." The table of 1815, however, simply lumps these fourteen poems with the twelve before them in a list of twenty-six separate sonnets with separate topics. The change in the presentation of the sonnets on liberty from 1807 to 1815 is, thus, from the (dangerous) appearance of a date-poem like Barbauld's, to the (safe) look of a series of timeless meditations on liberty. Since, moreover, the composite shadow-poem of 1807 is all about Britain's Gothic legacy—the "ancient English dower / Of inward happiness" localized in "hall and bower," the libertarian "charters" and chivalric code of the men of Kent, and English victory in an imagined rerun of 1066 (*MW* 286–90)—Wordsworth's careful removal of the markers of an historicist sensibility suggests an increasing anxiety to avoid the appearance of attempting, like Barbauld, to "date" the nation.

The dismaying alternative behind the letter to Christopher is, hence, that either Wordsworth or the unappreciative public—either the "Author" who has failed to "communicate," or the reading nation that has failed to grasp and to appreciate, the Gothic architecture of *The Excursion*—might be found deficient in both poetry and patriotism. Accordingly, Wordsworth's account of the suitably "enchanted" Bishop of London, and the "one opinion on the subject," represents a subtle coercion of Christopher to prove himself, and to save them all together, by recognizing the poem as an Anglican epic.

It is difficult to overstate the ideological significance of Wordsworth's "allusion" to Gothic architecture. Indeed, by 1814, Britain's Gothic patrimony had become deeply involved in questions of cultural and political identity. The notion that England was a "Gothic" nation had in fact been central to political discourse since at least the era of the Civil War, when republicans and levelers asserted the rights of the free-born Englishman on the grounds of descent from the Germanic Saxons, who had transplanted their pristine "*Gothique* Law" into Britain (Kliger 1952, 6). After the Glorious Revolution, historical and constitutional writers and periodicals like the *Gentleman's Magazine* constructed the Gothic as a consummately Protestant style. In 1695, William Temple, who was in his time both a servant of the Restoration and a close associate of William of Orange, published an *Introduction to the History of England* that pictured England as "one Branch of those *Gothick* nations" that had anciently come "Swarming from the Northern Hive," and that had absorbed subsequent invaders with minimal change to its government or its customs (Temple 1708, 44, 80, 134–38). In the 1730s, Richard Temple, first Viscount Cobham and leader of the opposition, built a Gothic "Temple of Liberty" at Stowe bearing the proud inscription, "I thank God that I am not a Roman"—in architecture, politics, or religion (Brooks 1999, 55). Baron Charles de Montesquieu's *Spirit of Laws* (1750) saw a "Gothic government"—"the best species of constitution" imaginable—yet subsisting in England (Montesquieu 1750, I, 233). The *Gentleman's Magazine*, meanwhile, set about the task of grafting the elite vogue for the Gothic onto the newly created public sphere.

Launched in 1731, the *Gentleman's* regularly reprinted the remarks of weekly journals on current affairs, and in December 1739 it carried articles from *Common Sense* lamenting the craze for architectural innovation among the gentry. Since, the anonymous author opined, architectural "Improvement" on the continent had "quite destroyed" its "ancient Senate-Houses," the proposed rebuilding of Parliament House should be done "intirely in the antient Gothick Stile, after one of those excellent Plans left us by our *Saxon* Ancestors" (*GM* 9 [1739], 635). Warmed by this rhetoric, *Common Sense* went on to equate "the bold Arches and the solid Pillars" of Gothic architecture with the solidity of the "old *Gothick* Constitution":

> Methinks there was something respectable in those old hospitable *Gothick* halls, hung round with the Helmets, Breast-Plates, and Swords of our Ancestors; I entered them with a Constitutional Sort of Reverence and look'd upon those arms with Gratitude, as the Terror of former Ministers and the Check of Kings. Nay, I even imagin'd that I here saw some of those good Swords that had procur'd the Confirmation of *Magna Charta*, and humbled Spencers and Gavestons...Our old *Gothick* Constitution had a noble strength and Simplicity in it, which was well enough represented by the bold Arches and the solid Pillars of the Edifices of those Days. And I have not observed that the modern Refinements in either have in the least added to their Strength and Solidity. (*GM* 9 [1739], 641)

According to Samuel Kliger, this was quintessentially "the Whig taste in the fine arts" (Kliger 1952, 27). The "Constitutional Sort of Reverence" needed to appreciate Gothic architecture operates here as a sort of alembic between the "constitution" of the individual and the constitution of the country. The reverential makeup of the ideal Whig subject is sublimated and altered, through the associations of Gothic architecture, into a national Constitution that commands reverence.

This imaginative Gothic constitutionalism was extended still further in the writings of William Blackstone, the preeminent common-law theorist of the eighteenth century. In his *Commentaries on the Laws of England* (1765–69), Blackstone conceived England's constitutional and legal history, with its descent from time immemorial and its gradual articulation through the common law, as resembling "an old Gothic castle, erected in the days of chivalry, but fitted up for a modern inhabitant" (Blackstone 1791, III, 268). "The moated ramparts, the embattled towers, and the trophied halls, are magnificent and venerable," he added, "but useless, and therefore neglected. The inferior apartments, now accommodated to daily use, are cheerful and commodious, though their approaches may be winding and difficult." The similarity here with the Gothic language of the Whig periodical *Common Sense* is purely superficial, and indeed it has much closer affinities with Horace Walpole's *Castle of Otranto* (1764), in which an exploration of labyrinthine architecture dramatizes and stands in for the explicit articulation of historical knowledge. Where *Common Sense* had spoken of "hospitable *Gothick* halls" as physical embodiments of an ongoing libertarian tradition, Blackstone speaks only of redundant "trophied halls," holdovers from a "Gothic" past that was for him, in James Watt's phrase, a "semi-imaginary division of history" (Watt 1999, 46). Indeed, as Gerald J. Postema notes, the Gothic figure is here used expressly to describe the common law process of making "legal fictions" (Postema 1986, 12). By reducing the Gothic to a set of apparently redundant features that invite a retrospective and ultimately fictional account of constitutional development, Blackstone disarmed it of its real historical association with radical politics. As the legal reformer Jeremy Bentham complained in his *Fragment on Government* (1776), "[H]e turns the Law into a Castle, for the purpose of opposing every idea of 'fundamental' reparation" (Bentham 1776, xxxii–xxxiv).

By the end of the eighteenth century the term "Gothic" had, as Michael Gamer notes, modulated into a crucial cultural marker. It was the watchword of the emphatically "masculine and antiquarian tradition" constructed by writers such as Richard Hurd, Thomas Warton, and Thomas Percy out of the relics of the national past (Gamer 2000, 49). It was also a major bone of political contention in the wake of the French Revolution; a period in which, as Wordsworth put it, the "meagre, stale, forbidding ways / Of custom, law and statute, took at once / The attraction of a country in romance" (*1805* X, 694–96). The question of national tradition and its bearing on the modern nation became increasingly important as the war with France intensified. As Daniel Abramson has recently argued, the twenty-year conflict with France increasingly undercut "the dominance of élite cosmopolitan classicism and fostered a more populist, cultural nationalism, oriented towards medievalism" (McCalman, ed. 1999, 266). Edmund Burke, one of the figureheads of this movement, avoided the Gothic theory in politics and explicitly rejected "the superstition of antiquarians." But his account of British liberty, with its "ensigns armorial," its "gallery of portraits, its monumental inscriptions, its records, evidences, and titles," is made in the very image of a Gothic hall (Burke 1987, 30). With neoclassicism subsequently finding its "most powerful benefactor" in Napoleon (Hearn 2003, 11), the Gothic progressively became identified—in books, newspapers, and magazines—as an essentially English, or at least, an essentially un-French, or "antiGallican" style.

The work of John Carter—architect, journalist, and renegade member of the Society of Antiquaries—provides a metonymy of this (conservative) culture of the Gothic. In 1814 Carter published the second installment of his monumental study, the *Ancient Architecture of England*. The Society of Antiquaries had already claimed in 1800 that Gothic was "properly...called English architecture, for if it had not its origin in this country, it certainly arrived at maturity here"

(Warton, Bentham, Grose, and Milner 1800, iii). But Carter went much further. He held that the "characteristic" pointed arch was a "growing style" whose stages could be traced strictly within England, and he inferred from the "Gothic" features of Malmesbury Abbey the existence of a rudimentary Gothic style in England at its foundation in AD 675 (Crook 1995, 42). Adopting the "immemorial" mentality of English common law—described by J. G. A. Pocock as an introspective view of the nation "making its own laws, untouched by foreign influences, in a process without a beginning" (Pocock 1987, 41)—Carter apparently placed the idea that Gothic was English beyond any possible foreign encroachment.

So when, as J. Mordaunt Crook notes, J. S. Hawkins published his *History of the Origin and Establishment of Gothic Architecture* in 1813, which "pointed out that France, in particular Suger's Saint-Denis [1144 AD] might well be the birthplace of Gothic, Carter grew splenetic…[A]n importation of the entire process, that miraculous integration of the Gothic system, seemed surely impossible" (Crook 1995, 42). His counterattack took place in the already heavily "Gothic" pages of the *Gentleman's Magazine*. Described by Hazlitt in 1823 as an "agreeable" repository of "useless antiquity" and "lingering remains" (*Edinburgh Review* [1823], 369), the *Gentleman's* had, as I noted above, been rhapsodizing on "the antient Gothick Stile" of "our *Saxon* Ancestors" since the 1730s. The political connotations of this "Gothic" stance became increasingly clear in the 1790s, when the magazine not only took a staunch editorial line against all attempts "to regovern the world," but also, as Kevin Gilmartin notes, invoked its own long duration, its lifetime's worth of steady social chronicling, and its miscellaneous aesthetic as the antithesis of French philosophy and its pretensions of "a new Aera in the history of the world" (Gilmartin 2007, 98, 111). Continuing to appear with a frontispiece of an imposing Gothic gate, which, as the magazine's preface for 1796 put it, gave the miscellany "promising Auspices" even in these dark times, the *Gentleman's* offered its "Variety" to "Men of deep reflection" and literary taste as a "Shelter…from the Tumults of the World" (qtd. in Gilmartin 2007, 111). And with Carter on board as "An Artist and an Antiquary" from 1799, its pages were increasingly dominated by Gothic architecture (Kuist 1982, 47; Clark 1962, 72–76). This shift was straightforwardly ideological. There was, Carter wrote in March 1799, no better way to "aid the general cause" against French "innovation" than to "stimulate my countrymen to think well of their own national memorials" (*GM* 69 [1799], 190). And in October 1813, the magazine's English Gothic regime turned militant as Carter threw down his "gauntlet of determined objection" and declared open war on Hawkins:

> [D]isplaying the British standard of the Pointed style of architecture against your anti-national flag of geometric phantasies, to conquer or fall in the attempt: but a Briton struggling for a Briton's rights, in defence of an art and science all his own, must never doubt or fear. I come! (*GM* 83 [1813], 321)

In February 1814, this "anti-national" denunciation modulated into the charge that in tracing the origins of the Gothic style to France, Hawkins was acting as a sort of architectural fifth-columnist. He was, Carter alleged, working "to give succour to his dear friends on the other side of the water, and disparage the questionable faculties of his poor countrymen here at home" (*GM* 84 [1814], 135). By April, the month in which Napoleon was dethroned and France received a new Constitution, "assimilated," in the words of the magazine, "to the British" (*GM* 84 [1814], 396), Carter was figuring Hawkins as a French agent captured and detained for reeducation:

> Mr. H. who has raised all his hopes in having the honour to establish the origin of Gothic on the land of our natural Enemies, must be compelled to humble his lofty propositions, and look in future with more veneration to the heretofore genius of his countrymen...(*GM* 84 [1814], 330)

To deny in the spring of 1814 that Gothic was English was effectively to side with the defeated Napoleonic regime, and implicitly to deny the legitimacy of a British-style constitution. In this light, Wordsworth's "gothic Church" of April 1814 looks overtly political. Promulgating an unwritten poetical constitution ("not...formally to announce a system") at the moment of victory over Napoleon's Continental System, Wordsworth announces *The Recluse* as an ideally nationalist poem; as the archetypal work of "a poet and an Englishman." He thus appears to stand in the avant-garde of the *Gentleman's Magazine*'s English Gothic campaign; to be, as Kenneth Johnston has suggested, an intellectual pioneer of the nineteenth century's Gothic Revival (Johnston 1984, xxiii). Augustus Pugin's call in the late 1830s and early 1840s for a more religious architecture and for truth in materials ("better to do a little substantially and consistently with truth, than to produce a great but fictitious effect" [Pugin 2003, 45]) is prefigured in Wordsworth's desire to construct his verse as the medieval churches had been built.

Wordsworth had been an occasional reader of the *Gentleman's* since the early 1790s, and he is quite likely to have come across Carter's articles on Gothic architecture while, in Dorothy's phrase, he "wasted his mind in the Magazines" (Wu 1993, 62 and 1995, 137–38; Pamela Woof, ed. 1991, 59). Whether or not Wordsworth took inspiration for his "gothic Church" from the *Gentleman's*, the magazine certainly saw him as a poet and an Englishman after its own heart. *The White Doe of Rylstone* (1815), a romance set in the remains of Bolton Priory, was a work whose "real pathos" proved Wordsworth's "high rank among the living Poets of his Country" (*GM* 85 [1815], 524). If Robert Southey had taken on the Gothic constitutionalism of the *Gentleman's* in his claim that the "tranquillizing sound" of "sabbath bells" and the sight of "the church and church-yard" were vital tools in forging national solidarity (*QR* 8:16 [1812], 337–38), then Wordsworth's poem went one better. It concludes with a complex prosopopeia whereby the "Sabbath bells" of ruined Bolton Priory are heard across the centuries to speak out a poignant plea for aid in the face of national division: "God us ayde" (*WDR* 142; ll. 1781, 1793). And if, as I have suggested, it is possible to detect a powerful resonance between Wordsworth's "gothic Church" and the *Gentleman's* English Gothic campaign, that resonance develops into a swelling chord in a letter of April 1816 to John Scott, in which Wordsworth attempts to approximate "the true British character" by imagining a series of responses to a series of images of the British constitution:

> Suppose the opposition as a body, or take them in classes, the Grenvilles, the Wellesleys, the Foxites, the Burdettites, and let your imagination carry them in procession through Westminster Hall, and let them pass thence into the adjoining Abbey, and give them credit for feeling the utmost and best that they are capable of feeling in connection with these venerable and sacred places, and say frankly whether you would be satisfied with the result. Imagine them to be looking from a green hill over a rich landscape diversified by Spires and Church Towers and hamlets, and all the happy images of English landscape, would their sensations come much nearer to what one would desire; in a word have [they] becoming reverence of the English character, and do they value as they ought, and even as their opponents do, the Constitution of the country, in Church and State. (*MY* II, 304)

As James Garrett notes, "[b]y shifting the burden of patriotism from overt act to intricate response," Wordsworth here circumvents loyalism of the merely conformist, flag-waving variety, and "establishes a new test for inclusion, one focused on the individual's response to an idealization of the local and specific," to "an imagined feudal landscape of Church and hamlet" (2008, 110). Reliant as it is upon an intricate inwardness that is ultimately unknowable and unquantifiable, this virtual proof of allegiance through a "becoming reverence" of constitutional imagery has a suspicious and an invasive quality that marks it as a historically specific product of what Thomas Pfau sees as the "paranoid" culture of the 1790s, especially as evidenced in the treason trials of 1794 (Pfau 2005, 146–90). These trials—which Wordsworth was vehement in denouncing at the time—saw the government prosecution construct treasons by imputing just such intricate chains of inward associations to a group of constitutional reformers belonging to the London Corresponding Society. In an instruction to the jury that has uncomfortable parallels with Wordsworth's imaginative test of allegiance, Judge James Eyre ordered the jury to treat any action toward reform as evidence of treason—narrowly defined by medieval statute as an imaginative design to kill the king—and to treat the invisible nature of the supposed "conspiracy" and the evanescent nature of the government's "evidence" of its existence as a point *against* the defendants:

> If...it should appear that it has entered into the heart of any man who is a subject of this country, to design, to overthrow the whole government of the country, to pull down and to subvert from its very foundations the British monarchy, that glorious fabric which it has been the work of ages to erect, maintain, and support, which has been cemented with the best blood of our ancestors; to design such a horrible ruin and devastation, which no king could survive, a crime of such a magnitude that no lawgiver in this country ever ventured to contemplate it in its whole extent...the complication and enormous extent of such a design will not prevent its being distinctly seen...(qtd. in Pfau 2005, 163)

In suggesting that an attack upon one of the bases of the "glorious fabric"—the monarchy—would result in the "overthrow [of] the whole government of the country," Eyre "shows th[e] myth of the ancient constitution to be acutely nervous and unstable" (Pfau 2005, 163). The supposedly monstrous, "enormous" and complex "design," is figuratively entangled with the "glorious fabric," cemented with blood, of the constitution itself—suggesting the unconscious perception by even the government prosecutors that the monstrosity is within the "Gothic" state itself. But the most important point is to note the similarity between Eyre, judging of the loyalty of the LCS by their imaginative associations, and parlaying the standard image of the constitution as a Gothic edifice into an image of the king literally perishing amidst its wreckage, and Wordsworth testing the loyalty of the "opposition" by way of their response to a politicized architecture.

Wordsworth's architectural constitutionalism is marked, then, by the oppositional politics of the 1790s. But his "becoming reverence" of the English "character" and "Constitution" is also a refinement of the longstanding *Gentleman's* depiction of a "Constitutional Sort of Reverence" as unfailingly communicated by the sight of England's patrimony of Gothic architecture. Fed back into literary culture through Wordsworth's poetry and prose—the landscape subservient to the "old Church-tower" at the end of *The Excursion*, and the "lowly pile" of the chapel of Buttermere, described in the prose section of *The River Duddon* (1820) as helping a "Patriot" to "cal[l] to mind the stately fabrics of Canterbury, York, or Westminster" and thus to visualize the "all-pervading...venerable Establishment" (270)—the association between Gothic architecture and the constitution was thoroughly naturalized by the 1830s. So much so, indeed, that the *Gentleman's Magazine*'s correspondent on the Westminster fire of October 16, 1834 felt, "as an antiquary and a British subject," "as if a link would be burst asunder in my national existence" as he witnessed the destruction of the "palladium of the English monarchy," the "giant of the Gothic age" (*GM* 2 [new series, 1834], 477). This invention of a personal "national existence" through the associations of Gothic architecture epitomizes the (Wordsworthian) culture of the Gothic, visible in its "pregnant moment" in 1814, struggling into life by 1816, and full-fledged by the 1830s.

But this is not the only story. To William Hazlitt, whose criticism has been well described by Tim Fulford as a "counterweight" to the "growing conservatism" of Wordsworth's imagination, the "Gothic" attitude adumbrated in *The Excursion* appeared wholly retrograde (Fulford 1996, 195). Hazlitt's review of *The Excursion*, mentioned earlier, had a second installment on 28 August. Focusing now on the poem's mixture of anecdote and "philosophy," on the way that it proceeds by, as Geoffrey Hartman puts it, "heap[ing] up exempla in the medieval manner" (1975, 319), Hazlitt's second review found it defective on the grounds that the "connection" between the "particular illustration" and the "general principle" it was intended to demonstrate was "more difficult to find out than to understand the general principle itself" (*The Examiner*, August 28, 1814, 555). Exploiting Wordsworth's refusal to "announce a system," and opening up the problematics of exemplarity and representativeness in the "narrative" procedure whereby the character of the Pastor supplements the "aery" philosophy of the Wanderer by "Giv[ing] us, for our abstractions, solid facts" (V, 634–39; Bushell, Butler, and Jaye, eds. 2007, 184), Hazlitt's review hereby effectively equated Wordsworth's unintelligible poetics with the discourse of casuistry. Casuistry, a species of moral calculus, was virtually synonymous in Britain with the reviled and ultra-"Gothic" Jesuit order that had been reconstituted by papal bull only weeks before.[2] Lest his readers miss the point that a poem that required or inculcated such moral sophistication in its readership must be much less wholesomely Anglican than it seemed, Hazlitt then harked back to the architectural analogy to align Wordsworth with the Gothic restoration at large. Wordsworth, out of sympathy with his own "memorable lines" on the French Revolution, was now perilously close to those maliciously hoping to "efface" its gains. Such a scheme, Hazlitt announced defiantly, was not to be achieved by "the chaunting of *Te Deums* in all the churches of Christendom" (*The Examiner*, August 28, 1814, 558).

Hazlitt's anti-Gothic rhetoric probably derives much of its angst from the knowledge that under his hero Napoleon the Revolution had become, as he later put it, at best a "burlesque" on "the Gothic [forms] of civilized Europe" (Howe, ed. 1930–34, XIV, 238–42). When in December 1804 Napoleon was crowned Emperor—an event Wordsworth likened to the mechanical operation of an "opera phantom" (*1805* X, 940)—it was in a Notre-Dame that had been decorated, as *The Annual Register* for 1804 slightly put it, "with all the sumptuousness which French ingenuity could devise" (1806, 185), with the whole façade "clad with a cardboard Gothic exterior" (Horne 2004, 39). And the Empire of 1804 was no sooner born than incorporated with the revived writ of Rome by Napoleon's order that "*Veni Creator* and *Te Deum*…be sung in all the churches" of Paris (*The Annual Register…1804*, 1806, 175–77). In a sense, then, Hazlitt's angry denunciation of Wordsworth's "Gothic" backsliding is simply the obverse of Johnston's sunny vision of his "Gothic" pioneering. Both views reflect the fact that Gothic was back with a vengeance, and that Wordsworth was highly attuned to the way the cultural wind was blowing.

For Hazlitt, however, Wordsworth's new stance was not simply a change for the worse but, as he put it in *The Spirit of the Age* (1825), a "dereliction" of his early commitment to "the primal movements of the heart":

> His later philosophic productions have a somewhat different character. They are a departure from, a dereliction of his first principles. They are classical and courtly. They are polished in style without being gaudy;

dignified in subject, without affectation. They seem to have been composed not in a cottage at Grasmere, but among the half-inspired groves and stately recollections of Cole-Orton. (Cook, ed. 1999, 351–52)

*Laodamia*, a poem that transposes the stoicism of the domestic, "Gothic" *Excursion* onto the ground of ancient Greece and Troy, is said to "breath[e] the pure spirit of the finest fragments of antiquity;" its "glossy brilliancy" arising "from the perfection of the finishing, like that of careful sculpture, not from the gaudy coloring—the texture of the thoughts has the smoothness and solidity of marble." This image of Wordsworth as a "fragment of antiquity" incongruously located in the British Lakes alludes to the controversial vogue for appropriating and domesticating the ruined artifacts of classical civilization—epitomized in the widespread condemnation of the actions of the Scots Lord Elgin in seizing and shipping home a collection of sculptures from the Parthenon, and given epigrammatic expression by Byron's friend, John Hobhouse's recording of the Acropolis graffito: "Quod non fecerunt Gothi, hoc fecerunt Scoti" (qtd. in St Clair 1967, 193). Indeed, Hazlitt's comments on Wordsworth here allude in detail to his earlier article on the Elgin marbles, in which he praised their realism and "vital" "chiar-oscuro," as against the "insipid mediocrity" (Cook ed. 1999, 281–88) of the neoclassical taste (shared by George Beaumont, Wordsworth's friend and the proprietor of Coleorton [Rovee 2006, 141]) that preferred the "smooth finish" of the British Museum's existing collection of "restored statues" (Thomas 2008, 83). Hazlitt thus figures Wordsworth as something like a Grecian statue cobbled together from the rubble of a ruined British monastery. The "smooth texture" of the surfaces of his "later productions" belies (even as it unwittingly betrays) their mosaic composition from the Gothic ruin of his self-"dereliction." For Hazlitt, Wordsworth's later productions cannot be understood, or seen for the tortured works of restoration and political dereliction that they are, without a grasp of the original structure from whose rubble they are made. In order, therefore, to make better sense both of Wordsworth's late Gothicism, and of what it meant to Hazlitt and other contemporaries, it is necessary to turn now to look in more detail at the role of the Gothic in the culture and politics of the 1790s and early 1800s.

## Jacobins and Goths

Custom and the customary were at the heart of political debate in the early 1790s. Tradition was claimed by Anti-Jacobins such as Edmund

Burke as something prescriptive of the existing social and political order, so that the written form of the law only expressed or declared a situation existing time out of mind. For the reformers who composed the LCS, meanwhile, tradition connoted something like a zeitgeist, an immense, unconscious, immemorial force dwelling amongst the people, a tide of change, which forever outstripped the written law, and with which the written law needed to be brought into line. As Susan Manly has argued, the struggle over custom was in large part literary: the centrality of custom to political discourse being an effect of the mid-eighteenth-century rise of the periodical press, which, through its instantiation of the public sphere, "irrevocably alter[ed] the relationship of government and the governed," with government by ostensible force shading insensibly into "a system purporting to take account of the customary usages accepted as legitimate by the masses" (Manly, 65). The periodical press thus represented a strictly virtual instantiation of public opinion; the political ambivalence of which is neatly captured in the statement of a correspondent for *The World* in 1757 that the rise of the periodical press had been a "revolution…in the kingdom of learning, which has introduced the levelling principle, with much better success than it ever met with in politics" (qtd. in Keen 2008, 211). As Paul Keen notes, the phrasing here leaves it open whether the press is democracy's "precursor" or its "alternative" (211). While their belief that the law was properly only an expression of the "deeper reality" of national custom meant that conservatives took the recording activities of the periodicals as an ongoing ratification of the law as currently constituted, radical thinkers, who followed Rousseau in viewing the written law as only the formal counterpart of the law of custom inscribed on the heart of the people, saw the ongoing rearticulation of that law in the pages of the periodicals as increasingly deserving of adequate political recognition (Manly, 65). The difference in emphasis between these two positions suggests that the political struggle of the 1790s was ultimately a struggle to make the law conform to the deep-structural new reality that had insensibly come into being over the preceding decades—radicals seeking to make concrete and real the newly created public sphere, and conservatives seeking to preserve that same virtual system of public consciousness, with all the advantages it conferred on the ruling elite. This contest was played out, as Kevin Gilmartin has argued, through the contrasting rhetorical routines of periodical publications on either side of the question:

> Where radical editors and journalists were busy promoting themselves as agents of public pressure for parliamentary reform, conservative

periodicals were far more cautious about advancing any direct claim upon established political institutions. Though aggressive and even reckless in their polemical style, they ranged themselves against the idea that the state should become more responsive to public opinion as it was increasingly conditioned and expressed in print. (Gilmartin, 103)

The *Anti-Jacobin* (1797–98), which calibrated its eight-month performance against the duration of the parliamentary term, and dissolved itself when Parliament sat, is only the most striking example of the tendency of conservative publications to present themselves as strictly auxiliary to government, in order to square the rhetorical circle involved in mounting an extragovernmental press campaign in order to recruit public opinion against the idea that public opinion had any bearing upon the legislature (Gilmartin, 120). John Reeve's loyalist "Association" (1792–94) articulated this vertiginous sense of the loyalist critical enterprise in the claim of its *Proceedings* that while it was "irregular" "[t]o associate in the forms in which *they* do," in order to "take cognizance of what is transacted by the Executive and the Legislative Powers," its own secondary enterprise was (somehow) entirely regular (qtd. in Gilmartin, 43). Admitting that any association had the effect of "intercepting...some of that force, and confidence of the people, which should pass on to their only true centre, the constituted Executive and Legislative Authorities," the Association nevertheless claimed that "where such an irregularity has been once permitted, and the balance of the system seems to be affected by it, the equilibrium perhaps cannot be more naturally restored, than by placing a counterpoise of the same sort on the other side." The rhetoric of the *Proceedings* veers thus between an abject admission of its own compounded illegitimacy—driven to cite illegitimate meetings and publications as a precedent for its own appearance—and a "Gothic" (if not positively alchemical) faith in the regenerative power of increasing reflexivity.

The debate over custom was thus played out in fairly explicit terms in the periodicals. In a society characterized by burgeoning literacy-rates, and in which a thinker like William Godwin could speak seriously of the "spirit of philosophy" having "infused itself" into the modern prose style by way of the periodical press, debates about material inequality and political representation were inevitably encoded as debates about language (Manly, 46–47, 80, 86). The medieval ballad tradition was central to this debate over the nature of custom and tradition. Where, for instance, Walter Scott's *Minstrelsy of the Scottish Border* represented the medieval ballad as a socially inert literary artifact, produced by an elite poet for an elite culture, and functioning as a "depositar[y]" of "tradition," the radical antiquarian Joseph Ritson regarded it as what Susan Manly calls "a repository of value, encapsulating historical and political knowledge" held in common amongst the people, and "revealing the capacity of common people to create lasting sources of pleasure and interest" (70). The vulgar or "Gothic" artifact and its interpretation thus assumed a central role in the construction of national culture.

In 1605, Richard Verstegan had remarked in his *Restitution of Decayed Intelligence* that the Normans "could not Conquer the English language as they did the land" (Verstegan 1605, 222), beginning the long tradition that Christopher Hill has called "linguistic Saxonism," the literary counterpart to the political theory of the "Norman Yoke" (Hill 1968, 79). Ideas about the Conquest altered in the wake of the welcomed invasion of the Glorious Revolution, and by the middle of the eighteenth century, Thomas Warton's *History of English Poetry* (1774–81) inverted Verstegan's view, dating English poetry to the Norman Conquest on the grounds that at that date a still recognizable constitution was established.[3] Warton's *History* envisaged the Conquest as a "mighty revolution [that] obliterated almost all relation to the former inhabitants of this island; and procured that signal change in our policy, constitution and public manners, the effects of which have reached modern times" (Warton 1824, I, 8). Since the Conquest crystallized England as a "policy," Warton argued that the poetry of the time before the Conquest could not properly be considered as *English* poetry. Poetry that does not posit a political constitution similar to that which obtains at the present day thus becomes, in the national-historical view, null and void.

Thomas Percy began to undo this reductive ratio between poetry and the constitution by taking a somewhat longer view. As I noted in the introduction, Percy envisaged a line of "lineal descent" from the Songs of the ancient Goths to the "Romances of Chivalry," which had, as Richard Hurd had suggested, devolved upon Spenser's *Faerie Queene*, and Percy argued that this "Gothic" literary tradition was cognate with a political inheritance of enlightenment and liberty. Nor was linguistic Saxonism without its supporters in the late eighteenth century. Though Joseph Ritson's *Select Collection of English Songs* (1783) admitted that the Conquest was a key moment in the development of the English language (Ritson 1783, xlv–xlvi), the disconnection between Saxon and "modern" England was, he wrote in response to Warton in 1782, a malicious lie:

> "[T]hat the Saxon poetry has no connection with the nature and purpose of 'your' present undertaking," is an assertion, one may safely

venture to say, as new as it is ill-grounded, and full of mischief. Though the great revolution produced by the Norman invaders effected "that signal change in our policy, constitution, and public manners," which has in its consequences "reached modern times," yet neither the Saxon people nor the Saxon tongue was thereby eradicated. You, Sir, have sometimes been a biographer; and did you ever find it necessary to commence the story of your hero at the 15<sup>th</sup> or 16<sup>th</sup> year of his age, and to assert that the time of his birth and infancy had no connection with the story of his life because, forsooth, he was become a very different person when grown up and sent to college, from what he was when he was born, breeched, and sent to school? (Ritson 1782, 2)

Ritson's linguistic Saxonism here undoes Warton's politically tendentious "biography" of the state. Simultaneously, the agitation for Parliamentary reform begun by Major John Cartwright's Society for Constitutional Information (SCI) in the 1780s was, as Nicholas Roe notes, undertaken in the name of the "great Founders" of the English Constitution, the Saxons (Roe 1988, 29). In 1786 one of the SCI's leading members, John Horne Tooke, published the first part of his etymological treatise, *The Diversions of Purley*, which emphasized the historicity of the English language—its "Anglo-Saxon and Gothic" roots—and argued for a direct connection between the post-Norman "corruptions" of the tongue and those of the state: the intertwined discourses of law and language generating similarly abstract accounts of densely historical processes, with formerly expeditious "abbreviations" construed as expressions of absolute relationship, mystified, and perpetuated beyond their original usefulness (Tooke 1786–1805, I, 136–37, and II, 18).[4] Meanwhile, David Williams, a leading British radical (and possible acquaintance of the young William Wordsworth at Paris in late 1792 [Davies 2002, 28–31]), brought to his honorific role as constitutional adviser to the French Convention the conviction that the Saxon constitution, descended from Montesquieu's "Gothic government," offered a model of "a political constitution, the best imagined and the most effectual that has hitherto been exhibited in the world" (Williams 1790, 41). But as R. J. Smith says, the "almost exclusively English stress" of Cartwright and the insular tendency of the SCI, served to "isolate Saxonism from its Gothic ally" (R. J. Smith 1987, 138). This divorce from the Gothic in the reform movement is captured neatly in the English Jacobin John Thelwall's cancelled self-defence in the 1794 treason trials, published after his acquittal as *The Natural and Constitutional Rights of Britons* (1795). Thelwall spoke of "the free and glorious Constitution of our Saxon ancestors" yet surviving in the Common Law, but mentioned the Goths only as a byword for barbarism (Claeys, ed. 1995, 21–22). Lawyers, he said, were "a race of men who have spread more devastation through the moral world than the Goths and Vandals, who overthrew the Roman empire." Meanwhile, conservative writers increasingly appropriated the Gothic to their own purposes. Sharon Turner's *History of the Anglo-Saxons*, researched and written contemporaneously with *The Prelude* between 1799 and 1805 (and certainly known to Wordsworth by 1822 [Gravil 2003, 38]), saw "our language, our government, and our laws, display our Gothic ancestors in every part" (qtd. in Kliger 1952, 9).

Political Gothicism was fast falling out of favor in the late eighteenth century. British radicals had, understandably, little time for a constitutional legacy that was, in the estimation of Tom Paine's *Common Sense* (1776), "noble for the dark and slavish times in which it was erected," but in the present represented at best only a partial freedom (Paine 1995, 7). The view from France, Paine wrote in *Rights of Man* (1791), was that "the portion of liberty enjoyed in England, is just enough to enslave a country by, more productively than by despotism" (Paine 1995, 128). According to Paine in 1792, the English representation was "Gothic" in a wholly negative sense, for it was vitiated by corporation towns, "Gothic institutions" that injured the "property and commerce" of large new urban centers such as Manchester, Birmingham, and Sheffield (Paine 1995, 275–76). The "English government" was indeed linked to the ancient "Goths and Vandals"; but only, Paine said (with a glance at the ongoing Parliamentary hearings on the conduct of the former Governor-General Warren Hastings), because the British in India and the barbarians in Rome were alike "destitute of principle," and both "robbed and tortured the world they were incapable of enjoying" (Paine 1995, 320).

Edmund Burke's *Reflections on the Revolution in France* (1790) thus appeared at a time when Gothicism had been largely abandoned by radical politicians in favor of the discourse of abstract rights. Burke seized the opening, attacking the French Revolution as the destroyer of "the age of chivalry," the system of manners that had, he said, "given its character to modern Europe" (Burke 1987, 66–67). This appeal to chivalry was legible as Gothic politics, for the two terms were frequently associated in the eighteenth century. The influential antiquary Thomas Percy, for example, saw chivalric manners "in embrio" among the ancient Goths (Percy 1775, III, viii). Burke's evaluation of chivalry as a progressive social phenomenon was clearly indebted to accounts of "*Gothic* Chivalry" by writers like

Percy and the Whig historian Richard Hurd (Hurd 1811, IV, 239), and he clearly alluded to the construction method of the Gothic cathedrals in recommending to France, whose constitution had been "suspended before it was perfected," the British constitutional method of "making the reparation as nearly as possible in the style of the building" (Burke 1987, 31, 217). The sole use of the term in the *Reflections* relates to the Universities of Oxford and Cambridge: they provide what is "in the groundwork" a "Gothic and monkish education," which nevertheless has been found, Burke says, "capable of receiving and meliorating, and above all of preserving, the accessions of science and literature" (Burke 1987, 88). The Gothic here is the "monkish": no term of approbation in the Protestant Whig tradition. But to Burke, a lifelong advocate of Catholic emancipation, who was widely rumored to be—in Paine's words—on a "journey to Rome" (Gibbons 2003, 32; Paine 1995, 93), the analogy between these "monkish" institutions and the Constitution was clear. Like the Constitution that observed "the method of nature" in its evolutionary growth, moving "on through the varied tenor of perpetual decay, fall, renovation, and progression," the Universities had been amended gradually over the centuries, "without altering the ground" upon which they stood (Burke 1987, 30, 88). Moreover, the Universities furnished not only the training grounds of the political class but also the parliamentary seat of the Prime Minister of the day, William Pitt. Working by the method of "philosophic analogy" that he recommended in government, Burke here names obliquely the Gothic Constitution.

The *Reflections* are "Gothic," moreover, in a variety of senses that an exclusive focus on the term itself will fail to comprehend. Emma Clery and Robert Miles suggest that Burke's imagery is self-consciously and literarily Gothic, deployed with intent to "evoke the immanence of the past within the present" (Clery and Miles eds. 2000, 229). For example, the pamphlet's image of the hereditary state "grasped as in a kind of mortmain forever" (Burke 1987, 29), advances the claims of the past on the present by "partially literalising the ghoulish [legal] tenet of 'dead hand,' transference of property to a corporation in perpetuity" (Clery and Miles eds. 2000, 229). Purely in debating terms, this figuration of the Constitution as a dead hand is of questionable wisdom, since it clearly invites Paine's powerful image of Burke scrounging after "musty records and mouldy parchments to prove that the rights of the living are lost" (Paine 1995, 95–96). But "partially literalised" as it is, the "mortmain" sounds a reservoir of supernatural menace beneath the notion of the immortal state that works upon the imagination more effectively than if the state presented only its daylight face of "the method of nature."

The image of the "mortmain" is, however, also legible as Gothic in a politically opposite sense. As Burke likely knew, the Leveler John Hare had, in the 1640s, pictured England yet suffering in the sepulchral grasp of the Norman Yoke. Hare's "Norman Yoke ideology" was, as Christopher Hill has shown, widely influential during the later years of the English civil war—underpinning, for example, the Regicide preacher Hugh Peter's sermon justifying Pride's Purge of December 1648 (Hill 1968, 79–80). Burke's awareness of this "ideology" is suggested by his invocation of Peter and his sermons in the *Reflections* as the forerunner of Richard Price and his sermon of November 4, 1789 to the Revolution Society that celebrated the "triumph" of the French over their king; a precedent that brought Burke intimations that Price might also emulate Peter in meeting an unquiet traitor's death (Burke 1987, 10, 57–58). Indeed, Hare's *St Edwards Ghost, or Anti-Normanisme* (1647) itself seems to haunt the *Reflections*. For in a phrase that strikingly prefigures Paine's counterblast to Burke, inciting the English to regenerate their government by removing the "yet disfigur[ing]...marks" of the "tyranny transplanted...from Normandy into England," complete with "the curfeu-bell" that "not a village in England has forgotten" (Paine 1995, 127, 220), Hare had pictured Normanism as a dead hand that needed finally to be removed. "[I]t is but the carcass of an enemy that we have to remove out of our territories," he wrote, "even the carcass and bones of the Norman Duke's injurious and detested perpetrations" (qtd in Hill 1968, 79). Burke's conservative image of inheritance as a mortmain or dead hand is thus, startlingly, itself inherited from the imagery employed by Saxonists, Gothicists, and Levelers in the 1640s. His graveyard Gothic figure, used ostensibly to defend hereditary monarchy in England, flirts perilously with precisely the Gothic politics that had abolished it less than a century and a half before.

In *Letters on a Regicide Peace* (1796) Burke became more explicit about the Gothic legacy in England and in Europe at large. Here he stated categorically that "the polity and economy of every country in Europe" derived ultimately "from the old Germanic or Gothic custumary, from the feudal institutions which must be considered as an emanation from that custumary...improved and digested into a system and discipline by the Roman Law" (Burke 1796, 110). Burke's figurative language of "digestion" here rather complicates than clarifies the historical field in view. The play between several incommensurate but overlapping temporal frames is a refinement of the appeal in the *Reflections* to "the old common law of Europe" (Burke 1987, 32), which subtly equivocated between the laws of the ancient Goths and those of Europe under feudalism. Burke's polemic of the 1790s thus operated as sort of literary-historical stereoscope, composing a single vision of illusory depth of the "system of Europe" from the overlapping images of the Romano-Gothic and Gotho-feudal periods.

The English Jacobin John Thelwall seized upon these references to the Goths in a manner that helps to explain Burke's reluctance to use the term. In *Rights of Nature* (1796), Thelwall repeated incessantly (no fewer than twenty-two times) the phrase "Germanic or Gothic custumary" as evidence of Burke's barbaric, feudal, popish, tyrannical, and emphatically unnatural mentality. "Mr. B's *Nature* and mine are widely different," Thelwall wrote:

> In my humble estimate, nothing is natural, but what is fit and true, and can endure the test of reason. With him the feudal system, and all its barbarous, tyrannical, and superstitious appendages, is natural. With him, all the gaudy, cumbrous fustian of "the old Germanic, or Gothic custumary" is natural; and all the idolatrous foppery and degrading superstition of the church of Rome are natural, also. (Claeys ed. 1995, 405)

This equation between the Gothic Constitution and the "superstition of the church of Rome" was an effect of Burke's disruption of the Whig identification of the Gothic with rational Protestantism. Refuting Burke, Thelwall further distanced himself from the radical Gothic theory. With a glance at Montesquieu's well-known comment that the "beautiful system" of the English Constitution "was invented first in the woods" (Montesquieu 1750, I, 230), Thelwall emphasized the barbaric and regressive connotations of the Gothic: "Mr. B. and his college...would drive us back into the woods, to learn the arts of civilization and government from the half-naked barbarism of the Goths and Germans" (Claeys ed. 1995, 479). "[T]he Jacobin," by contrast, Thelwall continued to argue, is a progressive who "looks forward to a state of society...more perfect." This prospective view of a "more perfect" future shows the influence of William Godwin's *Political Justice* (1793), which urged the perfectibility of mankind, and anticipated "complete reformation...not instant but future" through the "uncontrolled exercise of private judgement" (Godwin 1793, I, 222, 158). In 1796, at what Nicholas Roe has shown was the high-water mark of Thelwall and the reform movement's intellectual debt to Godwin (Roe 1988, 171–75), the distinction could not have been clearer between the prospective Godwinian and the retrospective, Burkean, Goth.

Wordsworth was familiar with the distinction. He probably read both Burke's *Letters on a Regicide Peace* and Thelwall's *Rights of Nature* in the spring of 1797 (*EY* 309; Roe 1988, 240; Wu 1993, 135), and he was already the author of an unpublished tract that opposed Burke with a Godwinian and perfectibilian view of government and society. In *A Letter to the Bishop of Llandaff*, written in 1793, Wordsworth followed Tom Paine in picturing the "philosophic lamentation over the extinction of Chivalry" in the *Reflections* as proof of Burke's "infatuated" mental state (*Prose Works* I, 35–36). Burke's "Gothic" image of the state "grasped as in a kind of mortmain forever" is then turned back upon its author:

> Mr Burke roused the indignation of all ranks of men, when by a refinement of cruelty superior to that which in the East yokes the living to the dead he strove to persuade us that we and our posterity to the end of time were riveted to a constitution by the indissoluble compact of a dead parchment, and were bound to cherish a corse at the bosom, when reason might call aloud that it should be entombed. (*Prose Works*, I, 48)

The image of the "mortmain"—a "dead hand"—is here hyperbolized as necrophiliac abomination. Burke appears condemned out of his own mouth by the failure of mental hygiene involved in the approving use of such grotesque and "Gothic" imagery.

If chivalry thus threatened moral depravation, then the Gothic tradition beyond it that even Burke hardly dared invoke must have seemed to Wordsworth still more suspect. On June 17, 1791 he wrote to his Cambridge friend William Mathews, then teaching at the Free School at Appleby Magna in Leicestershire (established at the end of the seventeenth century), congratulating him on the fact that his "school hours could not be complained of as being too much under what may be called a Gothic regulation" (*EY* 49). Wordsworth's subsequent posturings on the "unphilosophic" desire to attain learning without effort make it clear that by a "Gothic regulation" he means a rigorous dedication to study—something like a monastic rule, or the regime imagined in *The Prelude* at Cambridge "of old,"

> When, in forlorn and naked chambers cooped
> And crowded, o'er their ponderous books they sat

> Like caterpillars eating out their way
> In silence, or with keen devouring noise
> Not to be tracked or fathered.
>             (*1805* III, 460–467)

The Gothic here is the medieval and the unenlightened. Indeed, at a time when a Sunday School master could enforce discipline with a burning iron (Foakes 1989, 189); when the normal course of education could be described by the radical David Williams as one of "superstition," "mechanic order," bad diet and hypocrisy (Williams 1789, I, 59); and likened seriously by the Anglican reformer Andrew Bell to a regime of torture (Bell 1808, 3), the school as "Gothic regulation" has shades of the prison-house and the Spanish Inquisition. In 1812, Southey would bring the imagination of bad education as a "Gothic regulation" into hard focus, likening the Southwark schoolmaster Joseph Lancaster's enforcement of discipline through the public punishments of pillory, shackle, and cage to "making an auto-da-fe a raree-show for the people" (Southey 1812, 89). But it seems likely that Wordsworth's phrase is above all an allusion to Burke's "philosophic" characterization of the Universities—which he and Mathews had so recently left—as providers of a "Gothic and monkish education." When, three years later, on June 8, 1794, Wordsworth wrote to Mathews that he was "not amongst the admirers of the British constitution," founded as it was upon "[h]ereditary distinctions and privileged orders" (*EY* 123–24), he was clearly transferring the idea of a "Gothic regulation" back onto the British Constitution, identifying it as Gothic in a wholly pejorative sense.

The debate over the "Germanic or Gothic custumary" continues to echo in the Preface to *Lyrical Ballads* (1800). As Peter Mortensen has shown, the growing fashion for literary Gothic in the years of the Napoleonic Wars was widely seen as a symptom of cultural and political degeneracy (Mortensen 2000, 211–33). In his *Pursuits of Literature*, Thomas James Mathias, for example, asked:

> Shall nought but ghosts and trinkets be display'd,
> Since Walpole ply'd the virtuoso's trade,
> Bade sober truth revers'd for fiction pass,
> And mus'd o'er Gothick toys through Gothick glass?
>             (Mathias 1798, 404, ll. 545–48)

"For Mathias," Mortensen suggests, "as for many other representatives of the cultural establishment…the issue was clear: exoticist and primitivist sympathies betokened a dangerous, potentially un-English enthusiasm" (Mortensen 2000, 212). In precisely this strain, Wordsworth saw the way "frantic novels, sickly and stupid German Tragedies, and deluges of idle and extravagant stories in verse" were "driv[ing] into neglect" the "invaluable works" of "our elder writers" Shakespeare and Milton, as a symptom of a "degrading" national "thirst after outrageous stimulation" (*Prose Works*, I, 128–30). Shakespeare and Milton are pointedly *our* elders, *national* writers who embody a distinctive English sensibility and a sanative English literary tradition, aligned against the sickly "Germanic or Gothic" influence, and alongside "certain inherent and indestructible qualities of the human mind" (*Prose Works*, I, 130) that sound very much like the "essentially progressive" powers of *Political Justice* (Godwin 1793, II, 865). It seems clear, then, that at least until 1800 Wordsworth shared the view of Paine and Thelwall that a Gothic Constitution was a "degrading" and an "outrageous" thing.

There is a sense, however, in which the argument of the Preface to *Lyrical Ballads* constitutes a reconfiguration of Saxonism, and thus a covert rehabilitation of the Gothic. As Susan Manly has shown, Saxonism was by no means only an antiquarian pursuit; rather it gave a historically oriented expression to a proto-democratic defence of the lives and customs of the English commons. The ethos of commonality and collective independency usually attributed to the Saxons was still observable in "common rights economies, with common fields farmed in strips... with bi-annual public meetings to ratify the management of the fields, and the annual walking of the bounds" (Manly 2007, 82). The Saxons and their "Gothic" customs were not departed, but still subsisted among the common people. Uncannily, the commons *were* the Saxons celebrated by political theorists; not a past reality but a present *alternative* reality. An earlier time, an older historical clock, was still running in parallel with the clock-and-calendar-time, the "homogeneous empty time," of the modern commercial nation. This notion of different orders of temporality existing side by side was current in the Scottish Enlightenment theory of uneven development, whereby, as James Chandler summarizes it, nations "are recognized as existing in 'states' that belong at once to two different, and to some extent competing, orders of temporality":

> On the one hand, each society is theorized as moving stepwise through a series of stages sequenced in an order that is more-or-less autonomous and stable [but which] always implies a second temporality, one in which these different national times can be correlated

and calendrically dated in respect to each other.... [R]ates of historical change are measurable by comparing the progress of different societies with one another and are to some degree explicable by relating the state of a society with the "state of the world" at that same moment.... When one begins to locate a state of society within a given state of the world, one produces a "historical situation" for the actions of those who inhabit it. (Chandler 1998, 128)

This kind of anachronism—or, rather, diachronism, can presumably occur just as well within a single nation—an entity not yet fully theorized in the early nineteenth century. The persistence of the Saxons in the commons suggests that the paradigm-shift theorized by Benedict Anderson (1999, 9–36) from medieval and imperial/dynastic "simultaneity along time" to modern and national simultaneity across time was still incomplete in the 1790s. Consciousness of this fact would in itself serve as a way to produce the "historical situation," since the commons retained a "medieval" mindset that served to "date" the modern nation. Wordsworth's appeal to "the real language of men" and the "regular feelings" of rustics in the Preface to *Lyrical Ballads* is thus legible as a rather sophisticated attempt to establish the state of the nation in 1800 (*Prose Works* I, 144, 178). Correlating the "great national events which are daily taking place" in the metropolitan centers of the modern nation with the unremembered acts of rustics generates an historical coordinate for the nation as a whole (*Prose Works* I, 150). And the representative cipher of this coordinate is the reconciliatory figure of the (national) Poet, who "binds together by passion and knowledge the vast empire of human society, as it is spread over the whole earth, and over all time" (*Prose Works* I, 167). As Wordsworth explicitly claims in the "Preface," "[l]ow and rustic life was generally chosen, because in that condition of life"—a phrase interchangeable with "state of society" in the idiom of the Scottish Enlightenment—

> the essential passions of the heart find a better soil in which they can attain maturity, are less under restraint, and speak a plainer and more emphatic language; because in that condition of life our elementary feelings co-exist in a state of greater simplicity, and, consequently, may be more accurately contemplated, and more forcibly communicated; because the manners of rural life germinate from those elementary feelings; and from the necessary character of rural occupations are more easily comprehended; and are more durable; and lastly, because in that condition the passions of men are incorporated with the beautiful and permanent forms of nature.... Accordingly such a language,

arising out of repeated experience and regular feelings is a more permanent and a far more philosophical language than that which is frequently substituted for it by Poets... (*Prose Works* I, 144)

Wordsworth speaks here of permanence, "essential passions," "primary laws," and "elementary feelings." But the distinctive frisson of the passage comes from the way its essentialist view of "human nature" is interpenetrated by a thoroughgoing historicism, which charts diachronically the uneven development in various states of society of this capacity for permanence. This historicist sensibility is clearly visible in his conviction of "Poets" who imagine escaping from history into the "arbitrary" and "capricious" realm of art of being strangers to "the sympathies of men" (*Prose Works* I, 144). The language of "low and rustic life" is primordial not in an unhistorical Adamic sense, but in the sense that it is vitally connected to an underlying social reality in a circulatory process in which "language and the human mind act and react on each other" (*Prose Works* I, 140), and this originary language is pointedly said to "arise" from "repeated experience"—to embody in itself, that is, a process of historical development.

This large-scale historiographical project of "dating" the nation by writing poetry that attempts to reconcile in its own texture (the "Lyrical" *Ballad*) the uneven development of the national tongue, is acted out at the level of individual poems within *Lyrical Ballads*. In "We are Seven," for example, the young girl expresses a sense of community and simultaneity along time which is the very opposite of her interlocutor's bureaucratic mentality:

> Then did the little Maid reply,
> "Seven boys and girls are we;
> Two of us in the church-yard lie,
> Beneath the church-yard tree."
>
> "You run about, my little maid,
> Your limbs they are alive;
> If two are in the church-yard laid,
> Then ye are only five."
>
> "Their graves are green, they may be seen,"
> The little Maid replied,
> "Twelve steps or more from my mother's door,
> And they are side by side."
> (*MW* 83–85; ll. 29–40)

Her words are readily dismissed as exemplifying the "Gothick ignorance" of the common law mindset (Linebaugh 2003, 273). But the poem nevertheless closes with the girl persisting in her view of familial simultaneity along time, and the speaker conceding that "'Twas throwing words away" to continue to attempt her reformation. Wordsworth thus implies that the culture of the Gothic is a necessary corrective to the culture of politeness; necessary, that is, if the nation is to retain its historical equipoise, and not attempt rashly to dart into futurity, as had France.

By the time of the invasion panic of 1802, Britain's "Gothic" customary had, for Wordsworth, taken on a quite different meaning. The Gothic hall that had been imagined as the engine-room of British liberty by both *Common Sense* and by Burke also provided the location for Wordsworth's inventory of Britain's conceptual armory in the 1802 sonnets on liberty. It was, he wrote, "not to be thought of that the Flood / Of British freedom," flowing from "dark antiquity," and with the "freights of worth" of British trade around the earth, "Should perish" before the French blockade. Instead, he imagined Britain as a Gothic antitype to neoclassical France:

> In our halls is hung
> Armoury of the invincible Knights of old:
> We must be free or die, who speak the tongue
> That Shakespeare spake; the faith and morals hold
> Which Milton held.—In every thing we are sprung
> Of Earth's first blood, have titles manifold.
> (*MW* 276)

Milton and Shakespeare, formerly guarantors of a sane Englishness against sickly Germanic influences, are now archetypal Goths; and the "tongue," the "faith and morals," and the freedoms ("titles") of Britain are direct corollaries of the persistence of *Common Sense*'s "old hospitable *Gothick* halls" in the nation.

In a sonnet of October 1803, with war now rejoined, Wordsworth imagined Britain's Gothic liberty incarnate in the shape of the "Men of Kent": a chivalric host facing the French enemy with "glittering lance" and warlike "countenance" (ll. 6–7; *MW* 289). But the tradition of Gothic radicalism is in there too. Wordsworth's reference to how Kent did, "of yore, / . . . from the Norman win a gallant wreath; / Confirmed the charters that were yours before" (ll. 9–11), constitutes an allusion to Kent's preservation of the law of equitable inheritance (known as *gavelkynd*) that writers as various as the English Jacobin John Thelwall and the Elizabethan antiquaries Michael Drayton and Richard Verstegan traced back beyond the imposition of the so-called

Norman yoke to the Anglo-Saxons, and beyond them to the ancient Germans or Goths.[5] But the poem does not only allude to the Gothic relic of *gavelkynd*. Rather, it transforms Kent's local commonality into a universal spirit of national solidarity: "No parleying now! In Britain is one breath; / We are all with you now from Shore to Shore:— / Ye Men of Kent, 'tis Victory or Death!" (ll. 12–14). Wordsworth thus imaginatively threw off the Norman yoke, refitting the antique weapons in Britain's armory of thought for the struggle against Napoleon. The "last spot of earth," as he put it in the 1805 *Prelude*, "where freedom now / Stands single in her only sanctuary" (X, 981–82), Britain had become for Wordsworth a bastion of Gothic liberty at the edge of the world.

## Gothic Culture

The larger English Gothic cultural project was also articulated in Richard Payne Knight's *Analytical Inquiry into the Principles of Taste* (1805), which Wordsworth read in 1805–6 (Wu 1995, 124). Knight encouraged the violation of neoclassical canons on the grounds that in great art other, deep-structural, rules were at work. Gothic architecture, described in Horace Walpole's *Anecdotes of Painting* (1765–71) as the architecture of the passions (I, 114–15), provided Knight's prime example. Unlike "Grecian" architects, who worked by rule, Gothic architects "attend[ed] to effect only" (Knight 1808, 176). Where the "uniform proportion" followed by classical architects made even a "gigantic" cathedral like Rome's St. Peter's "appear smaller than it really is," Gothic architecture varied proportions so as to "extend the scale...afforded to the eye...for the admeasurement of the whole." Developing the observation in Edmund Burke's *Sublime and Beautiful* (1757) that when "the eye" is "not...able to perceive the bounds of many things, they seem to be infinite, and they produce the same effects as if they were really so," and also picking up Burke's account of the mind "hurried out of itself" by "crouded and confused" impressions (1757, 52–53, 49), Knight thus posited Gothic architecture as a material manifestation of the sublime.

Knight's influence is clearly visible in the description of a Gothic church—St. Oswald's, Grasmere—in book five of Wordsworth's *Excursion*. The space in this Gothic church is highly articulated, with a "confusion" that only enhances the impression of grandeur:

>Admonitory Texts inscribed the walls,
>Each, in its ornamental scroll, enclosed,–

>     Each also crowned with winged heads—a pair
>     Of rudely-painted Cherubim. The floor
>     Of nave and aisle, in unpretending guise,
>     Was occupied by oaken benches, ranged
>     In seemly rows; the chancel only shewed
>     Some inoffensive marks of earthly state
>     And vain distinction. A capacious pew
>     Of sculptured oak stood here, with drapery lined;
>     And marble Monuments were here displayed
>     Upon the walls; and on the floor beneath
>     Sepulchral stones appeared, with emblems graven,
>     And foot-worn epitaphs, and some with small
>     And shining effigies of brass inlaid.
>     –The tribute by these various records claimed,
>     Without reluctance did we pay; and read
>     The ordinary chronicle of birth,
>     Office, alliance, and promotion—all
>     Ending in dust…
>   (V, 154–73; Bushell, Butler, and Jaye, eds. 2007, 171–72)

Grasmere church seems larger than it really is because the whole cannot be scanned at once: the dense articulation and the legibility of its surfaces mean paradoxically that the church is not architecturally "legible," and hence it is incapable (unlike "Grecian" architecture) of deconstruction to its constituent parts. Moreover, Grasmere here becomes a literary church in a complex sense. Moving from an architectural to a linguistic paradigm, the passage becomes self-consciously literary in its resonances with the tradition of church and churchyard poetry; the "tribute…claimed" being precisely the "passing tribute of a sigh" (l. 80) implored by the "frail memorial[s]" (l. 78) in Thomas Gray's 1751 "Elegy Written in a Country Churchyard." Meanwhile, the church itself both invites and resists the act of reading. Instead of abstracting the collective memory of the local community, the sheer density of the "records" produces only an "ordinary chronicle" of quotidian existence, "Ending in dust."

Wordsworth's reference to "Admonitory Texts" arranged around the walls does nevertheless seem to associate the church with a sort of collective memory. As Frances Yates has shown, the primary method of memory training, exemplified by the first-century Roman rhetorician Quintilian, was founded upon an architectural metaphor, in which memorized materials were disposed around complicated imaginary buildings, and placed under icons. The act of recall involved navigating to the desired icons and requiring them to yield their contents, or, in Quintilian's phrase, "demanding what has been entrusted of them" (Yates 1984, 22–23). Wordsworth would have come across Quintilian's *Institutio Oratoria* at Hawkshead and Cambridge, and there are clear echoes of this classical technique of memory training in Wordsworth's poetry well before *The Excursion*. Perhaps the most intriguing instance is "Tintern Abbey," with its slow recreation of "the picture of the mind," which begins with an initial interrogation of "hedge-rows, hardly hedge-rows," and finds its resolution in imagining the mind of the poet's sister as "a mansion for all lovely forms" (*MW* 131–35; ll. 62, 16, 141).

On such a view, the notorious absence of the abbey itself within the poem is an effect of the putative identity of the abbey and poem: the two memory-structures so "deeply interfused" (l. 97) that they are invisible to each other. Indeed, Marjorie Levinson's well-known argument that the poem sees Wordsworth install himself as successor to the defunct monastic community (1986, 29–34) finds a suggestive echo in the fact that the classical techniques of memory training were adapted by medieval monasticism. As Robert A. Scott notes, this involved the creation of corporate mental structures—as at St. Gall, Riechenau, in the early ninth century, when those presiding over "moments of communal worship…summoned the image of [a] plan and invited monks to join in imaginary processions through it" (Scott 2003, 176–80). The key point to note is that the direction of influence here is from imagination to physical architecture. As Mary Carruthers puts it, the stone of the cathedral is actually "the 'imitation'" of a structure "previsualised in the manner of rhetorical invention and of meditation" (qtd. in Scott, 180). In similar vein, Yates notes Erwin Panofsky's argument that the Gothic cathedral resembles the "scholastic summa" with its "system of homologous parts and parts of parts,"' and finds herself struck by an "extraordinary thought":

> [I]f Thomas Aquinas memorised his own *Summa* through "corporeal similitudes" disposed on places following the order of its parts, the abstract *Summa* might be corporealised in memory into something like a Gothic cathedral full of images on its ordered places. (Yates 1984, 79)

Reading Yates on Aquinas, the equally extraordinary thought now arises that Wordsworth's Gothic analogy possibly means that he indeed held *The Recluse* in his head in the form of a Gothic church subdivided into parts. Such a view makes sudden sense of the 1814

Preface, ridiculed by the *Augustan Review* for its parts of parts, and the perplexing reference in the 1815 Preface to a "two-fold view" in "habitual" use. Indeed, the notion of "corporealising" memory in architecture was current not only in commercial memory-training publications, such as Gregor von Feinaigle's *New Art of Memory* (1813) with its "three-dimensional mnemonic scheme[s]" (Chandler 1998, 275), but also in writings by several prominent figures in the years around 1814. William Godwin, for one, had come to reevaluate the Gothic aesthetic, and to see Gothic architecture as a vehicle for the transmission of a forward-looking mentality through the unenlightened middle ages (Weston 2002, 449–50). In his *Life of Geoffrey Chaucer* (1804), Godwin wrote that of Greek and Gothic buildings, the Gothic

> are more religious. They possess infinitely more power to excite the passions, and generate an enthusiastic spirit. We admire the Grecian style of building; we feel more from the Gothic. The Grecian is like the poetry of an Augustan age; it is harmonious, uniformly majestic, and gently persuasive. The Gothic is like the poetry of a ruder and more daring period. The artist does not stoop to conform himself to elaborate rules; he yields to the native suggestions of his sublime and untutored fancy; he astonishes the observer and robs him of himself, and the heart of man acknowledges more occasions of sympathy, of affection and feeling in his productions, than in the laboured and accurate performances of a more enlightened age. (Godwin 1804, I, 229–30)

Coleridge concurred: his 1818 lecture on the "General Character of the Gothic Mind in the Middle Ages" argued that

> [t]he contemplation of the works of antique art excites a feeling of elevated beauty, and exalted notions of the human self; but the Gothic architecture impresses the beholder with a sense of self-annihilation; he becomes, as it were, a part of the work contemplated. An endless complexity and variety are united into one whole, the plan of which is not distinct from the execution. A Gothic cathedral is the petrifaction of our religion. (Raysor, ed. 1936, 7)

This developing account of the Gothic as the (English) style of the sublime has a close affinity with the eighteenth-century view of Shakespeare as a "Gothic" artist. As Nick Groom puts it:

> Shakespeare was conceived as an individual author and a national genius, built from conjectural emendation, minute editorial collation, and historical explication…[H]e was the origin of the definition of

English literature: a national poet, a Gothic genius whose linguistic copiousness displayed both an instinctive love of liberty and a dismissive contempt (or a total ignorance) of the tyrannical canons of neoclassical theatre and the Aristotelian unities. (Groom 1999, 11–12)

Constructed by "minute" accretions, Shakespeare is—to adapt Coleridge's phrase—the petrifaction of English poetry; and indeed Pope's figure of Shakespeare's works as "an ancient majestick piece of Gothick Architecture, compar'd with a neat Modern building...more strong and more solemn" (Warburton ed. 1747, I, xlv–xlvi), seems to underpin the comparisons between Greek and Gothic architecture made by Thomson, Walpole, Hurd and Godwin. The taste for Gothic architecture is developed out of a taste for "Gothic" poetry. Wordsworth's prose of 1814–15 shows, however, that the process could now work in reverse. After proposing to build his own Gothic church in the Preface of 1814, Wordsworth moved in the 1815 "Essay, Supplementary" to fabricate and to quote as typical of wrongheaded English criticism a description of Shakespeare as "a wild irregular genius, in whom great faults are compensated by great beauties" (*Prose Works*, III, 69). In fact, Wordsworth said, Shakespeare's heterogeneous materials "constitute a unity of their own, and contribute all to one great end"—and the "Germans only" had seen this truth.

There is a clear sense, then, in which Wordsworth describing Shakespeare is also describing the correct (German or Gothic) view of himself and his own works. Intriguingly, Coleridge's 1818 lectures on "the Gothic mind" posit not metropolitan Shakespeare but rural Wordsworth—described by Coleridge in January 1804 as living a "most august & innocent Life"—as the archetypal Goth:

> The Goths are free from the stain of hero worship. Gazing on their rugged mountains, surrounded by impassable forests, accustomed to gloomy seasons, they lived in the bosom of nature, and worshipped an invisible and unknown deity. Firm in his faith, domestic in his habits, the life of the Goth was simple and dignified, yet tender and affectionate. (Raysor, ed. 1936, 12)

Coleridge's thoughts in these lectures clearly run along lines already established in his collaboration with Wordsworth. His account of the Gothic cathedral as a "whole" whose "plan...is not distinct from the execution" expresses the very same notion of organic growth that lay behind his 1804 letter's full statement that "Wordsworth is a Poet, a most original Poet—he no more resembles Milton than Milton resembles Shakespere—no more resembles Shakespere than

Shakespere resembles Milton—he is himself," and that *The Recluse* would be "the first & finest philosophical Poem, if only it be (as it undoubtedly will be) a Faithful Transcript of [Wordsworth's] own most august & innocent Life, of his own habitual Feelings & Modes of seeing and hearing" (*CLSTC* II, 1034). Both august and Gothic—that is, on both sides of the Gothic/Grecian divide, Wordsworth is the synthesis produced from Coleridge's dialectic of English poetic "genius."

Given this enabling context, the Gothic analogy looks rather less like the deliberate offering-up of a curious poetic ruin to the antiquarian taste of the age than an attempted resolution of the cultural paradox, inherited from James Thomson's *Liberty* (1735–36), of Gothic historical vigor and Gothic aesthetic decrepitude. Indeed, Wordsworth's late comments upon the *Recluse* scheme insist upon preserving a distinction between a (rugged Gothic) fragment and a (shameful Gothic) ruin. The note on *The Excursion* dictated to Isabella Fenwick in 1843 addresses the "further labours" promised at the end of *The Excursion* with the reflection of the 1819 sonnet, "Malham Cove" that,

> 'Mid the Wreck of is & was
> Things incomplete & purposes betrayed
> Make sadder transits o'er thought's optic glass
> Than noblest objects utterly decayed.
> (qtd. in *FN* 91)

"Things incomplete" and "noblest objects...decayed" are not identical but rather antithetical. *The Recluse*, like the deliberately unfinished Temple of Philosophy near the grave of Rousseau at Ermenonville, which "invites philosophers of the future to 'restore' it to a finished state" (Thomas 2008, 51), brings "sadder" thoughts to the mind than a "decayed" ruin like, say, Tintern Abbey. But the sad "transits" of such fragments nevertheless retain a melancholic dynamism that is in pointed contrast to the static "decay" of the ruin. Even in this final recognition of the failure of *The Recluse*, then, Wordsworth still places the emphasis upon the effort of construction, upon the dynamic work of building, and forestalls the critical reflex that would make the project prematurely into a ruin. New Gothic churches had, after all, been a great rarity in 1814, owing to the overcapacity of existing medieval structures and the rigors of a wartime economy. But in 1818 Parliament had passed the Church Building Act and established a Commission that eventually oversaw the construction of over two hundred new churches, most of them Gothic (Brooks 1999, 227; Clark 1962, 94–95). In 1843, looking back on his proposal to build a church in poetry, and to build it in the Gothic style, Wordsworth could justifiably have seen himself predicting public policy, if not, indeed, in Shelley's near-contemporary formulation, making unacknowledged legislation for it.

Matters were, however, more complicated than such a retrospective view would suggest. Although the 1814 Preface to *The Excursion* was retained in every subsequent edition, the poem's intimate connection with the *Recluse* scheme was gradually obscured. The subtitle, "Being a portion of *The Recluse*" was removed from the title page of the 1836 edition. Coming as it does shortly before Wordsworth's confession to George Ticknor that *The Recluse* was now "beyond his powers to accomplish," and his renewed efforts to get *The Prelude* into a "state fit for publication" (qtd. in Jonathan Wordsworth, ed. 1995, xlv), it seems likely that this partial disappearing of *The Recluse* represents not only an attempt (like Lamb's in the *Quarterly* back in 1815) to emphasize the completeness and legitimacy of *The Excursion*, but, taking advantage of the "common knowledge...that Wordsworth was withholding a substantial poem for posthumous publication" (Gill 1998, 29), to begin to install *The Prelude* in the place of the missing *Recluse*. If this was the strategy, it was a resounding success. *Tait's Magazine*, for example, responded to the octogenarian poet's death in 1850 with the startling claim that "[h]aving the 'Excursion' before us, and knowing that the 'Recluse' is somewhere a *fait accompli*, we cannot (as in the case of Keats' unfinished 'Hyperion') create out of the unwritten works of Wordsworth anything like *un grand peut-être*" (17 [1850], 394). Several weeks earlier, the *Athenaeum* newspaper's "Weekly Gossip" section had included a notice to the effect that "Mr Wordsworth has left a poem, consisting of fourteen cantos, descriptive of his life, reflections and opinions, with directions that it should be published after his decease...In all probability this is the poem called 'The Recluse'—of which 'The Excursion' was avowedly published as an instalment" (May 18, 1850, 532). By 1850, the literary public was thoroughly prepared to take *The Prelude* for the "something evermore about to be" (*1805* VI, 542) of *The Recluse*.

When *The Prelude* finally made its appearance, however, it did so under an "Advertisement" that reprinted verbatim "the Author's language in the year 1814," from the potted history of the *Recluse* project to the analogy with Gothic architecture (1850, v–vi). Readers of *The Prelude* were thus actively encouraged to understand the poem in the archaeological terms already established by Hazlitt's review for the *Examiner*. Indeed, Hazlitt's successors at the *Examiner* borrowed Wordsworth's 1822 image of Cologne's perennially unfinished cathedral as "a Plan / How gloriously pursued by daring Man," whose "inspiring heat / Hath failed" (Jackson ed. 2004, 363), to figure the appearance now of *The Prelude* as the very fulfillment of Hazlitt's prophecy of the failure of *The Recluse*:

> This ambitious conception has been doomed to share the fate of so many other colossal undertakings. Of the three parts of his *Recluse*, thus planned, only the second (*The Excursion*, published in 1814) has been completed. Of the other two there exists only the first book of the first, and the plan of the third. The *Recluse* will remain in fragmentary greatness, a poetical Cathedral of Cologne. (*The Examiner*, July 27, 1850, 478)

Ironically, it is by confessing his failure with *The Recluse* by publishing *The Prelude* that Wordsworth substantiates the putative affinity between his poetry and great Gothic architecture. The final irony does not, however, belong to the *Examiner*. Thirty years later the building campaign spurred by the twin impulses of Gothic Revival and German unification would indeed bring about the final completion (six hundred years from its foundation) of the actual Cathedral of Cologne (Brooks 1999, 261–63, 401). This fate *The Recluse* could not possibly share. For while the image of the work as a "gothic Church" may seek, as Kenneth Johnston suggests, to convey the idea of construction "over long periods of time from common materials by anonymous workmen" (Johnston 1984, xxii–xxiii), *The Recluse* was a structure that none but Wordsworth could build.

If the meaning of the Gothic analogy was thus open to alteration by the gathering complexities of the culture of the Gothic, Wordsworth's late revisions to *The Prelude*—the "Anti-chapel" of his "gothic Church"—suggest a concern to adapt the analogy to those new meanings on his own terms. Book three of the poem already contained a suggestive description of Trinity College chapel with its "Antechapel, where the Statue stood / Of Newton, with his Prism and silent Face" (*1805* III, 58–59). Revising this part of the poem in 1838–39, Wordsworth altered the description of the "gloomy courts" of St John's to "Gothic courts," and he drew (as Jonathan Wordsworth notes [1995, 568n.]) upon the poet of Gothic vice and virtue, James Thomson's description of Newton stemming "The noiseless tide of time," in his famous further description of Roubiliac's statue as "The marble index of a mind for ever / Voyaging through strange seas of Thought, alone" (*1850* III, 62–63). Wordsworth thus memorialized Trinity's antechapel within his own poetic antechapel, and approximated the division of his poem into church and antechapel to Trinity's division into plain-glass antechapel and stained-glass choir. The impulse to do this may have derived not only from its affinity with the Gothic analogy, but also from its personal and political associations. It was in Trinity chapel that, as Nicholas Roe has suggested, Wordsworth probably heard his Cambridge contemporary John Tweddell deliver an oration in welcome of the French Revolution (Roe 1988, 15–16). The oration combined both Burkean and Paineite rhetoric, and contained an architectural analogy that strikingly anticipates Wordsworth's virtual church. Insisting in Paineite terms that it was not enough to have "a constitution in theory...[i]t must not only be a visible, but a tangible constitution," Tweddell proceeded to call not for a written codification of the law but for the cultivation by his listeners of a bizarre, hyper-real imagination, according to which "The fabric of our *real* constitution is that of a temple situated on an eminence" (Tweddell 1815, 106–7). The "real constitution" turns out to be tangible only in the form of a poetic figure.

If Trinity chapel thus materializes the Gothic analogy, then it seems plausible that Wordsworth intends to align *The Recluse* with the ethos of Cambridge—described in book nine of *The Prelude* as "something.../ Of a republic, where all stood thus far / Upon equal ground, that they were brothers all / In honour" (1805 IX, 228–31). But the notion of a building filled with refracted light also has quite opposite political associations. "[L]ike rays of light which pierce into a dense medium," Burke had written in his *Reflections*, abstract rights were necessarily "refracted from their straight line":

> Indeed, in the gross and complicated mass of human passions and concerns, the primitive rights of men undergo such a variety of refractions and reflections that it becomes absurd to talk of them as if they continued in the simplicity of their original direction. The nature of man is intricate; the objects of society are of the greatest possible complexity; and, therefore, no simple disposition or direction of power can be suitable either to man's nature or to the quality of his affairs...The rights of men are in a sort of *middle*, incapable of definition, but not impossible to be discerned...(Burke 1987, 54)

Wordsworth's 1814 Preface effectively transposes Burke's figurative argument to the domain of poetry: the "system" of this poem comprehending "Man, Nature, and Society" is highly complex, embedded within a "gross and complicated" mass of poetry, but though it is therefore incapable of being prescribed, is not impossible to be extracted. These two readings of the architectural analogy are, on the face of it, politically incompatible. Burke championed British mixed monarchy against French democracy. But it seems possible to reconcile them in the form—both monarchical and (imperfectly) democratic—of the House of Commons. Until the Westminster fire of 1834, the Commons sat in the upper gallery of St. Stephen's Chapel: a modified Gothic church, whose layout of chamber and lobby corresponded exactly to that of Trinity College Chapel.[6] Wordsworth was certainly familiar with this politicized architecture. Lines in book seven of the 1805 *Prelude* imply that during his residence in London he saw Pitt speak on several occasions (*1805* VII, 521–42), and the "Genius of Burke" passage added to the 1850 poem quite clearly places his younger self in the gallery as one who sat, saw, and heard Burke and Fox part company over the French Revolution in May 1791 (*1850* VII, 512–43; Johnston 1998, 255–57). There is also a tantalizing hint that the Gothic analogy is patterned directly on St Stephen's in the fact that Wordsworth added this second parliamentary scene to *The Prelude* in early 1832: the very moment at which we have the testimony of his daughter Dora for Wordsworth's habit of referring to the poem as "the 'ante-chapel'... to the 'Recluse'" (Moorman 1957–65, II, 501).

Wordsworth's addition of a second scene in St Stephen's in 1832 is highly suggestive of the patterning of the whole Recluse scheme after the unreformed Gothic constitution, since this was the very moment at which Reform threatened its destruction. For Coleridge, Reform in 1832 meant what, for Burke, Revolution in France had meant in 1790: that "England is—no more!" (Gilmartin 2007, 252; Burke 1790, 5). This link was perhaps signaled again in the decision of 1836 to remove the words "Being a Portion of The Recluse" from the title page of *The Excursion*. Coming as it did in the wake not only of Reform but of the destruction of St Stephen's by the Westminster Fire of 1834—which, as we have seen, the *Gentleman's Magazine* figured as the demise of the "palladium of the English monarchy," the "giant of the Gothic age," and as a threat to "national existence"—Wordsworth's removal of the reference to the *Recluse* scheme strongly suggests that the scheme was coextensive with the duration of the unreformed Gothic constitution. Just as the *Gentleman's* had tacitly acknowledged the deep association of its "Constitutional Sort of Reverence" with the maintenance of the unreformed constitution by beginning a "new series" immediately after Reform in 1833, and just as its chasmic vision of the Westminster Fire in the second number of that new series bore witness to the ongoing trauma of recognizing that its political-aesthetic model of the Gothic subject was now defunct and "burst asunder," so Wordsworth's amputation of *The Excursion* from the "Gothic" scheme can be seen as a traumatic registering of the fact that it has ceased to be politically viable or desirable. Reform had removed the need for the Burkean work of reconciliation and balancing by which the old order was maintained, and for which *The Recluse* had been designed to provide the aesthetic training.

The problem for this reading is the fact that, as I noted above, *The Prelude* was published in 1850 complete with the account of the *Recluse* scheme given in the Preface to *The Excursion*—suggesting that the whole "Gothic" matrix of *The Recluse* was felt to be necessary to a reading of *The Prelude*, even when the "Gothic" constitution was no more. However, the fact that, as I noted above, the periodical reviews of the poem took this cue to figure it as an antediluvian relic, suggests that the Preface was reprinted in 1850 precisely in order to mark the historicity of the poem, to signal its antediluvian nature. In other words, where Wordsworth originally intended the Gothic analogy to body forth a constructive act of constitutional solidifying, its meaning was altered for him by a changing cultural ambiance in which the Gothic became an object of nostalgia and of historical interest precisely in proportion as the Gothic constitution was dismantled. As the Gothicism of the Romantics modulated into the high medievalism of John Carter and Walter Scott and then of Kenelm Digby, and as this in turn gave way to the Arthurianism of a poet like Tennyson, the narrow ratio between Gothic architecture and the Gothic constitution was progressively widened. We can thus see the Gothic analogy as a sort of historiographical "moment"—a pivot point through which the force of Wordsworth's historical consciousness is transmitted with widening effect across the nineteenth century; a narrowly political original impetus gradually opening the door to a full-blooded culture of the Gothic.

This chapter has argued that the Gothic theory of the constitution was an important component of the Revolution controversy in the 1790s, and that its traces remain visible in the poetry and prose of Wordsworth and his fellow Lakers on into the nineteenth century. But I have so far only given an outline of the radical Gothic politics that is thus so effectively and creatively "Disowned by memory" (*1805* I, 643). In order to appreciate the original fullness of the Gothic position whose fragments are thus scattered across poems such as "Tintern Abbey" and *The White Doe of Rylstone*, we must therefore turn, and, in proper *Prelude* fashion, "Planting...snowdrops among winter snows" (1805 I, 644), measure back a course to the early 1790s, and to the more explicitly "Gothic" poetry of *Salisbury Plain* (1794).

CHAPTER 2

RADICAL GOTHIC:
POLITICS AND ANTIQUARIANISM
IN *SALISBURY PLAIN* (1794)

On November 5, 1793 the satirist James Gillray published a print entitled *The French invasion;—or—John Bull, bombarding the bum-boats*.[1] The print, also captioned "A new Map of England and France," fuses together in a single striking image the stock figure of "John Bull," the silhouette of the British Isles, and the famously rubicund visage of King George III. "John Bull," with the head of the king joined incongruously to a body patched together from the counties of England and Wales, leaps over the severed "head" of France, and hitches up his harlequin's costume to discharge ordural ordnance upon the invading "bum-boats." What, in late 1793, with a French invasion a real possibility, was the meaning of this scatological lèse majesté? The Gagging Acts of December 1795 would shortly make such images potentially treasonable; though prints like Richard Newton's *Treason* (1798), in which John Bull breaks wind upon a picture of the king, would continue to defy the law. Changing tastes determined that when Henry Bohn printed Gillray's *Works* in 1851, *The French Invasion* was among the "suppressed plates" consigned to a separate supplement (Bohn, ed. 1851, II, pl. 32). But the print's early audience was almost certainly more amused than scandalized. "[A] Grub Street print not void of humour," sniffed the connoisseur Horace Walpole at a similar Gillray of 1791 that depicted a high-society scandal as a volley of turds answering a cannonade of billets-doux (Gatrell 2006, 255–56). And, as Vic Gatrell has shown, the print participates in a more general outbreak of carnal humor around the turn of the century, with, for example, "national enemies like Napoleon, or grotesque faces" adorning the bottoms of Britain's chamberpots (Gatrell 2006, 184). Thus, for Gatrell, the scatology of *The French Invasion* quite simply "communicated aggression" (2006, 183). Similarly, the British Museum's *Catalogue of Political and Personal Satires* focuses on how "the King...strides across the ocean with great vigour" (George, ed. 1870–1954, VII, 41); while in the eyes of both Linda Colley and Vincent Carretta, Gillray's "fusion of the monarch and the kingdom" generates a new graphic language of British loyalism (Colley 1996, 210; Carretta 1990, 299–301).

But the print is keyed to contemporary events in ways that complicate such readings. As Richard Godfrey notes, the "British Declaration" encrypted in John Bull's feces is a direct reference "to a royal promise that the port of Toulon, then occupied by the British, would be ceded to France on the restitution of its monarchy" (Godfrey and Hallett 2001, 112). Indeed, with France depicted as something like the guillotined and rotting head of Louis XVI, and the caption pointedly proclaiming a "new Map" of England and France, the print is as much a satire (timed for Guy Fawkes night) on the widening constitutional gap between still-monarchical Britain and newly republican France as a loyalist "fusion" of king and country. Gillray echoes the common loyalist scheme of contrasting scenes of "conscious" and domestic British liberty with depictions of deranged and public French anarchy, but he contrives to subvert such loyalist readings too.[2] Where the king in his Northumbrian dunce's cap is seemingly divorced from his own body—his mien of gormless rectitude betraying absolutely no consciousness of his own incontinent "declaration"—the gigantic French head, squeezing its "Seine" eyes shut, can be seen at least to possess a unitary national countenance. Or, to put that in the terms of the ongoing Revolution controversy, the image can be seen to constitute an ironic commentary on Burke's claim that "you can better ingraft any description of republic on a monarchy than anything of a monarchy on republican forms" (Burke 1987, 110). The print may illustrate Burke's account of the French republic coming "into the world with the symptoms of death," with a system on which "institutions can never" soundly be "embodied...in persons" (Burke 1987, 161, 68), but it also burlesques Tom Paine's riposte that "to connect representation with...monarchy, is eccentric government" (Paine 1995, 233).

Gillray's image of an artificial body yoked to a natural head has a long genealogy in British political discourse—stretching back at least as far as Thomas Hobbes's *Leviathan* (1651). Hobbes's argument that social existence required the concentration of all "power and strength" in one absolute sovereign was memorably captured in Abraham Bosse's frontispiece depicting the state as a gigantic "artificial man" composed of a multitude of individual bodies beneath a single natural head (Morgan, ed. 1996, 650, 586). This representation was subsequently adapted in Aylett Sammes's 1676 illustrated history of ancient Britain, where, alongside a discussion of the despotic rule of the ancient British Druids and their "absolute power" of life and death, there appeared the handsome naturalistic head and the victim-filled framework body of "The Wicker Image" (Sammes 1676, 103–5).[3]

Separated by more than a century, the analogy between Sammes's wicker man and Gillray's incontinent leviathan is clearly far from exact. But with the proper representation of Britain "sacrificed" to the representation of the periodically "mad" king's "eccentric government," and with his rag-bag of a body hinting at the ongoing ritual of sacrificial burning every November 5, the Gillray print obliquely suggests that Britain in 1793 is reverting to a despotic dispensation similar to the one encoded in Sammes's wicker image. We do not need, however, to make so large an analogical leap. As Alan Liu notes, the imagery of sacrifice was current in British public discourse through newspaper coverage of the September Massacres (Liu 1989, 151). One report, of the Paris mob ordering a Swiss soldier carefully to "take off [the] head" of a "very handsome" "young Swiss officer," in order to put it "upon a pike...to the best advantage," indeed takes us very close to Sammes's wicker man (*The Times*, September 12, 1792, 2). Richard Gravil has suggested that the figure of the sacrificial wicker was echoed in the "more topical colossus" of Jacques Louis David's "National Unity" pageant of August 10, 1793, "in which a Herculean figure strikes down the Monster of Federalism" (Gravil 2003, 12). In Britain the absent Tom Paine was guyed and burned at Chelmsford in November 1792 (Foot and Kramnick, eds. 1987, 15). And from the first the British revolution controversy was keyed to the ambivalent image of immolation. Burke figured Britain as a "frame of polity" given "the image of a relation in blood," as an "oblation...on the high altar of universal praise" (Burke 1987, 30, 86). He denounced the Revolution, however, for acting as though the French were "a people of yesterday" (32)—for attempting, that is, to engineer one of what Rousseau had pictured as history's rare "epochs" when old regimes give way to "the horror of the past," "and when the state, set on fire by civil wars, is reborn, as it were, from its ashes" (Morgan, ed., 929).

Radicals like Tom Paine and Richard Price, meanwhile, hailed the demise of the ancien regime as the end of government by "priest-craft;"[4] the "complete History" of which, or "the art of...leading the people by the nose," the Whig polemicist John Toland had long before identified in "the History of the Druids" (Toland 1726, I, 8, 11–12), and which Thomas Percy had recently epitomized in the druidical practice, associated with belief in "the Metempsichosis, or a Transmigration of the soul," of making human sacrifices in "large wicker images" (Mallet, trans. Percy 1770, I, xvi–xvii). Priestcraft and Druidism were one and the same thing. Gillray, whose *Smelling out a Rat* of December 1790 imagined the long-nosed Burke magically sending forth his spirit to disturb Price in his republican "midnight calculations," was certainly alive to this vein of weird political imagery. Indeed, in the light of a series of subsequent prints that includes *Midas, Transmuting all into Gold Paper* (1797), whose William Pitt made out of money strongly recalls both the wicker and the leviathan, and *Destruction of the French Collossus* (1798), which to Gravil "suggests the wicker man" (2003, 268n), *The French Invasion* looks distinctly like an early rendering of Gillray's "druidical" imagination of contemporary events.[5]

But if a sense of "druidical" reversion was only latent in Gillray in the early 1790s, it was already fully developed in the imaginations of the young radicals Samuel Taylor Coleridge and William Wordsworth. Coleridge's "Religious Musings" (1794) segued from reflections on how the "sublime of man / Our noontide majesty" was "to know ourselves / Parts and proportions of one wondrous whole," to how this sense sublime was travestied in the "grisly idols" of "superstition," and to the renewal of such fratricidal sin in Britain's "fiendish" prosecution of the present war against liberty in France (ll. 126–92; Jackson, ed. 1985, 16–18). Wordsworth, meanwhile, who was likely already acquainted with Sammes's "Wicker Image,"[6] had had first-hand experience of the sacrificial imagery and the reality of the French Revolution. He had been resident in France throughout 1792, at Paris only "a little month" (*1805* X, 65) after the September massacres, and, as Alan Liu and Nicholas Roe have suggested, in uncomfortably close proximity to the simultaneous "outrages" around Orléans.[7] Wordsworth's republican pamphlet of June 1793, *A Letter to the Bishop of Llandaff*, anticipated Gillray and echoed Paine in characterizing Burke's defence of Britain's "mixed" government as "infatuated" eccentricity (*Prose Works* I, 36). And in late August 1793, following an abortive tour of the Isle of Wight with William Calvert, and a solitary northwestward trek across Salisbury Plain and past Tintern Abbey to visit Robert Jones in north Wales, Wordsworth began composing a poem, *Salisbury Plain* (1794), in which he recorded a terrifying vision straight out of Sammes, of "huge wickers," sacrificial altars "fed / With living men;" their "deep…groans" filling the "dismal" desert (ll. 424, 184–85, 182).[8] The horror of the ancient British past clearly seemed to Wordsworth and Coleridge to have returned upon Britain in 1794. But what did this imagined historical reversion mean to them? Was the wicker man friend or foe, a help or a threat? Was it the death-dealing harbinger of a new republican epoch, or a warning out of a despotic past?

This chapter seeks to answer these questions, and to begin fleshing out my argument for the radical Gothicism of early Romanticism, by reading *Salisbury Plain* as a Gothic poem in the sense of adapting the conventions of Gothic horror to a poetic articulation of the antiquarian stance of British radicalism in the early 1790s.[9] Recent work on the poem by Damien Walford Davies and Paul Wright has brought out strongly how it links ancient acts of murder with what Wordsworth later called modern Britain's "wars…against Liberty" (*Prose Works* I, 308), and shown how the poem dramatizes Wordsworth's increasing awareness of "threatened Englishness" and his abandonment of the "Celtic" and "Druidical" radicalism with which he aligned himself on his return from France in late 1792 (Davies 2002, 67; Wright 1998, 75–78). I suggest that this is not simply a negative "reactionary" turn; rather that *Salisbury Plain* sees Wordsworth respond to the dismaying affinities of both the Revolution and the British counter-revolution with druidical sacrifice by resorting to an older English tradition of "Gothic" radicalism. By bringing a range of historical material to bear upon the first text of the poem (also known as "A Night on Salisbury Plain"), and by reconstructing the materialist and antiquarian orientation of late-eighteenth-century radical thought, I hope to recover a fuller sense of the historical and political ideas encrypted in Wordsworth's evocation of the landscape of Salisbury Plain in 1793–94.

## Two Nations

Stephen Gill has characterized *Salisbury Plain* as a protest poem, part of the politically radical "crusade against the follies and corruptions hidden within the apparently ordered and just structure of English society" (*SPP* 5). At the poem's heart is an encounter between a nameless traveler, making his way toward "the troubled west" (l. 36), and a female vagrant, who tells him a tale of social injustice and familial collapse. In tracing her oppression, Gill suggests, Wordsworth suddenly perceived a link with "the reasons why...the country was plunging into an unjust war" against revolutionary France, and imagined "the disaster that threatens a country that has divided into two nations" (*SPP* 5). This disastrous division is worked out in the poem in terms of the female vagrant's account of the visitations of social injustice—enclosure, conscription and indigence—upon her family and upon herself, and in the indifference of those who abandon her "homeless near a thousand homes" (l. 386). But the division within Britain was not, for Wordsworth, a thing only of the present. Rather, it was articulated in the very fabric of the nation.

In the "Advertisement" to *Guilt and Sorrow* (1842), *Salisbury Plain* in its final form, Wordsworth recalled how, in late summer 1793, he had watched the fleet preparing for war from the Isle of Wight. Filled with forebodings of "distress and misery beyond all possible calculation," he then "spent two days in walking on foot over Salisbury Plain":

> The monuments and traces of antiquity, scattered in abundance over that region, led me unavoidably to compare what we know or guess of those remote times with certain aspects of modern society, and calamities, principally those consequent upon war, to which, more than other classes of men, the poor are subject. (*SPP,* 216–27)

It was, he continued, in such "reflections, joined with some particular facts that had come to my knowledge," that "the following stanzas originated."

Two facts about Salisbury Plain were particularly "unavoidable" in the late eighteenth century. First, as the location of Stonehenge, the Plain was the battlefield for competing accounts of British antiquity. One tradition, transmitted from Geoffrey of Monmouth via the chronicles of Holinshed, Speed, and Stow, held that it was built by the fifth-century British king Aurelius Ambrosius in commemoration of the so-called Treason of the Long Knives, when, at a peace conference, the Saxons under Hengist had treacherously captured King Vortigern and massacred the British nobility (Jones 1725, 14). For Inigo Jones, writing in 1620, Stonehenge was a Roman Temple (Jones 1725, 44). But the eighteenth-century orthodoxy, established in William Stukeley's *Stonehenge a Temple Restor'd to the British Druids* (1740), was that Stonehenge was the "metropolitan church" of the British Druids (Stukeley 1740, 10). It was a scene, Stukeley said, where "neither Roman nor English had place" (2). Wordsworth would have encountered scenes of druidical sacrifice, often located among the cromlechs at Stonehenge, in poems by Michael Drayton, Thomas Chatterton, and Erasmus Darwin.[10] And, as I noted earlier, he would very likely have known of the rival claims upon the monument through historical works like Aylett Sammes's *Antiqua Britannia Illustrata* (1676), which discussed both the Vortigern legend and the traditions of Druidical sacrifice (390–391, 104–5).

These strands of legend are woven at the conclusion to *Salisbury Plain* into an equivocal endorsement of the supposedly more enlightened present:

> Though from huge wickers paled with circling fire
> No longer horrid shrieks and dying cries
> To ears of Dæmon-Gods aspire,
> To Dæmon-Gods a human sacrifice;
> Though Treachery her sword no longer dyes
> In the cold blood of Truce, still, reason's ray,
> What does it more than while the tempests rise,
> With starless glooms and sounds of loud dismay,
> Reveal with still-born glimpse the terrors of our way?
> (ll. 424–32)

Wordsworth here associates two acts of mass murder that are also foundational moments in British history: human sacrifice was, according to Sammes, central to the rule of the ancient British Druids (104–5). Later, the Treason of the Long Knives marked the dawn of Saxon England (391). Both "Britain" and "England" are seen thus to be founded in blood; "still-born" in the "iniquity and disgrace" that eighteenth-century British radicals saw at the bottom of all old governments (Paine 1995, 220).

The second "unavoidable" fact about Salisbury Plain was that, as the location of Old Sarum, the deserted town that epitomized the problem of "rotten boroughs" in the late eighteenth century, it represented all that was perverted and corrupted in modern Britain. Old Sarum was represented in Parliament by two members, despite having, in the words of the *Analytical Review* for June 1792, "not a single house standing, nor person living within...[its] limits...to be represented" (173–74). "And does not the friends of the Constitution weep, and does not the enemies of the Constitution smile," asked the Edinburgh reformer Thomas Muir at his trial for sedition in 1793, "when they hear of such representation" (Muir [1793], 124). For Paine boroughs like Old Sarum were "Gothic institutions" in a wholly negative sense. They formed part of a labyrinthine system of government—defended by Pitt's government as a "virtual representation"—under which man was "thrown back to a vast distance from his Maker" and kept from his natural rights by "a succession of barriers, or sort of turnpike gates" tended by priests, aristocrats and kings. But if this "wilderness of turnpike gates" could be escaped, Paine argued, natural rights would be resumed, and today might appear as the day after the Creation (Paine 1995, 275, 118, 125, 118–19). Such wished for effacement is literalized in Wordsworth's *Salisbury Plain* as a "desart" in which "no line of mournful light / From lamp of lonely toll-gate streamed athwart the night" (ll. 116–17).

But this imaginative displacement of "Gothic institutions" does not usher in a revolutionary utopia. Rather, it works like the creative acts of remembrance that in *The Prelude* "throw back our life / And almost make our infancy itself / A visible scene, on which the sun is shining" (*1805* I, 661–63). In *Salisbury Plain* modern Britain is "thrown back" to the dark moment before the dawn of "English" history—before the Normans, before the Danes and the Anglo-Saxons, before even the Romans—in the prehistoric "infancy" of Celtic and Druidical Britain. This imaginative relapse of modern England into ancient Britain stems directly from Wordsworth's interpretation of contemporary events. The war, he wrote in *The Prelude*, "put forth" the "strength of Britain," but tore "at one decisive rent / From the best youth in England their dear pride / Their joy in England" (1805 X, 229, 276–78). The once-vibrant cult of England and of English liberty—epitomized in the agitation for reform by John Wilkes and his followers in the 1760s—here dwindles to the repetition of an empty name. For Anne Janowitz, this national fall causes the remote past and the immediate present to collide at Salisbury:

> For a man suffering his first real "revolution"—the political self-betrayal of his nation—what makes Salisbury Plain an apt place for Wordsworth to lose his way and have to wander for a few days is that this "other region," this terrain most unlike the fruitful country of nature's benevolence, is also England most *like* itself, since the monument Stonehenge is the marker of England's own antiquity. The birth of the nation is here mapped onto the same "spot" as the blasting of the nation. (Janowitz 1990, 96)

Adapting Freud, Janowitz calls this the "political source" of the poem's "uncanny" atmosphere—the making-strange of a "long familiar" England (1990, 93). This "political uncanny" arises from the way Wordsworth uses Stonehenge simultaneously to conflate and to distinguish the historically and politically distinct entities of

England and Britain; from his strong misreading of Stonehenge—where, to quote Stukeley again, "neither Roman nor English had place"—as a sign of *English* antiquity. Indeed, Janowitz's description of Wordsworth's poem resonates with a key literary-historical text from the period in a way that suggests still more strongly that *Salisbury Plain* sees Wordsworth mapping two separate cultures onto one another. For the passage from a "fruitful country" to a "desart" is (as Wordsworth would likely have known) the identical image that Hugh Blair used in his *Critical Dissertation on the Poems of Ossian* (1763) to distinguish the literary remains of the two ancient peoples of northern Europe, the Celts and the Goths, as represented within Britain by the Scots (and Welsh and Irish) and the English respectively.[11] "When we turn," Blair wrote, "from the poetry of Lodbrog to that of Ossian, it is like passing from a savage desart, into a fertile and cultivated country" (Blair 1763, 11). The shift in *Salisbury Plain* is, however, in precisely the opposite direction—from a world of "Refinement" and "soft affections" (ll. 28–29) to one "more fierce" and barbarous "than e'er assai[led] / The savage without home in winter's keenest gale" (ll. 35–36). Wordsworth's poem does not move from a sane "Celtic" present to a barbarous "Gothic" past. Rather, it moves from an England marked by the "distant spire" of the Gothic cathedral of Salisbury to a prehistoric British landscape, marked by Stonehenge, where "huge wickers" (l. 424), "fed / With living men" (ll. 184–85), make "To Dæmon-Gods a human sacrifice" (l. 427).

Significantly, Wordsworth's reversal of Blair's judgment is not original. In *Northern Antiquities* (1770), a text Wordsworth possibly encountered during his school days under Thomas Bowman, Thomas Percy turned Blair's charge of Gothic barbarism back upon the Celts.[12] As we have seen, a long tradition—from Richard Verstegan and Nathaniel Bacon, through Henry Saint John Bolingbroke and Richard Hurd—pictured the English government as descended, via the Anglo-Saxons, from the ancient German or Gothic polities described by Tacitus.[13] For Montesquieu, the exemplary British Constitution was a "Gothic government" (1750, I, 233). And for Percy it was no absurdity to speak of Gothic England: "[I]nstitutions," including parliament and judiciary, that had "existed among the Germans already in the time of Tacitus…followed the Saxons into England; and when the times of confusion had caused them to wear out of memory, the great Alfred immortalized his name by reviving them" (1770, I, 181–82). But, Percy wrote, "[t]he Celtic nations" from whom the poetry of Ossian supposedly came, "do not appear to have had that equal plan of liberty, which was the peculiar honour of all the Gothic tribes," adding:

> The [Druids among the Celts] frequently burnt a great quantity of human victims alive, in large wicker images, as an offering to their Gods. The Gothic nations, though like all other Pagans, they occasionally defiled their altars with human blood, appear never to have had any custom like this. (I, xii–xvii)[14]

*Salisbury Plain*'s visions of wicker images, "fed / With living men," thus engage in what Nick Groom has called the "battle," fought out on the "enchanted ground" of ancient poetry and antiquarian enquiry, between Celts and Goths, Macpherson and Percy, for control of Britain's national mythology in the late eighteenth century (Groom 1999, 62, 82). In 1794, Edward Williams (the Bard Iolo Morganwg) drew similar battle-lines in Wales. The true history of the Welsh Bards and Druids was, he claimed, everywhere "wilfully suppressed in favour of the wildest preconceptions and absurdest theories that could ever enter the brain of the most barbarous *Goth*" (Williams 1794, II, 8–9, and I, xviii). This "Gothic" assault continued unabated in works like Southey and Lovell's *Poems* (1795), in which "The Druid throng...fall[s] away" before warriors marching under "Gothic banners" to eradicate the bloody rites of the Celtic deities Tentates and Taranis ("The Death of Odin," in Lovell and Southey 1795, 107–8). Similarly, Walter Scott's *The Antiquary* (1816), stages a mock-heroic struggle during the invasion scare of 1794, in which the lowland antiquary Jonathan Oldbuck and his highland nephew Hector quarrel over the relative dignity of Scotland's Celtic and Gothic patrimonies, and in which Gothic textual relics collected by writers like Southey and Percy are given antiquarian priority over Macpherson's "English Ossian" in proportion as the "mighty and unconquered Goths" are accorded historical priority over "the bare-breeched Celts whom they subdued" (Scott 2002, 292–94, 464n). Wordsworth, reproducing similarly negative "preconceptions" about the Celtic Druids, was clearly part of this "Gothic" assault. Indeed, many years later, Wordsworth made explicit his self-imagination as a combatant in the literary-historical "battle." In a letter of May 14, 1829 to George Huntly Gordon, Wordsworth related how, while in Wales in 1793, his "poor English head" had been threatened with a "huge sharp pointed carving knife" by an intoxicated "Priest" who had believed himself, "an ancient Briton," insulted "on [his] own territory" by this "vile Saxon" (*LY* II, 77–79; Gravil 2003, 272). The humorous manner in which Wordsworth miniaturizes the Celtic/Gothic opposition only makes the anecdote the more telling. Reversing the Treason of the Long Knives, Wordsworth makes his younger self into a civilized Gothic Saxon in need of protection from the barbarous Celtic Briton, even as the comic register of the story makes it clear that the "Celtic" threat is now safely past. But if, as I have suggested, Wordsworth's *Salisbury Plain* poem of 1794 is patterned upon this Celtic/Gothic opposition, it takes what is nevertheless a much more ambiguous position. The poem contains a minority report on Druidical enlightenment: "Long bearded forms" initiate "vast assemblies" in the arcane science of astronomy (ll. 191–96). And indeed, the poem's nightmare of relapse into Druidical sacrifice is apparently a deliberate reversal and partial undoing of the Whig model of English history whereby, in the words of James Thomson's *Liberty* (1735–36), the successive invasions of the "Gothic nations" of Saxons, Danes, and Normans had transported Britain "from Celtic night / To present grandeur" (IV, 624–25, in Robertson, ed. 1908).

My argument up to this point has been that in *Salisbury Plain* Wordsworth envisages parallels between Britain's divided Celtic and Gothic inheritance and the divisions within the modern nation, and that in this fraught choice of inheritance he cleaved, ultimately, to the Gothic side. The rest of the chapter will explore how the poem sees Wordsworth constructing a new political identity that is at once radical and Gothic.

## England's Palladium:
## Salisbury Cathedral and Magna Carta

I want now to suggest that Salisbury Cathedral provides the key to Wordsworth's attempt, in *Salisbury Plain*, to articulate his troubled sense that grand, Gothic England was under threat. Salisbury was, as Danziger and Gillingham note, the first cathedral in England to be built entirely in the architectural style that would later be denominated "Gothic" (2003, 272). Its spire was, at 404 feet, the tallest in England—making it, in Michael Wiley's phrase, "the physical pinnacle of the state Church" (1998, 25). Moreover, Gothic architecture was under construction at the turn of the nineteenth century as a definitively English architecture. In 1800 the Society of Antiquaries would propose that the term "Gothic" be dropped and "English" substituted in its stead (Warton, Bentham, Grose, and Milner 1800, iii). The architectural style was also closely linked in the long eighteenth century with the ancient Goths themselves. In August

1809 the *Quarterly Review* noted Archbishop William Warburton's discredited surmise that

> the Goths...having been accustomed, during the gloom of Paganism, to worship the Deity in groves...ingeniously projected to make [their churches] resemble groves as nearly as the distance of architecture would permit: and...no attentive observer ever viewed a regular avenue of well-grown trees, but it presently put him in mind of the long vista through a Gothic cathedral; or even entered one...but it presented to his imagination an avenue of trees. (*QR* 2:3 [1809], 131)

Wordsworth was certainly familiar with Warburton's thesis by 1814, when in book five of *The Excursion* he described the Gothic church of St. Oswald's, Grasmere, as a "Pile, / ...large and massy," "crowded" with "pillars,"

> ...and the roof upheld
> By naked rafters intricately crossed,
> Like leafless underboughs, in some thick grove,
> All withered by the depth of shade above.
> (V, 148–53; Bushell, Butler, and Jaye, eds. 2007, 171)

If St. Oswald's thus put Wordsworth in mind of arboreal colonnades and ancient Gothic dwellers in houseless woods, then similar thoughts might well have occurred to him in the presence of Salisbury Cathedral. For, as he surely knew in 1793, Salisbury had recently been "improved" by James Wyatt: its choir screen was removed precisely in order to create (or to "restore") the long uninterrupted "avenue" of the nave (Clark 1962, 86). And the circle that makes avenue-like Salisbury an icon of England's Gothic legacy would have closed for Wordsworth when he read, by the summer of 1793, Montesquieu's assertion that the "beautiful system" of the English constitution "was invented first in the woods" (see Wu 1993, 101; and Montesquieu 1750, I, 230).

Wordsworth was thus well prepared at the time of his night upon Salisbury Plain to make a symbolic equation between the Gothic cathedral and Gothic England. Salisbury Cathedral indeed functions in the poem as a signpost, only to be instantly effaced from the view of one who, stranded near the "mountain-pile" (l. 82) of Stonehenge, must take "the wet cold ground" (l. 63) for his bed:

> The troubled west was red with stormy fire,
> O'er Sarum's plain the traveller with a sigh

> Measured each painful step, the distant spire
> That fixed at every turn his backward eye
> Was lost, tho' still he turned, in the blank sky.
> (ll. 36–40)

The implication of the spire in the established social order is shown in the fact that the everyman traveler genuflects toward it from persistence of habit even when it is "lost" from view. Although the ideological significance of the "loss" is somewhat obscured at first by the extremity of the traveler's predicament, it is subsequently made clear in the female vagrant's tale. Her memory of the "miserable hour" of her family's "trampling" by "Oppression" is also figured as a "last…surve[y]" of "the steeple-tower" of their village church, "Peering above the trees" (ll. 262–64).

Before I expand on the symbolic centrality of the "loss" of the cathedral to the rest of *Salisbury Plain*, it is important to note that it is likely to be based in the facts of Wordsworth's own trek of August 1793. As Kenneth Johnston notes in *The Hidden Wordsworth*, the Plain is hardly a plain at all, "but rather a vast expanse of swales, swelling ridges, and slopes, in which the walker is paradoxically more often out of sight of the horizon and his general whereabouts than he would be in climbing a mountain" (Johnston 1998, 347). "Southwest Prospect from Stonehenge," plate sixteen in Stukeley's *Stonehenge*, illustrates the point well: showing—what Stukeley also described (1740, 13)—"Salisbury steeple" visible above the horizon in the view from Stonehenge, but also showing the deep furrows in the landscape of the Plain.[15] The steeple is presumably "lost" to the traveler, then, not because darkness falls (the sky is pointedly "blank" and the sun does not sink until thirty-three lines later), or because it recedes over the horizon, but because the traveler is himself "out of sight of the horizon," in one of the folds in the landscape between the two monuments. Wordsworth indeed says as much: "each slope" the traveler "mounted seemed to hide / Some cottage" (ll. 55–56); and it is only when, standing "on a mound," he lifts his gaze from "the deep entrenched ground," that Stonehenge heaves into view (ll. 73–75). Having lost his bearings within the landscape, the traveler is also figuratively lost within the historical field that runs from the ancient Britain of Stonehenge to the Gothic England of Salisbury.

The loss of the spire is thus on one level flatly literal, but on another it is highly symbolic. Indeed, the spire is, as Wiley notes, a double absence—lost first to sight, and then also to sound (Wiley 1998, 20). When the female vagrant relates how "An old man beckoning from the naked steep / Came tottering sidelong down to ask the hour," Wordsworth adds in parenthesis, "There never clock was heard from steeple tower" (ll. 165–67). This awkward authorial steer—introducing what Johnston calls the "inexplicable" notion that a vagrant might be expected to have a watch (Johnston 1998, 347)— suggests that the absence of the "steeple tower" in *Salisbury Plain* is an important interpretative crux. This suggestion is borne out by the manuscript history of the poem. For in another draft (in DC MS. 2) of the female vagrant's story, the very same "steeple tower" is oppressively *present*:

> N[o] sound save her own steps she seemed to hear
> For ten long miles: from the Minster tower,
> The distant clock tolled out the morning's second hour.
> (DC MS. 2, 58ᵛ, in *SPP*, 290, 297 [fragment b, ll. 25–27])

This passage might be either early or late: Ernest De Selincourt suggests 1791, while Carol Landon favors 1795–96 (*SPP*, 288). Wordsworth either removes the originally present cathedral from the 1794 text, or inserts it in a later revision. But the important point is that the cathedral can be inserted and removed at will. The poem's Plain is thus less a real or an imaginary than a *virtual* topography. Like the political system of "virtual representation" in Burke's *Letter to Sir Hercules Langrishe* (1792), it is dependent upon "a substratum in the actual" (70). But it is also susceptible to manipulation for emblematic effects. Something similar is suggested by Wordsworth's prefatory comment in *Guilt and Sorrow* that "one or two" of "the features described as belonging to [the Plain]...are taken from other desolate parts of England" (*SPP*, 217).

The lost steeple tower of *Salisbury Plain* can thus be read as a poetically purposeful absence. Indeed, the spire's function here as a symbol of Gothic England is confirmed by the fact that its second "loss" involves the absence of the cathedral clock. For Salisbury's was the oldest working clock in Britain and perhaps the world, and had kept the hours in a detached Bell Tower at Salisbury from 1386 to 1790, when, during Wyatt's "improvements," it was moved to the steeple tower itself (Duley 1997, 6–7). In the early 1790s it therefore represented a recent break with the medieval (Gothic) past. Was this dislocation another of the "particular facts" that fed into *Salisbury Plain*? Wordsworth's phrasing is certainly suggestive, for it was only since Wyatt's demolition and relocation work that it would have been possible for the clock to be heard (or not heard) from the "steeple" or the "Minster tower" rather than the old Bell Tower. To Wordsworth, who was at Paris soon after the institution of the new Republican calendar in September 1792, this rupture could well have suggested a vision of the Plain as another country in which the old scheme of history was abolished. As the Gothic spire of Salisbury disappears, the accumulations of the recent past and the controlling narratives of English history are sloughed off to reveal a region that is precisely devoid of English history and its physical traces on the land.

But Salisbury Cathedral was not only a symbol or a synecdoche of Gothic England. It was also, as Wordsworth almost certainly knew, the repository of Magna Carta (1215). Signed in the presence of Salisbury's future architect, Elias de Dereham, the charter extorted from King John by the English barons was, as William Blackstone noted in his *Commentaries on the Laws of England* (1765–69), "sent to all cathedral churches" soon after its confirmation (Stroud 1996, 11; Scott 2003, 19; Danziger and Gillingham, 273; Blackstone 1765–69, I, 124). The cathedral, founded five years later, thus marked the historical moment that, as Anne Pallister notes, the late-eighteenth-century reform movement imagined as the return of Saxon England from its Norman eclipse (Pallister 1971, 64). In *The Great Charter and Charter of the Forest* (1759), Blackstone noted that "the archives of the dean and chapter of Salisbury" held one of only "three…originals" of Magna Carta "still existing" in England (Blackstone 1759, xvii).[16] The two other known originals were held at the British Museum in London, having come down to posterity by eccentric routes that ended in their presentation to the nation in 1700 by the grandson of the private collector Sir Robert Cotton. One copy was badly singed by a fire that broke out in 1731, and concerns for its continued legibility prompted an engraving—which, "carefully printed" by Blackstone (1759, xvii, 10–25), then formed the basis for the wider public fame of Magna Carta. The Salisbury manuscript was reclusive and sedentary by contrast. According to J. C. Holt, it "probably resides in the count[y] which obtained [it] in 1215," forming a steady fixture in the religious and constitutional history of England (1965, 313). Despite languishing long in the cathedral library, "buried," as Beriah Botfield says of many of the library's volumes, "in dust," Salisbury's charter remained unscathed (qtd. in Eward 1983, 7). And it remains, according to Harry Bailey's history of Salisbury's library, "the best preserved of the four remaining originals" (1978, 5). With Lincoln's copy in abeyance, and the better known of the Cotton manuscripts apparently perishing by inches, the Salisbury copy was, in the middle of the eighteenth century, one of only two wholly legible copies—and, at that, the best copy—of the foundational document of English liberties remaining in England.

The physical location of the original document of Magna Carta at Salisbury is vital for my reading of the political symbolism at work in *Salisbury Plain* because the charter was the closest thing Protestant England had to a holy relic, and because the dominant doctrine of the "virtual constitution" was deeply reliant upon such a "substratum in the actual." For the constitutional writer Samuel Johnson, the great charter was nothing less than the "Palladium of our Government" (Johnson 1700, 78): England's answer to the statue of the goddess Pallas, on the preservation of which, as John Lemprière's *Classical Dictionary* (1792) noted, "depended the safety" of ill-fated Troy. And a long tradition of English radicalism, from the Levelers to the Wilkesites, emphasized the physicality of Magna Carta, imagining it as the bricks and mortar, and as the robust but vulnerable body, of English law (Pallister 1971, 17, 59–60). Changing the metaphor, Blackstone's *Commentaries* envisaged the "great charter of liberties," with its provisions against arbitrary arrest and imprisonment, at the head of a stream of English liberty that flowed on through the Petition of Right (1628), the Habeas Corpus Act (1679), the Bill of Rights (1689), and the Act of Settlement (1701), up to his own day (Blackstone 1765–69, I, 123–24). The Habeas Corpus Act, proscribing imprisonment without trial, was not only the "stable bulwark of our liberties" but a "second *magna carta*" (I, 133). And with a nod to Johnson's image of Magna Carta as England's "Palladium," Blackstone added that "so long as this *palladium* remains sacred and inviolate," the "liberties of England cannot but subsist" (I, 343).

Wordsworth is likely to have been familiar with this characterization of Magna Carta, and to have understood it, like other British radicals, in urgently contemporary terms. In January 1794, the London Corresponding Society (LCS) republished the 1780 *Report* of the Society for Constitutional Information (SCI) on Parliamentary representation, arguing that "equal representation of the people, in the great council of the nation, annual elections, and the universal right of suffrage" were "transcendent" national rights, to be considered collectively as "the grand palladium of our nation" (LCS 1794, 6). This "transcendent" Palladium was grounded in the historical facticity of Magna Carta, for although the *Report* denied with Paine that such rights originated in "extort[ion] by violence from the hand of power," it asserted that they had been—as indeed Magna Carta had been—ratified by "the wisest princes of the Norman line" (6). This vision of Magna Carta and the national palladium took on a new urgency when, in May 1794, the Pitt government acted to crush internal dissent with the suspension of Habeas Corpus, and arrested and imprisoned members of the LCS and the SCI on suspicion of treason. When Wordsworth wrote to William Mathews on 23 May that this "enforcement" of government "doctrines" by "imprisonment" was "pregnant with every species of misery," he presumably had in mind not least Blackstone's prophecy that when Habeas Corpus—a "second *magna carta*" and English Palladium—should be violated, the liberties of England should cease to exist (*EY* 119). Indeed, this likelihood becomes a near certainty in light of the fact that Wordsworth had, only weeks before, borrowed a copy of the *Commentaries* from the library of his brother Richard (Wu 1993, 16).

The latent presence of the image of the Palladium in Wordsworth's view of politics in 1793–94 is made the more likely by its explicit presence in the writings of like-minded radicals. In October 1794, William Godwin's *Cursory Strictures* on the treason trials spoke of the 1351 statute of treason as "one of the great palladiums of the English constitution"—placing it, as John Barrell notes, among a set of hallowed "laws and institutions" that included the Grand Jury and Blackstone's "second *magna carta*," the Habeas Corpus Act (Barrell 2000, 302, 383). During the treason trials the LCS became itself a sort of Palladium: figured even by Pitt and the prosecution as an intelligent "political monster," an "*imperium in imperio*," and a "Corporation" that rivaled the government (Barrell 2006, 67–69). When in November and December, juries acquitted the LCS members Hardy, Thelwall, and Tooke, these streams of imagery met in Edward Williams' celebratory song, "Trial by Jury, The Grand Palladium of British Liberty" (reproduced in Davies 2002, 144). The image of the Palladium was of such currency in the milieu of British radicalism in the early 1790s that it seems fair to take Wordsworth's reference to its concrete manifestation in Salisbury Cathedral as symbolizing the presence on the land not only of the English Church, but also of the Gothic libertarian tradition—and to read *Salisbury Plain*'s vision of the cathedral as first "distant" and then "lost" as articulating a fear of the imminent demise of English liberty.

## Palladium Lost

Indeed, Magna Carta, the epitome of England and English liberty, was conspicuously "lost" at the time that Wordsworth trekked across Salisbury Plain. For Salisbury's Magna Carta was missing. Blackstone reported that "upon diligent enquiry made at that cathedral in

A.D. 1759, nothing of this sort could be found" (Blackstone 1759, xvii). And Blackstone's story of the vanishing Magna Carta at Salisbury was evidently well known, giving rise to two government enquiries into the manuscript's whereabouts in 1800 and 1806 (McKechnie 1914, 168). The charter was eventually rediscovered in the cathedral library at some point between 1806 and 1814—comfortably in time, in its role of Palladium, for Waterloo (McKechnie 1914, 168). But in 1793–94, with the disappearance of the manuscript widely put down to theft, and another copy singed by fire, there would clearly have been uncomfortable parallels with the theft of the Palladium that had precipitated the fall and firing of ancient Troy.[17] Salisbury without its Magna Carta would thus have been legible to Wordsworth in 1793–94 as the geographical location of a historical dislocation. It was a place where the continuum of English political history that Burke and Blackstone envisaged as an "entailed inheritance" from Magna Carta, through the Glorious Revolution and up to the present (Burke 1987, 29; Blackstone 1765–69, I, 123–24), was mis- and displaced; "thrown back" to allow the reflux of a more ancient dispensation. Or, to phrase that in terms likely to have been familiar to Wordsworth from his Cambridge contemporary John Tweddell's speech of cautious welcome for the French Revolution, such an "impairment" of the correspondence between the "beauteous edifice" of the Gothic constitution and its "tangible" origins would constitute an undermining of history so total as to turn the nation into a sort of Pandemonium, and to render the British (like the French) a people of yesterday, "destitute of any constitution at all, and...with no clue at hand to guide our bewildered imaginations through the intricate mazes of forlorn inquiry" in search of one (Tweddell 1815, 101–7).[18] Deprived of its "substratum in the actual" at Salisbury, there would be no "Gothic" middle way between the sanguinary poles of Celtic Druidism and abstract French radicalism.

Wordsworth's global encryption of this sense of reversion and recurrence in *Salisbury Plain* is worked out in detail in the parallel imagery of two of the poem's scenes. The first of these is the female vagrant's account of her experience of the American war, and the other is her third-hand account (attributed to "An old man," who had it of another "swain" [ll. 165, 173]) of a supernatural vision of long-dead warriors. For ease of comparison, I quote the two passages together:

> Of noysome hospitals the groan profound,
> The mine's dire earthquake, the bomb's thunder stroke;

> Heart sickening Famine's grim despairing look;
> The midnight flames in thundering deluge spread;
> The stormed town's expiring shriek that woke
> Far round the griesly phantoms of the dead,
> And pale with ghastly light the victor's human head.
> (ll. 363–69)

> [O]ft a night-fire mounting to the clouds
> Reveals the desert and with dismal red
> Clothes the black bodies of encircling crowds.
> It is the sacrificial altar fed
> With living men. How deep it groans—the dead
> Thrilled in their yawning tombs their helms uprear;
> The sword that slept beneath the warriour's head
> Thunders in fiery air: red arms appear
> Uplifted thro' the gloom and shake the rattling spear.
> (ll. 181–89)

The two passages differ in that the former is a catalogue of immediate affect, all but two of its lines discrete and end-stopped grammatical units, whereas the latter adopts a panoramic view and, with its heavy caesuras, implies ceremonial procedure: the colon in the penultimate line magically produces an army from the "groans" of the wicker and the "yawning tombs" that had gone before. In short, the distinction—truthfully preserved—is between the rough-edged perceptions of an individual traumatic experience and a legend much smoothed in the telling. In all the essential points of action and imagery, however, the two scenes are identical. The "groan profound" of noisome hospitals is answered by the "deep…groans" of the wicker man; "the bomb's thunder stroke" repeats for the gunpowder age a sword's "Thunders in fiery air;" "the griesly phantoms of the dead" are woken just like "the dead" that "Thrilled in their yawning tombs their helms uprear;" and the description of "ghastly light" showing "pale" from "the victor's human head"—a traumatized registering of *in*humanity—brings the sacrificial wicker firmly into the present day.

Modern war and ancient sacrifice are also virtually indistinguishable in their depredations. The female vagrant's husband is taken away to war when "with proud parade the noisy drum / Beat round to sweep the streets of want and pain" (ll. 300–301), so that those in "want and pain" serve as substitutes in battle for the powerful and proud. And in Wordsworth's likely source for the sacrificial practices of the ancient Britons, Aylett Sammes's *Britannia Antiqua Illustrata* (1676), the poor and the marginalized are literally consumed by the interests of a tyrannical social and political elite that, "exempted from the services of War...paid no Taxes as the rest of the people did," and wielded "absolute power" over life and death (103). "The *Druids* held an Opinion," Sammes wrote, "that the life of a Man, either in a desperate Sickness, or in danger of War, could not be secured unless another suffered in his stead, so that in such cases they either offered *Men* in sacrifice, or else vowed so to do after their delivery." This sacrifice took the form of "a *Wicker* Image" filled with criminals, and, if necessary, innocents too:

> In some places this Custome was observed, which, I suppose, was common to the *Druids* of *Britain* and *Gaul; They made a Statue or Image of a MAN in a vast proportion, whose Limbs consisted of Twigs, weaved together in the nature of Basket-ware: These they fill'd with live Men, and after that, set it on fire, and so destroy'd the poor Creatures in the smoak and flames*...(104–5)

The wicker man encountered in *Salisbury Plain* is thus a general image for the social and political injustices detailed in the poor female vagrant's tale. But it is also, I now want to move on to suggest, rather more than this. The resonance of the wicker image with similar images within Wordsworth's field of reference in 1793–94 makes it in fact an epitome of the contemporary ideas of British radicals on the underlying *causes* of political injustice.

## A Nation of the Dead: Reconstituting Wordsworth's Wicker Man

As Wordsworth is likely to have known, Salisbury Plain was traditionally the site of national assembly in Saxon times. According to David Williams's *Lessons to a Young Prince, by an Old Statesman* (1790), the Saxon constitution of Alfred provided that the "Mycle-Gemot," the "Folk-mot or Great Assembly of the Nation by its deputies...should ever meet annually on Salisbury Plain" (84). Wordsworth probably read the *Lessons*, which treated Burke as the "pious muse" of despotism (Williams 1790, 27), as one of the "master pamphlets of the day" (*1805* IX, 97). And Damien Walford Davies has raised the intriguing possibility that, since both men moved among the Girondin faction in Paris, and had possible common acquaintances in the Gironde leader Jacques Pierre Brissot and Henri Grégoire, Constitutional Bishop of Blois and "author of the French Republic," they may even have met in Paris in late 1792 (Davies 2002, 28–31;

Roe 1988, 43, 66–69).[19] What Davies calls "Williams's great admiration for…the Saxon constitution" (2002, 32) can thus be glimpsed behind Wordsworth's wish, as he quit France in December 1792 and "Reluctantly to England…returned," for the advent of "one paramount mind" to "quell" Robespierre and the Jacobins, "clea[r] a passage for just government, / And le[ave] a solid birthright to the state, / Redeemed according to example given / By ancient lawgivers" (*1805* X, 179–88).

Recently returned from France at the time when he walked across Salisbury Plain, the contrast between its "desart" scene of ancient national assembly and the "tumult [and] intrigue" (*1805* X, 134) in the National Assembly must have seemed to Wordsworth particularly sharp. Indeed, he might have seen Salisbury as a place where Britain's lack of a National Assembly to match that actual in France was vividly apparent. The context of Williams's reference to national assemblies at Salisbury in the days of Alfred was a discussion of how, by following an example that had fallen into disuse in England, the workings of the French National Assembly could be improved (Williams 1790, 42–47, 82). The constitution of Alfred, Williams had written, adapting Thomas Hobbes's account of the state as an "artificial man," had "all the necessary properties and effects of an organized body." "Tythings" of ten freemen, analogous to "capillary vessels" in a natural body, made annual elections to the "Hundreds," the level of local government, which in turn elected "Commanders & Magistrats of Counties." Parallel to these "graduated elections" was the "Myclegemot," or annual assembly of all freemen at Salisbury, analogous to "the seat of the mind," the decisions of which were passed into law through the "Wittenagemot," the legislature composed of "King, Barons, Bishops &c." These laws were enforced in turn by the combined executive power of Church and King. By this arrangement, Williams said,

> [t]he head and the extremities are united; not by occasional elections, or by pretended delegations of national power. The whole surface of the body, by minute subdivision, is formed to receive and transmit instantaneous impressions, external and internal; all the parts are held to their office by the general force, without commotion and without violence…(42–43)

In effect, therefore, "[t]he Mycle-gemot of Alfred was…the Nation," and, Williams added, "the members at a signal could have produced the nation in arms on Salisbury Plain" (Williams 1790, 89–90).

In this light, Wordsworth's vision on the Plain of an army whose "red arms appear / Uplifted thro' the gloom and shake the rattling spear" (ll. 188–89) can be seen as an attempt similarly to "produce" the nation: an attempt that proves monstrous and abortive in proportion as the actual modern representative is distorted. Salisbury Plain, doubly represented in Parliament, has in Wordsworth's poem only one dwelling ("the dead house of the plain" [l. 126]) and only two (vagrant) dwellers. Still at the end of the eighteenth century the country bore the marks of its history of violence. "The English nation," Williams wrote, "is not arranged, constructed, or organized into a political body" as was its Alfredian forbear. It operated, rather, on the principle that "the people when assembled (and they were never assembled) were every thing: when they had made their election, they were nothing." Parliament was thus no more than a "pretended representation," and elections to the representative strand of the constitution, the House of Commons, were, Williams added, fraudulent. Even "[t]hey who are said to possess the privilege" of voting "are controlled or directed in the exercise of it, by various orders affecting to be their superiors." The motions and "ideas of this pretended body therefore do not originate in the external senses," and hence

> [a] factitious body is generated within the society, which assumes the denomination of the state: but not being in sympathy with all the parts, often acts in direct opposition to the general feeling, inclination, or interest, which is the actuating principle or fundamental law of every free community. (Williams 1790, 47–48, 75–76)

A "factitious body" without senses is precisely the condition of the wicker man, which was literally a "body...generated within the society" of the ancient Britons in the interests not of the "general feeling" but of what Sammes called the "absolute power" of the druids. There is thus a direct analogy between the wicker man as visualized by Sammes, with a realistic head yoked to a merely symbolic wickerwork body, and Williams's Parliament that had placed itself at the head of the nation, on the principle that "the people...were nothing."

That Wordsworth drew just this analogy in 1793/4 is strongly suggested by the argument against Britain's "mixed" system in his *Letter to the Bishop of Llandaff* of summer 1793. In a government founded upon monarchy, Wordsworth wrote, "the will of a single being" has "a weight which, as history shows, will subvert that of the whole body politic" (*Prose Works* I, 41). By contrast, in a republic like that toward which France was working, such corruption would be mitigated by the regular changing of heads:

> [A]s soon as a people has chosen representatives it no longer has a political existence except as it is understood to retain the privilege of annihilating the trust when it shall think proper and of resuming its original power. Sensible that at the moment of election an interest distinct from that of the general body is created, an enlightened legislator will endeavour by every possible method to diminish the operation of such interest. (*Prose Works* I, 37)

When Louis XVI, the so-called King of the French, had failed to identify himself with the "general body" of France, the National Assembly had only observed justice in "annihilating" him. Indeed, no other course was possible: "Pure and universal representation," Wordsworth wrote, "cannot…exist together with monarchy…They must war with each other, till one of them is extinguished" (*Prose Works* I, 41). In Britain, meanwhile, the fact remained "that the king *and* lords *and* commons, by what is termed the omnipotence of parliament, have constitutionally the right of enacting whatever laws they please, in defiance of the petitions or remonstrances of the nation" (*Prose Works* I, 47). The "mixed system" of British government here forms a compound body diametrically opposed to that of the people.

*Salisbury Plain* employs the same antithetical imagery. If, Wordsworth declaims in the closing stanzas of the poem, the ministry continues to think that "Exile, Terror, Bonds, and Force may stand" against the (French) "herculean mace / Of Reason," then not only is it irremediably consigned to "Wisdom's porch," but must indeed be "Insensate" (ll. 514–15, 544–45). Wordsworth thus concurs with Williams's account, and Gillray's contemporary images, of Britain being in the very opposite condition to France. For Christopher Rovee, Gillray's *French Invasion* is an illustration of the "violent wrenching of social multeity into national unity" in contemporary Britain, which exposes the "fantas[tic]" nature of the British body politic (Rovee 2006, 19). The French National Assembly furnished by contrast what Williams called an example of "a society organised into a political body, to which the head and limbs would be vitally annexed." And if both countries continued in their divergent courses, he prophesied, "[t]he difference of the French and the English Nation will be, that of an organised body acting for itself, and a passive mass acted upon" (Williams 1790, 119, 92–93). It would be the difference, in short, between a living Palladium and a deathly Wicker Man.

*Salisbury Plain* is animated, then, by its psycho-dramatic staging—inflected by the actual pageants and stagings of the French Revolution—of what Wordsworth's "Home at Grasmere" would later call a scene "Of two brave Vessels matched in deadly fight/ And fighting to the death" (ll. 930–931, in Darlington, ed. 1977, 96–99). It is a renewal of Thomson's Whiggish Manicheism that pitted "Celtic" darkness against "Gothic" light. This "Gothic" history was more conventionally narrated in the eighteenth century as a march of progress. As Linda Colley puts it, John Wilkes and his followers envisioned English history as a "centuries-old struggle for liberty…[a] pilgrimage towards habeas corpus, trial by jury, freedom of election and the liberty of the press" (Colley 1996, 111). The geography of Salisbury Plain provided Wordsworth with an analogous march of progress. In the words of Stukeley's *Stonehenge*, "six miles south of Stonehenge is Salisbury, a mile nearer is Sorbiodunum, or old Sarum, by the side of which passes the Roman road" (1740, 9). Stukeley moves south in space and forward in time from Stonehenge to Salisbury, passing Old Sarum by "the Roman road." Wordsworth and his traveler significantly undertake this journey in reverse, walking from Salisbury, past old Sarum and Stonehenge, and toward Wales, land of the "ancient Britons." If English history was, for Wilkes and Blackstone, a (southeastern) march of progress past such significant landmarks as habeas corpus and trial by jury, then the traveler's (northwestern) journey past these other national-historical landmarks is, figuratively, a march of *regress*, back down the straight "Roman road" of history.

## Distant Spires

*Salisbury Plain* does not close, however, on this regressive note. Rather, the female vagrant's final despairing statement that "no earthly friend / Have I, no house in prospect but the tomb" (ll. 392–93) is immediately answered by the return of Salisbury's Gothic cathedral:

> She ceased. The city's distant spires ascend
> Like flames which far and wide the west illume,
> Scattering from out the sky the rear of night's thin gloom.
> (ll. 394–96)

"Celtic night" is banished. Though "human sufferings" (l. 399) are not forgotten, the female vagrant and the traveler are now returned to "housed" society in the shape of a welcoming "lonely cot" (l. 417).

The "apparently ordered and just structure of English society," in Gill's phrase, is symbolically restored. It is upon this basis that the poem now turns toward the future, and concludes with a Spenserian vision of "Heroes of Truth" (l. 541) pursuing a new quest to destroy every trace of Pride, Error, and Superstition, and to establish Reason's reign. But the "eternal pile" (l. 549) of Stonehenge, the "monument of heathenism" against which, almost a hundred and fifty years earlier, Hugh Peter had urged General Fairfax to send the Army of Parliament (Watts 1985, 111), is exempted from this imagined assault. "[P]ursue your toils," Wordsworth exhorts the "Heroes of Truth," "till not a trace / Be left on earth of Superstition's reign, / Save that eternal pile which frowns on Sarum's plain" (ll. 547–49). If we ask why this should be—why Wordsworth eschews the iconoclastic "rigour pitilesse" of Sir Guyon in his Spenserian model (*Faerie Queene* II, xii, 83)—an answer is perhaps to be found in the fact that Stonehenge marks, in its mute historical facticity, the gory historical point at which Gothic England begins. In pointedly allowing the monument to stand at the very end of the poem, and to transmit its resonances both backward across the text and outward into a still unregenerate society, Wordsworth positions himself as a historical rather than an apocalyptic poet. As Wordsworth would have been well aware in 1794, Edmund Burke had framed the issue between radicals and loyalists in just these terms, asking: "Is our monarchy to be annihilated, with all the laws, all the tribunals, and all the ancient corporations of the kingdom? Is every landmark to be done away in favour of a geometrical and arithmetical constitution?" (Burke 1987, 47). Stonehenge, standing for a Burkean sense of the reality of history, for the irreducible quantum of Englishness in the poet, thus provides Wordsworth with a seal against a *real* reversion to the Druidical past; against "the bare idea of a Revolution"—from which, as Wordsworth wrote to William Mathews only two months after *Salisbury Plain* was completed—he now recoiled in horror (*EY* 124).

The conclusion of *Salisbury Plain* can thus be read as articulating a contradictory position in which a rational assertion of a radical freedom to act coexists with an overarching and inhibiting consciousness of historical embeddedness; a synthesis of Burkean and Paineite impulses that anticipates Marx's paradox that "[m]en make their own history, but...under circumstances directly encountered, given and transmitted from the past" (Marx 1977, 15). Looked at in this way, *Salisbury Plain* becomes legible as a text that gestures toward a dialectical analysis of the historical predicament of the British subject in the late eighteenth and early nineteenth centuries, representing in miniature what Ian Duncan has called the generalized shift in the period from an "Enlightenment understanding of 'culture' as economic and moral improvement (requiring the abolition of unevenness) towards the Romantic conception of it…as medium for the preservation of 'unevenness' in aesthetic forms of value" (Duncan 2007, 98). For Duncan, a text like Scott's *Waverley* (1814) represents one stage in this transition, "encod[ing] the formation of a distinctively modern kind of national subjectivity, in which the knowledge of our alienation from authentic cultural identities accompanies our privileged repossession of them as aesthetic effects," while a text like *The Antiquary* (1816) accumulates "thick description of an everyday social surface of manners and conversation" to generate a sense of the "profound, organic inertia of common life that resists the totalizing force of historical change" (Duncan 2007, 98, 139–40). To put that another way, Enlightenment "alienation" from tradition is the necessary precondition for its Romantic "repossession" in the form of an apparently continuous and organic national culture; a repossession so deeply imbued in historicism and so inventive in the use of anachronism that it supplants the parent culture of the Enlightenment, and seems itself to have priority. The end of *Salisbury Plain* adumbrates this process. Wordsworth abolishes all traces of "Gothic superstition" in a fantasized apocalypse of Enlightenment, but he then allows Stonehenge (the ultimate stubborn particular) not only to withstand "the totalizing force of historical change," but to stand as a final, resonant, image for all that has been lost. In a process similar to Stephen Greenblatt's account of the artwork living on and becoming a historical "wonder" through its ongoing absorption of its circumambient social context (Greenblatt 1990, 89–90), Wordsworth's exceptional preservation of Stonehenge represents a deliberate condensation of history into a single legible cultural sign; a "repossession as aesthetic effect" of an unrecoverable past, which becomes in turn the very basis of the possibility of recreating a purified Gothic culture.

This chapter has argued that *Salisbury Plain* delivers a critique of the cultural and political state of Britain in the early 1790s that is both radical and Gothic. It has argued that Wordsworth identified the illiberal actions of the Pitt government with a "Celtic" legacy, and the republican cause both at home and in France with an opposite "Gothic" inheritance. But I do not want to suggest that this is by any means a clear-cut distinction. It is substantially complicated by Burke's rival claim to the Gothic constitution, and by the uncertainty as to whether France will indeed become a healthy Palladium, or remain—as in 1793–94 it clearly was—a wicker man of Terror and sacrifice. Wordsworth certainly did not rest content with *Salisbury Plain*'s symbolic reassertion of England's Gothic legacy. The revision of the poem that produced "Adventures on Salisbury Plain" (1795–99) dispensed with the eschatological frame entirely, and added in its place a melodrama centered upon the previously unspecified guilt of the traveler. As late as 1798, "Adventures" was one of the poems under consideration for the publishing enterprise that eventually produced *Lyrical Ballads* (1798). Instead, *Lyrical Ballads* saw yet another incarnation of the material from *Salisbury Plain*. Wordsworth here exploited the literary and historiographical possibilities of the fragment: presenting the female vagrant's tale shorn of its frame of uncanny landscape and supernatural vision as though deliberately to heighten the effect of her helpless enmeshment within the political and historical narratives that describe her predicament. Where in 1794 the female vagrant's suffering is symbolically cured by the return of the Gothic cathedral, the 1798 poem imagines no such immediate restitution:

> She ceased, and weeping turned away,
> As if because her tale was at an end
> She wept;—because she had no more to say
> Of that perpetual weight which on her spirit lay.
> (ll. 267–70, in Butler and Green, eds. 1992, 50–58)

Explicit politics makes way for pathos, and the poetry is certainly the better for it. The long final line has a rhythmical roll and uplift that speaks of both the permanence of suffering and of the boundless human potential to sustain it. But in its own way the abbreviated poem makes a still stronger political statement. Denying the reader any refuge from present suffering in long historical views of ascent from "Celtic night" to present Gothic grandeur, Wordsworth makes of the female vagrant's narrative a much more direct criticism of modern Britain. Moreover, the poem's fragmentary form performs at the level of style the work of historical condensation that the earlier poem had routed through the closing meditation upon the eternal pile frowning on Salisbury's endless plain. The final line of the fragment poem absorbs into itself the rich cultural metaphoricity and the powerful sense of historical burden (a "perpetual weight" and a *perpetual wait*) that in the full text of 1794 had been figured explicitly in the pendant cromlechs of Stonehenge.

The supernatural frame of *Salisbury Plain*, meanwhile, was recycled as a spot of time in the 1805 *Prelude*. Here again the Gothic restoration of *Salisbury Plain* is denied. Rather than unjust government it is now Wordsworth himself who is the Druidical figure responsible for the return of "Celtic night." "I called upon the darkness, and it took" (*1805* XIII, 327), he says, and it seems to indicate a renewed ease with Druidism that what follows is a balanced vision of Druid sacrifice and Druid enlightenment quite different from the earlier poem. This is not to say, however, that the rematerializing of the Gothic cathedral of Salisbury at the poem's conclusion is an anomaly in his poetry. It points suggestively toward the half-present, half-absent Gothic architecture of "Tintern Abbey," and toward the "gothic Church" of the 1814 Preface, which seems, in its very typicality, to dwell just beyond the horizon of the material. It also looks forward to the architectural constitutionalism of Wordsworth's prose pamphlet of 1809, *The Convention of Cintra*, which is the subject of the next chapter.

## Coda: The Purest Style of Gothic

I want to conclude this chapter with a word on *Salisbury Plain* and "Tintern Abbey"—or, to give the poem its full title, "Lines, Written a few miles above Tintern Abbey, On revisiting the banks of the Wye during a tour, July 13, 1798." With its detailed specification as a poem that looks back across the "five years" gap that has intervened since the last "tour" that had brought the poet to the Wye valley, "Tintern Abbey" clearly refers back to 1793, to the trek that had taken Wordsworth from Salisbury Plain to Wales, and hence to the political and imaginative materials of *Salisbury Plain*. Indeed, "Tintern Abbey" outdoes even the "Female Vagrant" fragment in its sublimation of the explicitly historical content of the earlier poem. As in *Salisbury Plain*, Wordsworth here orients himself in relation to a symbolically resonant Gothic edifice. The Reformation-era ruin of Tintern Abbey was frequently described as an epitome of the Gothic style. Henry Wyndham called it "an elegant specimen of the pure Gothic, constructed upon one plan, and in one stile" (qtd. in Heath 1793, iv), and Richard Warner's *Walk Through Wales* (1798) noted that the various "vestiges" still observable at Tintern together proved "that the purest style of Gothic architecture was observed in the structure of the great church and the contiguous edifices" (232). As in *Salisbury Plain*, too, the Gothic edifice appears in "Tintern Abbey" only to vanish from view: the abbey materializes on the *textual* horizon of the title, but is entirely absent from the text of the poem itself. In thus alluding to "the purest style of Gothic," but averting its gaze from the ruin in order to attend instead to a subterranean "music of humanity" (l. 92), "Tintern Abbey" can be seen to continue *Salisbury Plain*'s project of virtualizing Gothic architecture and of recovering a lost "authentic cultural identity" as an "aesthetic effect." Tim Fulford has argued that sound was key to the aesthetics of Romanticism because its transmission through resonance meant that it baffled rationalist investigations of origins in nature and in history (Fulford and Hutchings, eds. 2009, 182). Wordsworth's evocation of an unlocatable music and a mysterious "burthen" (l. 39) in the historically dense landscape of the Wye valley thus works to evoke paths of historical transmission that are not directly *known*, but are subliminally *felt*; that are felt in proportion as they are *not* articulated. This art of virtual remembrance and creative forgetting is perhaps the most important legacy of the radical antiquarian experiment of *Salisbury Plain*.

CHAPTER 3

# "By Gothic Virtue Won": Romantic Poets Fighting the Peninsular War

> *Our Spain is a Gothic edifice, made up of morsels, with as many forces, privileges, legislations, and customs, as there are provinces. Public spirit does not exist in her at all. These causes will prevent the establishment of any government solid enough to be able to unite our national forces.*
>
> —trans. from M. de Pradt 1816, 360

So wrote the Marquis of Urquijo to General Cuesta on April 13, 1808, as King Ferdinand VII of Spain, who had come to his father's throne through the intrigues of Napoleon, now sleepwalked toward his own forced abdication at Bayonne. Urquijo was a prominent member of the Spanish faction, styled *afrancesados*, who sought to effect constitutional reform by cooperating with the French. And if his image of Spain as a "Gothic edifice" has interesting affinities with the architectural imagery deployed by British writers such as Edmund Burke and William Wordsworth in the 1790s, his picture of national decrepitude resonates still more powerfully with Napoleon's self-image as the scourge of the "Gothic edifice" of old Europe. Heir to the "rhetoric of national unity" employed by the revolutionaries of 1789 in their campaign against the "byzantine" structures of the ancien regime (Garrioch 2005, 19), Napoleon sought consistently to present his imperial enterprise as a progressive campaign against what Burke had designated "the old Germanic or Gothic custumary" of "every country in Europe" (1796, 110). The "Germanic body" of the Holy Roman Empire, described by Burke as "a vast mass of heterogeneous States, held together by [a] heterogeneous body of old principles" (Burke 1797, 19) had been right at the top of Napoleon's list. Banishing its "shadow" with the formation of the pro–French Confederation of the Rhine after Austerlitz in 1805–6, Napoleon informed the Elector of Würtemberg that the old imperial congress, the Diet of Ratisbon, was "no more than a miserable monkey-house" (Petre 1993, 10; Fisher 1903, 104). By removing its component states from this "monkey-house" and placing them in what Talleyrand told their representatives would be "a more prosperous and flourishing condition," the new federation would, in the words of its constitutional treaty, secure the peace "for which experience has long proved…that the Germanic constitution can offer no sort of guarantee" (Lucchesini, trans. Dwyer 1821, 358, 376–77). Thus the "Germanic body" itself was destroyed. But the rhetoric of the struggle survived. Indeed, it was in his campaign of 1808–9 in what Burke had called the "nerveless country" of Spain (1797, 31) that Napoleon's campaign against the Gothic order found its fullest and most imaginative expression.

There was no lack of material on Spain to feed such an imagination. From 1807 to early 1808, Napoleon received reports from his agents in Spain that the country was in an unimaginably "ruinous state," with a national structure "in the last stages of exhaustion" (qtd. in Lovett 1965, I, 31). Always diligent in researching his intended conquests, Napoleon may also have seen the former French ambassador Jean François Bourgoing's *Tableau de l'Espagne Moderne* (1807), which pictured Spain as a "medley": a "labyrinth" of overlapping and obsolescent institutions from the time of Ferdinand and Isabella rather than a modern unitary nation like France (Bourgoing 1808, I, 170–172 and II, 2). "I am," Napoleon wrote to Talleyrand as his plans for the conquest of Spain began to take shape, "the heir of Charlemagne" (qtd. in Oman 1902–30, I, 1). The French empire was the direct successor to a European order a thousand years moldered into ruin. In destroying the remaining "morsels" of that wreck, the Emperor of the French would reset the epochal clock of a continent. On 19 April, the eve of Ferdinand VII's arrival at Bayonne, Napoleon's view of Spain as a contemptible "Gothic edifice" snapped sharply into focus: "The interests of my House and of my Empire demand that the Bourbons should cease to reign in Spain! Countries where monks [rule] are easy to conquer!" (Johnston, ed. 2002, 204).

Throughout the rest of 1808, Napoleon continued to wage an ideological campaign against Spain's "Gothic edifice." On 25 May, as revolts broke out across the occupied and kingless nation, Napoleon pronounced that a "bad administration" and an old monarchy had led once-glorious Spain to its present "perishing" state, but that he would be its "regenerator" (qtd. in Lovett, I, 123). Writing to his brother Joseph in late July, Napoleon imagined himself as a strongman leveling Spain's old "Gothic edifice" with the dust: "I shall find in Spain the Pillars of Hercules, but not the limits of my power" (*Confidential Correspondence* 1855, I, 340). The Pillars of Hercules, the two summits on either side of the straits of Gibraltar, represented the limits of the ancient world. They had been created, according to the retelling of Homeric legend in John Lemprière's *Classical Dictionary* (1792), when Hercules cleaved Mount Atlas in two with his mace: connecting the Mediterranean with the Atlantic even as he divided Europe and Africa. Wrapped around with the Latin motto "*Plus Ultra*," the pillars had been a symbol of the Spanish empire since at least the time of the Holy Roman Emperor Charles V (Woodcock and Robinson 1988, 26). Napoleon, finding them in Spain, thus figures himself as a second Hercules, demolishing obstacles and remaking the old world at will. But his imagery of Herculean demolition is haunted by other, more disturbing, associations. There is a long history of typological confusion between the Pillars of Hercules and the pillars of the temple of Dagon that the Judaic strongman and deliverer Samson pulled down around his own ears—falling, in the words of John Milton's *Samson Agonistes*, "among [the] slain self-killed" (l. 1664). Napoleon's boast of irresistible regenerative mission in Spain thus resounds with the distant thunder of an imagined self-immolation.

By July 1808, the myth of Napoleonic invincibility had indeed begun to tumble in upon itself, with crushing defeat at Bailén in mid-July, and a general insurgency sapping the energies of the French armies. In Britain, Leigh Hunt, editor of the weekly liberal paper *The Examiner*, tapped directly into the lethal undercurrent of Napoleon's Herculean rhetoric. French conquest in Spain could only come, Hunt wrote in early July, by "the most awful bloodshed," and "one or two such conquests of his refractory allies would go a great way to conquer himself" (July 10, 1808, 434). Within days of Hunt's prediction the siege of Zaragoza commenced: a struggle that would ultimately claim the lives of more than thirteen thousand French troops, and consume throughout the summer of 1808 the energies of a force that, as Charles Oman notes, "Napoleon at [its] commencement...would have supposed to be equal to the task of conquering...the whole eastern side of the Iberian Peninsula" (I, 162).

But the worsening situation in Spain would elicit from Napoleon an only increasingly strident language of wreck and renovation. The Emperor's speech of 9 December to the Corregidor of Madrid proclaimed that "feudal rights" were "abolished," and that "henceforth everyone may...give free scope to his industry" (qtd. in *The Annual Register for the Year 1808*, 282–84). These "feudal rights," Urquijo's "morsels," were the true tyranny: "As there is but one God, so should there be in a state but one judicial power. All peculiar jurisdictions were usurpations, and at variance with the rights of the nation; I have abolished them." In the place of the Gothic state Napoleon pledged "a king and a free constitution." Or, if the citizens of Madrid continued the resistance that had begun with the revolt of *el dos de mayo*, he threatened to "govern Spain, by establishing as many viceroys in it as there are provinces." He would govern, that is, in contempt of the Gothic establishment of "privileges, legislations, and customs": whether by implementing liberal reforms, or by abolishing the state and its Gothic partialities altogether. Either way, the "Gothic edifice" was scheduled for demolition. And whatever their feelings about its destroyer, political progressives of every stripe looked forward to the event as to the birth of the public domain that Spain seemed so signally to lack (Lovett, II, 558, 590–601, 430).

The shift in the meaning of the Gothic from 1808 to 1814, from Spain to Britain, and from Urquijo and Napoleon to Wordsworth, could hardly be more pronounced. With *The Excursion* described as part of "the body," the unpublished *Prelude* likened to an "Antichapel," and the "minor Pieces" of *Lyrical Ballads* and *Poems, in Two Volumes* (1807) compared to "little Cells, Oratories, and sepulchral Recesses," *The Recluse* was indeed, like Urquijo's Spain, a "Gothic edifice made up of morsels" (1814, viii–x). Far from confessing a lack of "public spirit," however, Wordsworth implicitly offered his "gothic Church" as a means of imagining the public realm. As we have seen, the 1814 Preface pointedly refused to engage in public controversy by prescribing a "system" of any variety—a clear rebuke, seen in this context, to both systemic "Jacobinical" philosophy and the Continental System of Napoleon—and left the "attentive Reader" to "extrac[t] the system for himself." But a "gothic Church" is, after all, nothing but an architectural "system," and Wordsworth's language clearly implied that he imagined it possessing real systematic integrity. When the "minor Pieces" already published were "properly arranged," they would be seen to fulfill specific structural functions, like the "Cells" and "Oratories" "ordinarily included" in Gothic churches. The "attentive Reader," moreover, would not need to await the author's statement of this proper arrangement. For if the extant parts were related *systematically* to each other and to the whole, then by implication the plan of the whole might be "extracted" from the interrelationships between those parts—just as the hard-headed Dr Johnson had speculated in 1775 that the "general form" of the ruined monastery of Aberbrothick could be "conjectured" from a survey of the "parts yet standing" (Levi, ed. 1984, 40)—and *The Recluse* might thus already be "read."

This kind of proleptic "reading" has a public dimension because it posits both author and "attentive Reader" as mentally adequate to think in abstract terms and to combine disparate parts into complex wholes: the very attributes, as John Barrell has shown, that were widely held to qualify one for participation in public life in late eighteenth- and early nineteenth-century Britain (Barrell 1992, 41–61). To grasp the plan of the fragmented "gothic Church," the reader must make an effort of synthetic imagination that manifests his public spirit, and that therefore helps to instantiate the public realm. The "gothic Church" of *The Recluse* is thus diametrically opposed to the "Gothic edifice" of public absence that Urquijo and Napoleon saw in Spain. This chapter will seek to show that this alteration in the meaning of the Gothic is a function of Wordsworth and his contemporaries' response to the Napoleonic invasion of Spain and the resulting British intervention. I will be arguing, furthermore, that this alteration is directly observable in Wordsworth's prose tract dealing specifically with Spain and the Peninsular War, *The Convention of Cintra* (1809).

The tract's title refers to the armistice agreed between the British and French armies at Cintra, Portugal, in August 1808, the unfavorable terms of which prompted public outrage when they became widely known in Britain. Wordsworth professed himself "cut to the heart" when he heard the news, adding, significantly, "I have not suffered so much upon any public occasion these many years" (*MY* I, 267). He responded by writing *Cintra*. Robert Southey, with whom Wordsworth tried and failed to arrange a county meeting to protest against the Convention, noted on 22 November that his neighbor had gone home to "ease his heart by writing a pamphlet" (qtd. in *Prose Works* I, 197). The vessel for this discharge from Wordsworth's "cut...heart," *Cintra* holds approximately five thousand lines of rhetorically strenuous and ideologically fervent prose. Coleridge complained admiringly that it was "all in hot tints—that the first note is pitched at the height of the Instrument, & never suffered to sink...that the Attention is kept throughout at it's utmost Strain & Stretch" (*CLSTC* III, 214). But such attention is amply repaid. Its powerful feelings still fresh long after its historical moment, the pamphlet was, as Mary Moorman notes, reprinted in 1915 to "strengthen national enthusiasm for the war against Germany" (Moorman 1957–65, II, 154). In place of the proverbial "marshal's baton" of the Napoleonic soldier it may then be that, as J. R. Watson has speculated, "some soldier on the battlefield of the Somme...had Wordsworth's tract in his knapsack" (Watson 2003, 127). No more appropriate fate could be imagined for a work in which, as I will show, Wordsworth sought to match and to surpass the self-reliance of the French armies with a moral rearmament of the British soldiery.

Wordsworth worked at *Cintra* continuously for more than half a year (November 1808 to May 1809), assisted by Samuel Taylor Coleridge and by Thomas De Quincey, who oversaw its eventual publication on 27 May. Over this period Wordsworth extended the scope of the work from a series of essays to an independent book. Two installments appeared in *The Courier* (on December 27 and January 13, 1809), but the essay format was abandoned shortly thereafter, since, in the words of Wordsworth's "Advertisement," "the pressure of public business" rendered it "improbable that room could be found" in the paper for regular publication of "matter extending to such a length" (*Cintra*, ll. 14–16).[1] Outpaced by events, but convinced that the lapse represented by the Convention held lessons for individual and national renewal and demonstrated "the paramount efficacy of moral causes" in international affairs (l. 4633), Wordsworth proceeded to place the Convention and the struggle against Napoleon, as Southey had predicted in November 1808, "in a more philosophical point of view than any body has yet done" (qtd. in *Prose Works*, I, 197).

This chapter will argue that in *Cintra* Wordsworth adumbrates a progressive Gothic politics that mediates between his past radical and his future loyalist political sympathies. The second half of the chapter will demonstrate how *Cintra* develops the Gothic language of reform coming out of Spain for the purposes of domestic reform. But I begin with an account of how Wordsworth and his Spanish and British contemporaries came to conceive the Peninsular War in specifically Gothic terms.

## The Cortes Will Be Assembled...

Napoleon's speech of December 9, 1808 to the Corregidor of Madrid was, as I have suggested, aimed directly at the private interests and "peculiar jurisdictions" of the old Gothic constitution in Spain. But his vacillation between promise and threat reflected the insecurity of his conquest, which was the direct result of the development through 1808 of precisely the "public spirit" that both he and Urquijo (now Minister of State in Joseph Bonaparte's puppet government of July 1808) had seen as lacking in the country. Following the forced abdications of Charles IV and Ferdinand VII in May, and in anticipation of the coronation of Napoleon's brother Joseph, late June saw the publication of a "Manifesto" by José de Palafox, Governor and Captain General of Aragón, which urged national unity, and asserted the "elective right" of the nation against Joseph I as king (reprinted in *The Times*, June 29, 1808, 2). Simultaneously, the Supreme Junta of Seville issued a set of "Precautions" that called for the creation of "three Generalissimos" to "act by common accord" in a guerrilla war (a "war of partisans") against the French. The document, reprinted in *The Times* for July 5, 1808, also stated clearly the ultimate aim of the war:

> Ferdinand VII being restored to the throne, under him and by him the Cortes will be assembled, abuses reformed, and such laws shall be enacted as the circumstances of the time and experience may dictate for public good and happiness. (4)

The assembly of the Cortes, the Spanish parliament, appears here as a panacea for reform and the redress of public grievances. But as Jan Read suggests, "[t]o describe the Cortes" of the early nineteenth century, "which worked on a regional basis, as a 'parliament' is perhaps misleading; it was rather an assembly of representatives from the three estates—clergy, nobility and commons—with very limited advisory powers" (Read 1977, 57). The limitations of the Cortes were fully exposed in Jean François Bourgoing's account of modern Spain, published in Paris in 1807 and in London in 1808 (I, 167–72). Bourgoing noted that the Cortes was now assembled only for ceremonial functions, and that the full national Cortes had not in fact been assembled since 1713. As a force in the life of the nation, it existed now only in the "shadow" form of an impotent and unrepresentative eight-member committee. Nominations to this committee, moreover, did not proceed on a view of Spain as a unified nation, but of her major subdivisions.[2] Hence the "shadow" Cortes only reproduced in microcosm the "medley" of rival administrations and jurisdictions that was modern Spain. As such it was the very epitome of the public absence and local partiality that *afrancesados* like Urquijo diagnosed in the old Gothic regime. This was also the received view of the Cortes in turn-of-the-century Britain. In December 1789 *The Times* pictured Spain as "the most despotic kingdom in Europe," with the Cortes, once guarantor of "more power and privileges" than the English Parliament, now "in a great measure abolished" (December 19, 1789, 4). Reduced to a heap of "feint remains...under the absolute control of the king," the Cortes clearly had, from a British perspective, only a bad eminence among the decayed "morsels" in Spain's tottering "Gothic edifice."

The war aim of restoring the Cortes was, then, a seemingly regressive pledge of allegiance to Spain's old Gothic order—characterized by the liberal weekly *The Examiner* as a "polity...[without a] parallel in the world for despotism" (June 19, 1808, 385). Days after "Precautions" was published in Britain, however, *The Times* proclaimed "Glorious News from Spain" (July 11, 1808, 3) that appeared to confirm its revolutionary motive power. The occupying French armies of Dupont and Lefevre, and the squadron at Cádiz had been defeated and "routed" by the armies of a national uprising. "All the provinces of Spain," the paper reported, "are under arms, and propose to assemble the General Cortes, or Grand Council of the Nation." The modest proposal in "Precautions" of assembling the Cortes under the king had, with a further augmentation of public spirit, revealed its latent revolutionary potential. Rather than the decrepit "morsel" of the ancien regime, the Spanish patriots were clearly proposing to restore the Cortes to something like its original full-bodied form; a formidable body like the English Parliament, or a Gothic National Assembly. In this cause, moreover, the patriot armies led by Palafox and Echavania had given "no quarter," treating the French, according to the orders of Palafox, as "guilty of high treason."

In the light of this redemption of the "Gothic" Cortes, the apparently outlandish charge of France's "high treason"—the definitive civil crime—takes on a particular significance. The actions of Napoleon were clearly treacherous. He had occupied Spain and Portugal under what "Precautions" called "the mask of friendship," in what Wordsworth called a time of "profound peace" (*Cintra*, l. 1529); a "peace" the more "profound" because in the midst of general war. Napoleon was thus guilty of treason in the sense that his betrayal of his allies constituted what Wordsworth's late additions to his revolutionary verse play, *The Borderers* (1842), would call a "plot, against the soul of man" (V.iii.2113). But in the view of Spanish patriots like those composing the Supreme Junta of Seville, France was guilty less for her violation of present-day alliances than for her violation of the traditions and historic usages of Europe. The French had, the Junta said in "Precautions," dealt with "horrible perfidy...with all Spain," and "if they rule over us all is lost, Kings, Monarchy, Property, Liberty, Independence, and Religion." By contrast, Spain had "many times mastered [France], not by deceit, but by force of arms"; and where the French threatened no less than everything, the Spanish had "made her Kings prisoners," and no more. The French might, with the morbid growth of their public spirit, have changed into principled atheists, rapists and thieves, but, "Precautions" announced, "we are the same Spaniards, and France, and Europe, and the World shall see, that we are not less gallant, nor less brave than the most glorious of our ancestors." "Precautions" was echoed from Cádiz by one Dr Ruiz, for whom the French, outcasts from both religion and human society, had in their depredations on Spain reached a level of ferocity and barbarism that posterity would find it hard to credit (Ruiz 1808, 11–12). But now, he wrote, "the Spanish nation, which has in nothing degenerated from its ancient valor and patriotism, and which is the same today as it was in the time of the Huns, Vandals, Goths, Saracens and Romans, has arisen to take a just and Christian vengeance." France was held by Spanish patriots to be guilty of a crime against the ancestral order of Europe; an order yet honored in a Spain that, despite its staging of epoch-making struggles between "Goths, Saracens and Romans," was immemorially the same.

But for the Spaniards to view this crime as *treason* depended upon their sharing substantially the perspective of Edmund Burke, whose *Letters on a Regicide Peace* (1796) pictured Europe before the French Revolution as a "Commonwealth" of nations linked less "by papers and seals" than by "religion, laws, and manners," by "resemblances, by conformities, by sympathies" in "customs...and habits of life," that was "virtually one great state" (108–10). The present war in Europe was for Burke "a *civil war*...between the partisans of the antient, civil, moral, and political order of Europe against a sect of fanatical and ambitious atheists which means to change them all" (144). Jacobin France had broken with all the "usages...of this civilized world," and "made a schism with the whole universe" (111–12). Not quite "the whole universe," what Burke really saw the Jacobins rebelling against was an ancestral order that was specifically Gothic: "[T]he polity and economy of every country in Europe," he wrote, derived ultimately "from the old Germanic or Gothic customary...improved and digested into a system and discipline by the Roman Law" (110). The present war was, hence, a civil struggle between Revolutionary France and Gothic Europe, and it was only on some such view of the Napoleonic war that Spain could meaningfully level at France the charge of *treason*. Or, to put that in less reductive terms, the charge of treason against Napoleon was not simply a charge of generalized treachery to human nature, nor simply an allegation of a crime against the old Gothic order, but a claim that he had sinned against both at once, for human nature and the Gothic order were one and the same thing.

The Supreme Junta's *Manifiesto de la nación española a la Europa*, promulgated on January 1, 1809, suggests that the Spanish patriots indeed saw the issue in just these Burkean terms. Taking a view identical to that of Burke on the "balance of Europe" (1796, 130), the Gothic order assaulted by Regicide France, the *Manifiesto* declared that now was the time for all the "Sovereigns of Europe" to take "[w]ar to the French" in order to "re-establish the equilibrium which [they] had achieved at the cost of so many combinations and so much blood" (qtd. in Lovett, I, 326–27). France had usurped legitimate sovereignty and had destroyed the "equilibrium" or "balance" of Europe. When in June 1808 the Spanish patriot army treated the French armies as "guilty of high treason," then, it acted as the loyal army of the ancient and immemorial Gothic constitution in Spain and in the "one great state" of Europe beyond.

This potent language of Gothic opposition had, as Richard Herr has shown, been brewing in Spain since the middle of the eighteenth century, with the development of a liberal history that traced the nation's decline to the destruction of the medieval constitution and the Cortes. In 1780 Gaspar Melchor de Jovellanos told the *Real Academia de la Historia* that the Spanish constitution, "established under the Visigoths between the fifth and eighth centuries," merited at least partial resurrection in the present (see Herr 1969, 341–42). The Cortes, the epitome of Spain's decrepit "Gothic edifice," was right at the heart of this antithetical language of Gothic restitution; for, Jovellanos said, the feudal system of government, dividing the nation into various isolated parts, "would have made our constitution variable and vacillating, if the Cortes, established since primitive times, had not reunited the parts that composed it for the settlement of affairs that interested the general good" (qtd. in Herr, 342). Jovellanos was keen, however, to situate Spain's Gothic inheritance in a wider European context. As Herr notes, Jovellanos saw the ultimate source of Spain's Gothic constitution in "the laws of the Germanic tribes described by Tacitus and Caesar" (Herr, 342), the very sources that underpinned the seventeenth-century theory of the Gothic Constitution in England. Spain, in this view, was the sister-nation of Gothic England.

Even before the French invasion, then, Spanish liberals were well-equipped with a language of Gothic opposition. Something of its power against the ancien regime in place before 1808 can be gauged from the comment of Godoy, "Prince of Peace" and *de facto* monarch, that "Our own annals, from the time of the Goths, offered dangerous examples" to his enemies (qtd. in Herr, 337). And against Napoleon, who brought along an aggressively new constitution, the Gothic language was deployed to devastating effect. Indeed, the resistance to Napoleon, whose pragmatic conversion to Islam during the Egyptian campaign of 1798 earned him the Coleridgean moniker "Ali Buonaparte," was readily assimilated to the Spanish mythology of *reconquista*, the struggle to reconstitute the Visigothic kingdom lost by King Rodrigo to the Moors in 711.[3] In the Constitution subsequently promulgated at Cádiz in March 1812, the Cortes claimed to have synthesized into one "fundamental law" the "political laws," the "venerable uses and customs" and the ancestral religion of the nation (qtd. in Lovett, II, 451). The nation reserved the right, according to the constitutional preamble, to "destroy with one blow all the fundamental laws if the public interest...demanded it" (qtd. in Lovett, II, 450). But such radical ideas were cast in terms of tradition and historical precedent: the preamble claimed, for example, that the doctrine of popular sovereignty was established in Spanish law by the election of a new king to the vacant throne of Aragón as long ago as 1412 (Lovett, II, 435).

Thus, in the uprising on the Peninsula, the decrepit Gothic order that Napoleon had contemptuously overthrown in Spain and throughout Europe now returned, embattled, against him. In April 1809 Calvo de Rozas, a leading Spanish liberal, demanded the convocation of the Cortes, epitome of the "Gothic edifice," precisely for the direct antithesis it offered to the Napoleonic system. "Since," he wrote, "the oppressor...promise[s]...a constitutional regime aimed at correcting the abuses from which we have suffered, let us face him with a system directed at the same goal, but let us undertake this with better faith and in the framework of legality" (qtd. in Lovett, II, 424).

This oppositional attitude took graphic form in an anonymous Spanish print of late 1808, "La Gratitud al Inventor Ingles del Toro Español," reproduced on the cover of the first edition of this book. The print shows Spain in the shape of Hercules, assisted by England as a sort of maritime Mars, slaying the Napoleonic Hydra, against a background composed by the shattered Pillars of Hercules and a Gothic edifice. Above their heads, Ferdinand VII appears as the "Sun of Spain," who purges off the fog of Napoleonic proclamations and propaganda.[4] The same antithesis was staked out on the country's battlefields. Encamped with his armies outside Madrid in early December 1808, Napoleon demanded the surrender of the indefensible city only to have his troubled self-image as a mountain-cleaving destroyer returned upon him with grim intent. "Gothic" Samson to his classical Hercules, the citizens of Madrid declared that they were "ready to bury themselves under the ruins of their town rather than surrender" (qtd. in Lovett, I, 309). Such rhetoric seemed to warn that if the "Gothic edifice" must come down, then, like Milton's Samson among the Philistines, not only the city or the Spanish nation but Napoleon and the French Empire would be crushed in the catastrophe. One Captain in Seville, urging all Spaniards to the defense of their "*Arquitectura política*," put the point quite explicitly ("Manifiesto Político," 1808). Of the available models of such patriotic acts, he wrote,

> I will only praise the feat of that Hebrew Hercules, of that Israeli Captain, Samson. This hero, for the defence of his country, was not afraid to surrender his life to the cruel files of death. The same palace that had been the scene of the festivals of the Philistines became the terrible barrow of their funeral exequies. (trans. from "Manifiesto Político" in *Papeles Varios*, I, 8)

In the event, Madrid held out for only two days, but its declaration of unyielding resistance had already been made good at the siege of Zaragoza in the summer of 1808. There, General Verdier's peremptory order to capitulate had met with a chilling invitation from José de Palafox to "War to the knife," and in both the first siege of the summer and the second siege of the winter, the defenders of Zaragoza had fought the French house to house, sustaining and exacting massive casualties, before the city finally fell (Read, 75–77, 132–33). The ferocity with which such Spaniards prosecuted the cause of the King and the Cortes seemed to the London *Times* to demonstrate the "perfect ubiquity of patriotic sentiment and active valour throughout the country" (July 11, 1808, 3). And a Gothic constitution might still connote, in Urquijo's phrase, "privileges, legislations, and customs," but in the national uprising, Spain's very defects now became instinct with "public spirit."

It was a strange transformation, not least in the view from Britain. For the "old and venerable" British "castle" (Burke 1987, 31) that Edmund Burke and his conservative auxiliaries had sought to defend against the influence of the French Revolution was surely related to the revolutionized "Gothic edifice" in Spain. The chivalrous order that Burke had imagined dying in the streets of Paris at the close of the old century seemed to have arisen in the new century to combat its Napoleonic antitype, the Continental System. And the very language of reaction and conservation was now, by a sudden reverse, the language of revolutionary reform and of the people. While Spanish liberals such as Calvo de Rozas clamored for the convocation of the Gothic Cortes, their preceptor Jovellanos affirmed both the radical doctrine of national sovereignty and the Burkean tenet that the Spanish Constitution, like that of every country in Europe, depended upon "ancient and constant custom" (Jovellanos 1858–59, I, 598). With Spanish liberals setting this example, what better time for British reformers to take stock and to articulate, in the wake of revolutionary disappointment in the 1790s, that apparent oxymoron, a progressive Gothic politics?

## "Sounds Like History in the Land of Romance": British Imaginations of the Peninsular War

J. R. Watson has described the Spanish uprising against Napoleon in 1808 as "a turning point," a moment of "sudden hope," in which reform-minded "British "patriots," who had been at first troubled by the justness of the war" were able finally to come into alignment with the national effort, and to "rejoin," in Margaret Russett's phrase, "nationalist and republican rhetoric" (Watson 2003, 124). The dramatist and leading opposition Whig MP Richard Brinsley Sheridan called the uprising an opportunity "to strike a bold stroke which might end in the rescue of the world" (speech on "Affairs of Spain" on June 15, 1808, in Sheridan 1816, V, 369). As Deirdre Coleman has shown, the reform-minded *Edinburgh Review* took the "*Spanish* revolution" to extend "a much better prospect of reform in England" now than had the French Revolution before it (Coleman 1989, 144–61). The hopes raised in the early 1790s had seemed, the *Edinburgh* said, "to hide for ever" after they were betrayed by the unwinding of the Revolution (13 [1808], 222–23). But recent events in Spain meant that "we can once more utter the words *liberty* and *people*, without starting at the sound of our own voices, or looking round the chamber for some spy or officer of the government." In the light of a new revolutionary dawn, the *Edinburgh*'s language implied that the old Jacobin need no longer, like the (Gothic) ghost of old Hamlet, start "like a guilty thing / Upon a fearful summons" (*Hamlet* I. i. 129–30), but might pass on to his heir his knowledge of the rottenness in the state. Warming to its argument, the *Edinburgh* triumphantly turned the charge of guilt by implication back on "spies" and "officers of the government." The British supporter of Spain and Portugal must accept "that he has been espousing the popular side of the greatest question of the present day; that he has been praying most fervently for the success of the people against their rulers; that he has, in plain terms, been, as far as in him lay, a party to revolutionary measures."

Not all reactions to the news from Spain were quite so bold or quite so straightforward. The ghost of old Hamlet behind the *Edinburgh*'s feeling of new fire in revolutionary embers was also the ghost of Wordsworth's "Ode, Intimations of Immortality," published in *Poems, in Two Volumes* in 1807. Not for "Delight and liberty, the simple creed / Of Childhood" had Wordsworth raised "The song of thanks and praise":

> But for those obstinate questionings
> Of sense and outward things,
> Fallings from us, vanishings;
> Blank misgivings of a Creature
> Moving about in worlds not realiz'd,
> High instincts, before which our mortal Nature
> Did tremble like a guilty Thing surpriz'd…
> (ll. 139–50; *MW* 297–302)

A former French sympathizer, avowed republican and quondam democrat, Wordsworth in 1807 still celebrated revolutionary "worlds not realiz'd." The "Fallings from us, vanishings" that in the *Edinburgh* were only "Blank misgivings" of revolutionary betrayal were for the poet of the "Ode" intimations of the other world in which it was not the revolutionary spirit but quotidian "mortal Nature" that was a spectral alien. But the gradual loss of this border-crossing capacity was proof of the growth through suffering of the "philosophic mind" (l. 189). Wordsworth was not, one year later, likely to be interested in undoing the long process of reconciliation to "what remain[ed] behind" (l. 183) by simply reverting to old political sympathies. Nevertheless, Wordsworth in 1808 remained in favor of reform. He had long since been in "recoil" from "the bare idea of a Revolution" (*EY* 124). But he was indeed on the "popular side" of the question. In late March 1809 he told Daniel Stuart, then in charge of publishing *Cintra*, that "a thorough reform in Parliament" was "absolutely wanted in this Country," and he shared with Francis Wrangham his expectation that the pamphlet would "create me a world of enemies, and call forth the old yell of Jacobinism" (*MY* I, 296, 312). However, where the *Edinburgh* contrived a blanket pardon for "revolutionary measures" of the past, Wordsworth, whose imaginative identification with the Spaniards was such that he would later lobby Stuart and De Quincey to get his pamphlet translated into Spanish (*MY* I, 297, 303), sought to develop the Gothic language of reform daily issuing from revolutionary Spain.

This effort took its first, fragmentary, form in a poem begun in the ferment of June 1808, "A few bold Patriots, Reliques of the Fight"—sometimes known, after the name of its hero, as *Pelayo*. As Carl H. Ketcham suggests (1989, 498), Wordsworth probably drew both the historical material and the inspiration for this prophetic fragment from an early version of Robert Southey's *Roderick, Last of the Goths* (1814)—a poem I will return to below. But it is also a product of the Gothic imagination of the struggle developed by the Spanish patriots. Leading the "Reliques" of King Rodrigo's "crush'd...Gothic sovereignty of Spain" into an Asturian refuge from the conquering Moors, the prince Pelayo tells his "little band" of "Christian Warriors" (ll. 1–13) that their retreat is only prelude to a glorious reconquest—when, like a gathered storm that "Breaks forth and spreads in ravage o'er the plain," they "shall...descend and quell / The astounded Infidel" (ll. 1–13, 33–35; Ketcham, ed. 1989, 49–51). There is an unmistakable echo here of the standard description of the Gothic conquest of Rome as a swarm or a deluge.[5] Pelayo's prophecy also has a specifically Spanish flavor, however, looking forward to the *reconquista* completed in the fifteenth century. But, startlingly, Wordsworth proceeds to ignore this fact, and reaches instead across an entire millennium to bind Pelayo's prophecy upon the exact present:

> Thus spake Pelayo on his chosen Hill;
> And shall at this late [ ] the Heavens belie
> The heroic prophecy
> And put to shame the great Diviner's skill?
> (ll. 51–54)

Subject once more to a "foreign Tyrant" (l. 62), Spain is, Wordsworth implies, still bound at this late hour to redeem its Gothic inheritance. Indeed, it is precisely the corruption in Bourbon Spain of the legacy bequeathed by Pelayo that has "invited" the "malignity" of the Napoleonic invasion:

> Alas, not unprovoked those Tempests low'r,
> Not uninvited this malignity.

> Full long relinquishing a precious dower
> By Gothic Virtue won, secured by oath
> Of king and people pledged in mutual troth,
> The Spaniard hath approached on servile knee
> The native Ruler; all too willingly
> Full many an age in that degenerate Land
> The rightful Master hath betrayed his trust.
> Earthward the Imperial flower was bent
> In mortal languishment;
> This knew the Spoiler whose victorious hand
> Hath snapp'd th'enfeebled Stalk and laid its head in dust.
> (ll. 66–78)

"[L]aid...in dust," the redemption of "degenerate" Spain can only come through a new access of "Gothic Virtue"—through, more specifically, a renewal of the "mutual troth" between "king and people" of the sort that the proposal to reconvene the Gothic Cortes seemed to promise.

Wordsworth was by no means alone among British writers and poets in imagining the struggle in these Gothic terms. Spain had long been seen by literary Britons as the place where the terms Gothic and Romance became interchangeable. Thomas Warton's monumental *History of English Poetry* (1774–81), for example, saw Romance entering Europe via the Moorish conquest of Spain, and spreading thence in a Europe already well "seasoned" by "the poetry of the Gothic Scalds" (Warton 1824, I, lxxiii). This association was not lost upon Southey, the leading Hispanist of his generation, who had recently published translations of the Spanish Romances *Amadis of Gaul* (1803) and *Palmerin of England* (1807). In August 1808, at the very moment British troops were committed in Portugal, Southey published his *Chronicle of the Cid*, a translation and redaction of a range of medieval texts on the Spanish hero, and, Southey claimed, a "fine [text] for *touching* upon" the "present Spanish affairs" (Southey 1855, 245). The *Cid* contained a "Scene in the Cortes" that Coleridge pronounced "superior to any equal Part of any Epic Poem, save the *Paradise Lost*," with its depiction of the "deep, glowing, yet ever self-controlled, Passion" of the Spanish hero (*CLSTC* III, 136), and Southey hoped that the poem, the "most ancient and most curious piece of chivalrous history in existence," would perform some service in helping on the present constitutional "crusade" against Napoleon (Southey 1855, 226, 236–45). On August 16, Southey wrote in just this vein to his brother Tom, then serving aboard HMS *Dreadnought*, reporting Walter Savage

Landor's "noble" departure to fight on the peninsula, and picturing the struggle there against Napoleon as

> something like the days of old as we poets and romancers represent them,—something like the best part of chivalry,—old honours, old generosity, old heroism are reviving,—and the career of that cursed monkey nation is stopt…(qtd. in Bainbridge 2003, 148)

The "monkey" jibe, employed by Napoleon in his rhetorical demolition of Germany's old Gothic order, is hurled back at the French Emperor by the revival of that very order in Spain. Southey's language also resonates powerfully with James Gillray's exactly contemporary print celebrating the battle of Bailén, *Spanish-Patriots attacking the French-Banditti, Loyal Britons lending a lift* (August 15, 1808), in which a French "monkey" army engages in a quite literal "war to the knife" with a crusader force that seems to have stepped straight out of the "Gothic" middle ages, and that is led by a resolute British redcoat.[6] The cartoon exemplifies what Diego Saglia calls the tendency of British responses to the war in Spain to define the country

> as a cultural geography caught between past and present through the lasting effect of its ancient traditions on the contemporary. [N]ot only was Spain construed as a transparent historical palimpsest, but it appeared so imbued with its own tales that it was imagined as a land divided between reality and fiction. (Saglia 2000, 59)

Wordsworth certainly took part in this half-fictionalization of Spain. His sonnet of April 1809 on the captured Palafox, "Is there a power that can sustain and cheer," pictures Spain as both an "injured Country" and "a stage / Whereon deliberate Valour and the Rage / Of righteous Vengeance side by side appear" (Ketcham 1989, 55, ll. 6–8)—a phrase that would serve equally well as caption for Gillray's cartoon, or for the Spanish print mentioned earlier, "La Gratitud." Indeed, the Spanish uprising seemed to come ready-formed as a Gothic romance, fitted perfectly to the ideology of "loyalist Gothic"—of martial prowess rather than of political liberty—that, as James Watt has shown, was developed by writers such as Clara Reeve in the late eighteenth century, and that flourished throughout the war with France in the works of Anne Radcliffe (Watt 1999, 42–69). *England and Spain* (1808) by Felicia Hemans worked in precisely these "loyalist Gothic" terms. The poem associated the martial heroes of British history—Arthur, Alfred, Richard I, Edward III, and Henry V—with the British forces on the Peninsula, and imagined the Spanish resistance as a restoration of the "Gothic reign" of the "Genius of chivalry": a living version of "deeds of yore" that until now had "Live[d] but in legends wild, and poet's lore!" (Hemans [nee Browne] 1808, 14–15). Britain and Spain are here Gothic allies against Napoleon. Similar ideas informed even the antiwar poetry of Lord Byron. Although, as Simon Bainbridge has argued (2003, 170–179), Canto I of Byron's *Childe Harold's Pilgrimage* (1812) generally reacts against the "loyalist" poetry on the conflict, his vision of the fallen as "broken tools, that tyrants cast away / By myriads," is only one movement in a deeply ambivalent poem that begins with a description of Spain as a "renowned, romantic land!" and that then picks up the legend of Pelayo as Spain rallies to the "standard which Pelagio bore," when the invading Moors dyed Spain's "mountain streams with Gothic gore" (Byron 1812, 29, 25; Canto I, stanzas xlii and xxxv).

Nothing better illustrates the British investment in the Gothic imagination of the war, however, than the fact that poets as different as Southey, Landor, and Walter Scott, all took the specifically Gothic legend of Roderick as their subject. Landor's *Count Julian* (1812) told a republican tale of the collapse of the old national order (see also Saglia 2000, 76–115). Scott's poem, *The Vision of Don Roderick* (1811), meanwhile, followed upon a sense of chivalric and Romantic rebirth very similar to that evinced by both Southey and Gillray. In a letter to his brother Thomas of June 1808, Scott expressed his wonder that "all the places mentioned in Don Quixote and Gil Blas" were "now the scenes of real and important events." "Gazettes dated from Oviedo, and gorges fortified in the Sierra Morena," he wrote, "sounds like history in the land of romance" (qtd. in Watson 2003, 124–25). Scott's *Vision* was also keyed to the "Gothic" imagination of Spain as Samson. At Napoleon's treachery, Spain's "Valour woke / . . . As burst the awakening Nazarite his band, / When 'gainst his foes he clenched his dreadful hand" (Scott 1812, 56 [stanza xliv], 61 [stanza li]). And the final subjugation of Zaragoza was, Scott wrote, the winning not of the city but of only "her children's bloody tomb" (stanza li).

If, as J. R. Watson has suggested, the collaboration of Wordsworth, Coleridge, Southey, and De Quincey on *Cintra* saw the development of "a kind of 'Lakers' view of the matter" (2003, 127), it was, like Scott's, a "view" strongly inflected by the rhetoric of the Spanish patriots. Coleridge's *Letters on the Spaniards* in *The Courier* from late 1809, for example, developed a Gothic imagination of the conflict in his answer to those "Anti-iberians" who asked despondingly what the Spaniards were fighting for. The question, he says, "unfairly attribute[s] to the Spaniards a want of [national] feelings," or presumes that "a nation's sufferings" are limited "to visible and bodily evils." But, Coleridge continues, quoting himself from *The Friend*,

> could we bring within the field of imagination, the devastation effected in the moral world, by [Napoleon's] violent removal of old customs, familiar sympathies, willing reverences, and habits of subordination almost naturalised into instinct…could [we] give form and body to all the effects produced on the principles and dispositions of nations by…the soul-sickening sense of unsteadiness in the whole edifice of civil society; the horrors of battle, though the miseries of a whole war were brought together before our eyes in one disastrous field, would present but a tame tragedy in comparison. (Erdman, ed. 1978, III, 83–85)

If the Spaniards fight, Coleridge implies that it is because their imaginations have indeed grasped this "devastation;" because they have perceived the need to rebalance "the whole edifice of civil society." Engaged on "the field of imagination" as much as on the recent "disastrous field[s]" of Ocaña and Alba de Tormes, they "give form and body" to the imagination of the conflict as a resurrection of the old Gothic order.

Southey's *Roderick, Last of the Goths* delivers a similar pro-Iberian polemic through a retelling of the legend of the demise of the ancient Gothic kingdom of Spain through the civil war and foreign invasion occasioned by King Rodrigo's rape of Florinda, daughter of the potentate Count Julian. Then, as now, "from all sides the miscreant hosts move on," threatening "the walls" then of "Salduba,"

> Now Zaragoza, in this later time
> Above all cities of the earth renown'd
> For duty perfectly perform'd.
> (XVIII, 298–315, in Fitzgerald, ed. 1909)

The resistance to Napoleon is thus seen as one more stage in a Spanish tradition of resistance and *reconquista* that was, as I have shown, a Gothic legacy. Indeed, Southey seems to have made a conscious decision to focus on the specifically Gothic components of Spain's *reconquista* mythology. As Saglia notes (2000, 82, 91), he originally intended to write a poem on the "native" Pelayo, representative of the mythic original Spaniards, "that most ancient and heroic race" that had resisted Romans, Carthaginians, Greeks and Goths alike (*Roderick*, VII, 140–143). The focus of the finished poem, however, is upon the fall and redemption of the Visigothic king Roderick—a pointedly Anglicized Rodrigo. This suggests that Southey's concern is rather with the Gothic legacy that Britain and Spain share than with Spanish history as such. Indeed, the redemptive plot of Roderick returning from exile to assist the "native" Pelayo invites an allegorical reading in which Roderick represents a formerly sinful Britain that now brings a fresh access of "Gothic Virtue" to Spain. The reconstitution of Burke's international Gothic order is, moreover, explicitly imagined by Pelayo, who sees his mission as the repair of the ravages of this "portentous age," which "As with an earthquake's desolating force, / Hath loosen'd and disjointed the whole frame / Of social order" (XIII, 176–79). Like that other Gothic scion young Hamlet, it is his commission to put the time back into joint.

My argument to this point has been that the Spanish revolt against Napoleon was widely—if by no means exclusively—imagined as a revival of the old "Gothic" and "chivalric" order, and that this phenomenon was common to both Spain and Britain. I have also been arguing that writers and artists of both nations harnessed this imagination to preexisting national mythologies. In Britain, certainly, the revolution allowed old narratives about both Britain and Spain to be cast in a redemptive light, particularly in the texts produced by Wordsworth, Coleridge, Southey, and Scott. But my account so far has not reckoned with the sudden crisis precipitated by the Convention of Cintra, or with the tract Wordsworth wrote in response. The next section will argue that *The Convention of Cintra* epitomizes the redemptive power of the imagination of the struggle in Spain as a revival of the Gothic order. But I want first to give a brief account of the Convention itself.

As in the days of the French Revolution, Wordsworth and those contemporaries who found new hope in the Spanish uprising were laboring for an adequate language "beneath / The breath of great events" (*The Prelude* [1805], X, 943–44). August 1808 saw new alliances with Spain and Portugal take effect as the British Government, with the full support of the Whig Opposition in Parliament, and only light raillery from the liberal press, launched an expedition on the Iberian Peninsula. After an inconclusive victory at Vimiero in Portugal, however, in late August the British Generals accepted the French offer of an armistice, shortly formalized as the Convention of Cintra. The terms of the Convention provided for the safe escort and transportation of the defeated French armies from Portugal to France by the Royal Navy, and the surrender of all forts to the British. The departing French were to make no reparations, and French citizens remaining in the country were placed, along with Portuguese collaborators, under the protection of the British army (*Prose Works*, I, 350–357).

News of the Convention was received with disbelief and horror at home. *The Times* was still hoping against hope that "misconception exists in some quarter" on 16 September (2), but by the 27th it was expressing "with all the warmth of indignation" and all "the bitterness of grief" the "feeling of the British public" that by the Convention "our honour…had been debased," "our interests…sacrificed, our rights surrendered, and the lustre of our arms sullied" (2). Looking over the Convention on 17 September, *The Examiner* professed bewilderment: "the head turns in confusion through the maze of our military politics, and the reader is dragged from error to error, from stupidity to stupidity, till his faculties become numb, and he is converted into a mere mass of astonishment" (606). By 25 September, however, this "astonishment" had hardened into shame and anger over "our late disgrace" (607). Few participated in these sensations of degradation and betrayal more strongly than Wordsworth.

## *The Convention of Cintra*: Revaluing the Spanish Gothic

By the time he came to write *The Convention of Cintra* in 1808–9, Wordsworth had already followed a long and tortuous course of revaluing the Gothic. As we have seen, his opposition to Britain's "Gothic regulation" across the 1790s gave way in the 1800s, and particularly in the 1802 sonnets on liberty and the later books of *The Prelude*, to a stylistic and ideological opposition to Napoleon, and a view of Britain as the "last spot of earth where freedom now / Stands single in her only sanctuary" (*1805* X, 981–82). *Cintra* continues this development. There is, Wordsworth says, a principled opposition in the British people to "the spirit of selfish tyranny and lawless ambition," which had been shown in the opposition of the "immense majority of the people" to the government's liberticidal war back in 1793 (*Cintra*, ll. 89, 91–92). But since the French "subjugation of Switzerland" in 1798, Wordsworth claims, the roles of Britain and France had been reversed (l. 79). With the spirit of tyranny now "undeniably embodied in the French government" (ll. 95–96), Wordsworth implies that Britain has replaced France as the spirit of liberty incarnate, as it were, by default.

The change of allegiance had long remained, however, an "afflicting alternative" (l. 132). Thrown into alignment with their government not by any change in its moral or political complexion but rather by a "revolution in circumstances," the condition of the British people "savoured too much of a grinding restraint—too much of the vassalage of necessity" (ll. 127, 134–35). Clearly, the "alternative" was particularly "afflicting" for former French sympathizers and republicans like Wordsworth because the reconcilement required was not simply with a particular administration, but with the whole unreformed system: still in 1808–9 a "decay[ed]...machine of government," "checked and controul[ed]" in "its constitutional motions" by "illegitimate forces" (ll. 3326–28). Still, that is, too Gothic in the pejorative sense. In the language of the *Letter to the Bishop of Llandaff* (1793), the British people desiring reconciliation with their government "were bound to cherish a corse at the bosom, when reason might call aloud that it should be entombed" (*Prose Works*, I, 48). The process of mortification had, indeed, already begun, with "grinding constraint" generating rather a "despond[ing]...deliberate and preparatory fortitude—a sedate and stern melancholy" than fresh libertarian fervor (*Cintra*, ll. 134–38).

To complete the transfer of the cause of liberty from France to Britain would require nothing less than a complete transvaluation of the once reviled and still unreformed Gothic Constitution. But this is precisely the prospect that the Spanish uprising seemed to offer. "[F]rom the moment of the rising of the people of the Pyrenean peninsula," Wordsworth says, "there was a mighty change; we were instantaneously animated" (ll. 142–44). Wordsworth's language of "instantaneous animation" alludes both to his own earlier image of the British government as a noxious "corse," and to what Nicholas Roe has shown was the analogy drawn by radical thinkers like Joseph Priestley and John Thelwall between the animating power of "electrical fluid" in organized matter and the renovating virtue of political information in the state (Roe 2002, 92–93, 101–19). If Britain could be "animated" by a spark from the Spanish conflagration, the body of the Gothic Constitution might indeed be safely "cherish[ed] at the bosom," joyfully embraced rather than grimly clasped.

*Cintra* opens, however, with an attitude toward prerevolutionary Spain that is almost indistinguishable from Urquijo and Napoleon's condemnation of the "Gothic edifice." Spain's "old Monarchy" was "imbecile even to dotage," "destitute of vigour" even in its determination "to prop up the last remains of its own decrepitude;" precisely the "worn-out" structure that Napoleon had taken it to be (ll. 3114–16, 3140, 1214). But Wordsworth is keenly alive to the fact that Napoleon had not properly abolished the Gothic structure. Rather, "presuming on its decrepitude," the "tyrant" had, "through the real decrepitude of [the] Government," "perfidiously enslaved" the Spanish nation (ll. 178–80). Napoleon's installation of a "solemn puppet" on the Spanish throne was a piece of constitutional surgical theatre: an attempt to "remove the old heart, and put a new one into the bosom of the spectators" (ll. 4060–64). Reviving the graveyard Gothic imagery that he had employed in the *Letter to the Bishop of Llandaff*, Wordsworth pictures the decrepit "old Monarchy of Spain...taken laboriously and foolishly by the plotting Corsican to his own bosom" (ll. 3114–17). The "plotting Corsican," cherishing the "corse" of the Gothic state at the bosom, exposes himself to the contagion of its "imbecil[ity]." Indeed, in giving artificial life to the Gothic order that he had stripped of the last weak lendings of legitimacy, Napoleon had, Wordsworth said, quoting the Junta of Seville from *The Courier* for September 15, 1808, "compelled" the nation "to take up arms and to choose itself a form of government;" "working blindly" thus "against his own purposes" (ll. 3158–61, 3121). By this symbolic transferral of Gothic "imbecility" the roles of France and Spain (and her allies) are reversed. "[D]isburthened of a cleaving curse," of "the incumbrance of superannuated institutions," Spain is in precisely the condition of France in 1789, whereas France is ossified under a tyranny that "sickens at the sight" of anything "endued with such excellence" and genuine original power (ll. 3135, 3148–49, 4416–18, 4437–39). Indeed, in thrall to a man whose mind is of such "barbarian impotence and insolence" that it lags, "in moral sentiment and in knowledge, three hundred years behind the age in which it acts," and bound together in a "frame of polity" that "possesses the consistency of an ancient Government," Napoleonic France is, Wordsworth implies, less enlightened and more negatively Gothic even than Spain before 1808 (ll. 3759–62, 4563–64).

Wordsworth recognized, however, that Spain's devout Catholicism rendered the country irredeemably Gothic in the negative sense in the eyes of many of his contemporaries. "[M]any of my countrymen," he wrote, had seen "[t]he superstition...which prevailed" in Spain and Portugal as a "stain" upon them, and been "checked" in "their hopes for the cause" (ll. 2905–10). "Even their loyalty" to Church and King was, Wordsworth confessed, "such as, from our mixed constitution of government and other causes, we [i.e. the British people] could not thoroughly sympathize with" (ll. 192–94). Britain's "mixed constitution" is here the (progressive) opposite of Gothic loyalism in Spain. And indeed the "mixture" in the British constitution of the state and the Anglican Church, with (until 1829) the attendant legal disabilities for Catholics, meant that no "loyal" Briton could "thoroughly sympathize" with the religious and political "loyalty" of the Spaniard. Wordsworth thus registered the continued prevalence in Britain up to 1809 of the mythology—what Diego Saglia calls the "Black Legend" (Saglia 2000, 40–52)—of Spain as an evil Catholic power whose Inquisition thirsted for Protestant blood. Two prints—James Gillray's *Spanish-Patriots attacking the French-Banditti* (August 15, 1808), and George Cruikshank's *The Noble Spaniards* (July 20, 1808)—epitomize the way such anxieties about Spanish Catholicism haunted the imagination of the war as the revival of "chivalry." As I noted earlier, Gillray's print pictures the French as wholly degenerate. Even the least simian of their number uses his rifle as a club. But though the enemy of the Gothic order is thus dealt his own "monkey" medicine, the Spaniards are not thereby reciprocally transformed in Gillray's eyes into noble Goths. An incongruous army, their (British-supplied) cannon "manned" by aristocratic ladies, a monk, and a dueño in doublet and hose, they are less "the best part of chivalry" than the hopeless thralls of the ossified forms of despotic government and Catholic superstition. In Simon Bainbridge's terms, the Spanish patriots here are "representatives of an *ancien régime* alliance of monarchy and papacy" (Bainbridge 1995, 105). Their loyalty is redolent more of medieval fanaticism than of enlightened independence. The "Loyal Brito[n]," however, is represented quite differently. Pointedly situated between the two armies, he too fights a "war to the knife," but in a markedly unfanatical manner, and with a modern rifle and bayonet rightly used. Representing the happy medium between two kinds of throwback—"monkish" Spaniards and "monkey" Frenchmen—the Briton supports, without "thoroughly sympathiz[ing] with," the Gothic cause of Spain. Cruikshank's print, meanwhile, manifests the residual power of the "Black Legend" both in its ambivalent subtitle ("Britannia assisting the Cause of Freedom all over the world, *whither Friend or Foe*" [my emphasis]) and in its depiction of the lurking presence in the rear of the Spanish army of a group of black-cowled monks.[7] Britain's purer Gothic effort is expressed, meanwhile, in the forms of a sword-wielding British soldier and a heavenly Britannia, who showers military matériel down upon Spain and proclaims her support for any "Nation that has spirit to throw off the yoke of the Tyrant of France." Thus, as much as in Southey's *Roderick*, these cartoons make the Spanish conflict into the backdrop for a British narrative of Gothic redemption. They are the more clearly exercises in militaristic chauvinism for the fact that, as Mary George notes, even by the time of the Gillray print, "[n]o English soldier had yet set foot in *Spain*" (George, ed. 1870–1954, VIII, 662; my emphasis). Indeed, Spain in these cartoons already provides what Saglia, speaking of the period following the Spanish collapse at Corunna in January 1809, calls a "counter-text" for the clearer articulation of a British "nationalist narrative" (Saglia 2000, 66). With all the negative connotations of the Gothic concentrated in the Spanish other, the Briton becomes the Goth purified and reinvented for the modern age.

Wordsworth was determined to rescue the Spanish patriots from such libels—though, as I will show, overcoming his reservations regarding Spain's Catholicism required a much more strenuous act of imagination. In a letter of December 3, 1808 congratulating Francis Wrangham on his recently published sermon, *The Gospel Best Promulgated by National Schools* (1808), Wordsworth begged to differ with Wrangham's opinion that Spain, "a brave but sluggish kingdom shaking off her lethargy of centuries," fighting Napoleon "with a heroism worthy of her most chivalrous period," was nevertheless only "devoting herself for a Bourbon in chains, and the crumbling relics of the Inquisition" (Wrangham 1816, II, 118). "This," Wordsworth wrote, "is very fair for pointing a sentence, but it is not the truth":

> They have told us over and over again that they are fighting against a foreign tyrant who has dealt with them most perfidiously, and inhumanly, who must hate them for their worth, and on account of the injuries they have received from him, and whom they must hate accordingly; against a ruler over whom they could have no control, and *for* one whom they have told us they will establish as the sovereign of a *free* people, and who therefore must himself be a limited monarch. (*MY* I, 278)

However, in another letter to Wrangham of late March 1809, Wordsworth substantially undermined this view with his worry that to constitute Catholicism as the Established Church in Ireland, "upon the plea of their being the majority merely," "implies an admission on our part that their profession of faith is in itself as good as ours, as consistent with civil liberty" (*MY* I, 313). If hers was a faith of dubious consistency with civil liberty, then the struggle of Catholic Spain for a limited monarchy like Britain's was surely fundamentally flawed. Wordsworth was well aware of the contradiction, and that Wrangham would think him "fair game upon the Catholic Question." This was not least, perhaps, because Wrangham would likely have seen the parts of *Cintra* by now published in *The Courier*, in which Wordsworth parlays typical anti-Catholic sentiments into an argument that Spain's

Catholic establishment is positively germane to her new alliance with Britain against France.[8] "If," he wrote,

> in the sensations with which the Spaniards prostrated themselves before the religion of their country we did not keep pace with them—if even their loyalty was such as, from our mixed constitution of government and from other causes, we could not thoroughly sympathize with...in all these things we judged them gently: and, taught by the reverses of the French revolution, we looked upon these dispositions as more human—more social—and therefore as wiser, and of better omen, than if they had stood forth the zealots of abstract principles, drawn out of the laboratory of unfeeling philosophists. (*Cintra* ll. 190–200)

It is thus precisely the Gothic constitution of Spain that makes her suitable as an ally for Britain. Wordsworth concedes that Spain's revolutionary vitality is vitiated by a "mixture of superstition." But, he insists, established forms and superstitions should be imagined not as impediments to national regeneration, as constraints upon the "mass fluctuating with one motion under the breath of a might[y] wind," but rather as obsolescent vessels or "organ[s]" that "must...necessarily [be] transmuted" and vivified by that same "mighty wind" (ll. 2900–2901, 2937, 2912). The "corse" of Spain's Church and state, still bearing the Gothic trappings of a more armorial age, might yet show its face above ground:

> The chains of bigotry, which enthralled the mind, must have been turned into armour to defend and weapons to annoy...And the types and ancient instruments of error, where emancipated men shewed their foreheads to the day, must have become a language and a ceremony of imagination; expressing, consecrating, and invigorating, the most pure deductions of Reason and the holiest feelings of universal Nature. (ll. 2915–22)

Wordsworth's renascent Gothic order has learned the lessons of Enlightenment and the French Revolution, cloaking "a language and a ceremony" over the "pure...Reason" which is its bedrock. "[A]ncient instruments of error" are thus "converted...to instruments of nobler use" by the spirit that is in them rather than by any alteration in their outward appearance (ll. 3017–18). Like Burke's English, with their "powerful prepossession towards antiquity," and their preference rather "to continue the prejudice, with the reason involved, than to cast away the coat of prejudice, and to leave nothing but the naked reason" (Burke 1987, 28, 76), Wordsworth's

Spaniards have a constitutional "predilection for all established institutions" (*Cintra* ll. 418–19). The declarations of the various Juntas of Spain and Portugal indeed constitute a grand invocation of "elder ancestors":

> The Biscayans are called to cast their eyes upon the ages which are past, and they will see their ancestors at one time repulsing the Carthaginians, at another destroying the hordes of Rome; at one period was granted to them the distinction of serving in the van of the army; at another the privilege of citizens. "Imitate," says the address, "the glorious example of your worthy progenitors." The Asturians, the Gallicians, and the city of Cordova, are exhorted in the same manner. (ll. 839–46)

This passage is particularly suggestive of Wordsworth's identification with the Gothic tenor of the Spanish war-effort, for the Asturians were, as Bourgoing had noted in *Modern State of Spain*, "regarded as the descendants of the ancient Goths, who took refuge in the mountains of their province, and never submitted to the yoke of the Moors" (Bourgoing 1808, I, 161). An apocryphal proclamation of May 8, 1808 of Ferdinand VII, formerly Prince of the Asturias, now a prisoner at Bayonne, made clear reference to this Gothic myth in exhorting the "Noble Asturians" to throw off a "foreign yoke" and restore his "right," as, "in worse circumstances," "[y]ou once saved Spain" before (qtd. in *Gentleman's Magazine*, Vol. 78, June 1808, 542). Indeed, the centrality of this Gothic pedigree in the rhetoric of Spanish independence is reflected in José Muñoz Maldonado's 1833 history, which noted that Asturias, the "refuge" in which "Don Pelayo...salvaged the remains of the Gothic monarchy; this land...inhabited by an indomitable race, was the first that raised the cry of independence" (trans. from Maldonado 1833, I, 193). Wordsworth had, as we saw earlier, already written a poem on Pelayo's salvaging of the old Gothic monarchy. *Cintra* does not mention the more explicitly Gothic legend of Roderick. But the ancestral exemplars of heroism he does cite are taken directly from the larger Spanish mythology of *reconquista* that, as Joseph F. O'Callaghan has shown, pictured a genetic continuity between the unified Gothic kingdom of Spain of the seventh century and the sovereign nation constituted in the late fifteenth century (O'Callaghan 2003, 4–7). Situating himself squarely on this "Gothic" ground, Wordsworth commends the fact that

> [t]he names of Pelayo and The Cid are the watch-words of the address to the people of Leon; and they are told that to these two deliverers of their country, and to the sentiments of enthusiasm which they excited

in every breast, Spain owes the glory and happiness which she has *so long* enjoyed. (*Cintra* ll. 835–39)

Wordsworth's own attempt to stimulate "sentiments of enthusiasm" in *Cintra* is thus clearly legible as an attempt to recuperate and aggressively to employ—as the Spaniards themselves were doing—a specifically Gothic legacy. According to Wordsworth, the "predilection for all established institutions" leads to a uniquely Spanish application of the advice in Edward Young's *Conjectures on Original Composition* (1759) to imitate the ancients but not their works. "Let us," Young had written,

> build our Compositions with the Spirit, and in the Taste, of the Antients; but not with their Materials: Thus will they resemble the structures of *Pericles* at *Athens*, which *Plutarch* commends for having had an air of Antiquity as soon as they were built. (Young 1759, 22)

The Spaniards of *Cintra* pointedly depart from Young in reusing ancient "materials." But in Wordsworth's view the Spanish imagination of continuity with the Gothic past generates a new, historical, form of originality:

> [T]hey...express a rational hope of reforming domestic abuses, and of re-constructing, out of the materials of their ancient institutions, customs, and laws, a better frame of government, the same in the great outlines of its architecture, but exhibiting the knowledge, and genius, and the needs of the present race, harmoniously blended with those of their forefathers. (*Cintra* ll. 987–93)

In evidence of this syncretic and creative mentality Wordsworth quotes the Junta of Seville's "Precautions" on the assembly of the Cortes, singling out for emphasis the words "*the Cortes will be assembled, abuses reformed*" (l. 945). "Things," Wordsworth and the Junta continue, "which we Spaniards know how to do, which we have done as well as other nations, without any necessity that the vile French should come to instruct us, and, according to their custom, under the mask of friendship, should deprive us of our liberty, our laws, &c. &c." (ll. 947–51). "Precautions" sounds a straightforward nationalistic note: the French enemy is "vile," and Spain derives peculiar national glory from its unique constitutional history. But the sense of national superiority in this passage seems to derive as much from a Burkean contempt of the sort of constitutionalism that France in 1808 represents, and has recently represented, as from simple anti-French feeling. More importantly for my reading of *Cintra*'s Gothic politics, it seems likely that such contempt for French constitutionalism resonated in Wordsworth's mind with his knowledge of the ancient and supernational provenance of the Cortes: a provenance he would have known through the antiquarian writings of Thomas Percy.

Between the years 1797 and 1798, Wordsworth read or reread Thomas Percy's *Northern Antiquities* (1770), a translation of Paul-Henri Mallet's two treatises (published in 1755 and 1756) on the history of ancient Denmark (Wu 1993, 93). The account Percy and Mallet gave of the religion and government of the North was, Peter Mortensen has suggested, the most important text for the sudden surge of interest in all things Nordic in the late eighteenth century (Mortensen 2000, 213). Not only Nordic, but specifically Gothic—for where Mallet's French original conflated the legal and religious practices of Celtic and the Germanic peoples, Percy's translation argued that they were "*ab origine* two distinct people, very unlike in their manners, customs, religion and laws," and that the Danes were no Celts but archetypal Goths (Mallet and Percy 1770, I, iv). The deep imprint left in Wordsworth's mind by the book's Gothic lore can be seen in his plan—adumbrated in the preamble to *The Prelude*—of writing an epic poem on the Norse god Odin, "Father of a race by whom / Perished the Roman Empire" (*1805* I, 188–89). Wordsworth's phrase is a compression of the "poetical" supposition offered by Percy and Mallet (and later echoed in Gibbon's *Decline and Fall* [1777, I, 294]) that Odin, defeated and driven north by the Roman armies of Pompey, inspired the northern peoples with an undying hatred of Rome; and that when, half a millennium later, the Empire fell to his Gothic progeny, it was the fulfillment of his revenge (Mallet and Percy 1770, I, 67–68).[9] Wordsworth, working on the preamble some time around January 1804, might well have seen in the figure of the fugitive and vengeful Odin, "obliged...to go seek in countries unknown to his enemies, that safety which he could no longer find in his own" (Mallet and Percy, I, 59–60), a model for his earlier self.[10] At the outbreak of war in 1793, he became himself a fugitive, "cut off" (*1805* X, 257) in spirit from Britain and in body from France, the home of his personal and political hopes. And when, hearing "prayers...offered up / Or praises for our country's victories," he, like Odin, "Fed on the day of vengeance yet to come!" (X, 268–74).

Odin's presence in *The Prelude* of 1805 indicates that his legend—and hence the matter of *Northern Antiquities*—was still in Wordsworth's mind six years after he read the book, and only four years before the writing of *Cintra*. Indeed, there is a clear echo of the preamble's fervent desire to "summon back from lonesome banishment" a "little band of yet remembered names" (I, 172–77) in the prophecy of the *Pelayo* fragment that his "little band" will return triumphant from their wild "retreat" (ll. 12, 20). This would put *Northern Antiquities* center-stage in Wordsworth's thoughts as late as June 1808. It is probable, then, that when he read the call in "Precautions" for the assembly of the Cortes, it was in the knowledge that Mallet and Percy numbered it among the modern descendants of the "general assemblies" or "States General" of the ancient Goths. The Cortes was, they said, the Spanish equivalent of the "witenagemot" or Parliament in England, and the "Champs de Mars" of the French (Mallet and Percy 1770, I, 178). The proposal in "Precautions" to reconstruct the Cortes was therefore plainly legible to Wordsworth as a plan to rebuild the Gothic constitution. In the light of Edmund Burke's powerful contemporary analysis that opposed Britain's Gothic government to "speculative philosophy" in France, this was not merely matter for antiquarian research. France had gone wrong, Burke said, at the precise moment when it had elected to abolish rather than to restore and reform the "old states," the Estates-General last convened in 1614 (Burke 1987, 31). Spain clearly seemed to Wordsworth to have imbibed this Gothic wisdom, with its intention of reconstructing the Cortes from the "material of...ancient institutions, customs, and laws." His approval of "Precautions," with its plan of convoking the Cortes, thus constitutes a declaration of sympathy not only with the Spanish people but also with the country's Gothic institutions, what the Spanish Deputation at Bayonne had called the "old system of laws" (*Cintra* l. 743), that Napoleon and his Spanish collaborators sought to destroy. Like Young's Plutarch commending the "structures of *Pericles* at *Athens*," Wordsworth approves above all the Spanish Revolution's instant "air of Antiquity." It is the formulation of a progressive Gothic politics.

In the various ways that I have been suggesting, then, the events in Spain in 1808 were legible to Wordsworth in terms of a struggle between Goths and Jacobins that was the very mirror image of the early years of the French Revolution, with the Goths now playing the role of Liberty incarnate. Aligning Britain with Spain and against France, *Cintra* first pictures British liberty in terms of venerability and originality; the terms, that is, of the Gothic Constitution:

> [L]iberty—healthy, matured, time-honoured liberty—this is the growth and peculiar boast of Britain; and nature herself, by encircling

with the ocean the country we inhabit, has proclaimed that this mighty nation is to be for ever her own ruler, and that the land is set apart for the home of immortal independence. (ll. 2384–88)

This "immortal independence" is the positive corollary of Burke's unsavory conception of the "mortmain," a partnership between the generations that creates a permanent state. Seen through the lens of the Convention of Cintra, however, Britain's "immortal independence" begins to look like a rag-bag of musty precedent and moldered tradition that is an active obstacle to the fresh effusion of liberty in Portugal and Spain. Wordsworth laments the narrow military view of the situation on the Peninsula taken by the generals who signed the Convention (ll. 1141–46), and exhorts the British government that ratified and honored it to a more comprehensive view of the national good:

> [T]he true welfare of Britain is best promoted by the independence, freedom, and honour of other Nations; and...it is only by the diffusion and prevalence of these virtues that French Tyranny can be ultimately reduced. (ll. 3819–22)

Combating Napoleon requires, that is, an imagination of the conflict like that of the Spaniards themselves, as the renovation of the "Gothic edifice" of government. Just as the pressure of a feared invasion in 1803 had served in "To the Men of Kent" to transform the Kentish relic of *gavelkynd* into a transcendent national solidarity, so the impetus of the Napoleonic "evil" in Spain is imagined as an opportunity to reform the old Gothic order of Europe into a neo-Catholic utopian community:

> The true sorrow of humanity consists in this;– not that the mind of man fails; but that the course and demands of action and of life so rarely correspond with the dignity and intensity of human desires: and hence that, which is slow to languish, is too easily turned aside and abused. But—with the remembrance of what has been done, and in the face of the interminable evils which are threatened—a Spaniard can never have cause to complain of this, while a follower of the tyrant remains in arms upon the Peninsula. Here then they, with whom I hope, take their stand. There is a spiritual community binding together the living and the dead; the good, the brave, and the wise, of all ages. We would not be rejected from this community; and therefore do we hope. (ll. 4807–14)

But the signing of the Convention seemed to show precisely the failure of such a hopeful imagination in Britain, which had behaved "as if it had been our aim to level to the ground by one blow this long-wished-for spirit" (ll. 988–91, 1216–17). *Cintra* thus engages directly with the widespread Gothic imagination of the war, but extends it to implicate Britain as both a Napoleonic leveler of Gothic edifices and as a "Gothic edifice" itself: the government's depraved actions reveal its divorce from the sympathetic imagination and the public spirit of the British people. Appropriately enough, then, Wordsworth moves to adopt a stance similar to that of Paine taunting Burke in 1791 for relying on "musty records and moldy parchments to prove that the rights of the living are lost" (Paine 1995, 95–96). When Spain rose against Napoleon, generating "new authorities, which...were truly living members of their body, and...organs of their life," Britain should have fostered the growth of the national spirit that animated the new body politic, or "ought at least to have stood at an awful distance" (*Cintra* ll. 3212–20). But instead "the heads of the British army and nation...stepped in with their forms, their impediments, their rotten customs and precedents, their narrow desires, their busy and purblind fears," and confounded the Spanish cause by signing the Convention of Cintra (ll. 3218–22).

Wordsworth's language is very close to John Thelwall's "dreadful warning to old establishments" in *The Rights of Nature* (1796) that new opinions prevail over old "because there is an incalculable distance between the energy and enthusiasm of a new conviction, and the science and mechanism of ancient habits" (Thelwall 1995, 426–27). "Because," as Burke had recognized and feared in his *Letters on a Regicide Peace*, "it is the former, alone, that rouses the full force of intellect and valour, and 'suffers not a particle of the man to be lost'" (Thelwall 1995, 426–27; Burke 1796, 70). In *Cintra* the ancient constitution is "rotten," and its charnel-house reek proves noxious to the young body of Spain. In the language of Wordsworth's attack on Burke's notion of the "mortmain" or "entailed inheritance" in *A Letter to the Bishop of Llandaff*, Spain was again "bound to cherish a corse at the bosom, when reason might call aloud it should be entombed" (*Prose Works*, I, 48). Or, to adapt book ten of *The Prelude* on the Napoleonic travesty of the French Revolution, when in Spain "the sun /...rose in splendour, was alive, and moved / In exultation among living clouds," British liberty, "a gewgaw, a machine," brings about a catastrophe in which the living light of liberty "Sets like an opera phantom" (*1805*, X, 936–41). Liberty of the British variety is pictured in *Cintra* as a poor substitute for the spontaneous overflows of revolutions and national uprisings. The Gothic inheritance proves a dead hand if not inspired by a more comprehensive benevolence.

## *Cintra*, Burke, and Gothic Politics

I want to move now to explore in more detail the Gothic idiom developed in *Cintra*, with particular attention to the role of Burke in Wordsworth's formulation of his own Gothic politics. At the conclusion of the pamphlet, Wordsworth expresses a hope that the "chiefs of the Spanish people may prove worthy of their situation" by following an eminently Burkean method of nature:

> [T]hough heads of a nation venerable for antiquity, and having good cause to preserve with reverence the institutions of their elder forefathers—they must not be indiscriminately afraid of new things. It is their duty to restore the good which has fallen into disuse; and also to create, and to adopt. Young scions of polity must be engrafted on the time-worn trunk: a new fortress must be reared upon the ancient and living rock of justice. (ll. 4926–34)

Here the two central conservative metaphors of the Gothic hall and the sheltering oak are formally equivalent, balanced on either side of a colon. Furthermore, they become literally intertwined by taking on each other's characteristics. The artificial fortress is "reared" like young. And the organic tree suffers with built architecture the ravages of time; its growth through the "grafting" of "young scions" mimicking the accretive mode of ecclesiastical Gothic architecture. From this interfusion comes a hybrid structure in which, paradoxically, the perennial newness of nature bestows on revivalist architecture the gravity of antiquity:

> Then would it be seen, while the superstructure stands inwardly immoveable, in how short a space of time the ivy and wild plants would climb up from the base, and clasp the naked walls; the storms, which could not shake, would weather-stain; and the edifice, in the day of its youth, would appear to be one with the rock upon which it was planted, and to grow out of it. (ll. 4935–40)

Architecture takes on the organic properties of the oak, appearing to grow seamlessly out of the rock. Indeed, the "fortress" does not simply appear here as a convincing mock antique, but as a structure without origin, or at least without human origin and agency. Just as William Blackstone's account of the English law played on the historical associations of Gothic architecture but also turned the Gothic into the material of fiction, so this constitutional building in Spain recalls the ancient style of architecture but does not affect to be from any particular period;

deriving, rather, from the "semi-imaginary division of history" that the middle ages were for Blackstone (Watt 1999, 46). To quote Young on Plutarch again—a passage that is surely in Wordsworth's mind as he writes of an edifice naturalized "in the day of its youth"—the new fortress has a vague "air of Antiquity as soon as [it is] built." It is like a growth of nature, like an evolving tradition: it is immemorial.

Wordsworth's imagery here is itself of a piece with the Spanish conflict, anticipating the concern of the delegates to the Cortes of free Spain to reconcile reform with regard for tradition and for constitutional continuity. As I noted earlier, the Cádiz Cortes framed its radical claim to the right to set aside "fundamental law" in "the public interest" in terms of historical precedent and Gothic tradition. It thus represents a classic example of the phenomenon that Eric Hobsbawm calls "the invention of tradition," whereby a set of new or hitherto unconscious practices—here a national constitution practically identical with the aggressively modern Napoleonic system—is so formulated in relation to a (usually factitious) historic past as to appear hallowed by customary usage from time immemorial (Hobsbawm and Ranger, eds. 1983, 1–14). But as Gabriel Lovett suggests, though the Cádiz Constitution "preserv[ed] some links with Spain's past," it "was quite different in spirit and form from Spain's historical legislation" (Lovett, II, 451). In other words, its "tradition" was obviously "invented": it failed to "become tradition" in the manner of Wordsworth's immemorial fortress. And it was at just this point that the enemies of the Cortes attacked. When Ferdinand VII returned to claim his throne in 1814, he clothed himself in the language of tradition the better to expose the modern figure of the Cádiz Cortes inside its doublet and hose. In opposition to Cádiz, which had confected a spurious popular sovereignty from antiquarian fantasy and democratic principles, Ferdinand proclaimed on May 4, 1814 that his "sovereignty" was "established by the Constitution and the laws by which the Nation has lived for a long time" (qtd. in Lovett, II, 830).

At the touch of this rival Constitution and its uninvented tradition, which seemed to have behind it all the reactionary forces in Spain, the "Gothic" Cortes at Cádiz dwindled into dust. By May 11, 1814, many of the leaders of the Cortes were in jail, and by 25 May Arthur Wellesley could report that the king's "measures" had effected "the overthrow of the Constitution" (Lovett, II, 829, 832, 840). With the Cortes fell much of the sense of Britain and Spain's "Gothic" commonality. *The Christian Observer* for April 1815 urged the government to stipulate that Britain's participation in the renewed effort against Napoleon was on the understanding that in expending

> blood and treasure for the freedom and independence of Europe...she shall not be made to contribute, in any degree, to the renewal of a French Slave Trade; to the re-establishment of the papal power; to the revival of the order of the Jesuits; or to the rekindling of the fires of the Inquisition. (271–22)

*The Annual Register* for 1814 characterized as "perplexed" all those "who...expect a regular progress towards melioration in governments":

> [T]hey must be severely mortified by the total failure of the great experiment of that kind conducted with apparent success by the Spanish Cortes, which has terminated in a cruel persecution of all the friends of light and liberty in that country, and the restoration of the Court of Inquisition, and all the other supports of civil and ecclesiastical despotism...and particularly from the revival of an order [the Jesuits] rendered odious to all the liberal of their own communion, by their servile devotion to the pontifical court, and their dark and subtle policy. (iv–v)

This historical "failure" of an "experiment" conducted on a pattern so similar to Wordsworth's constitutional manifesto, calls into question the structural soundness of *Cintra*'s own account of the efficacy of tradition. Indeed, I want to move now to argue that the immemorial fortress is in fact a radically unstable image, and that the conservative typology of *Cintra* is legible as a critical reflection upon all such "inventions of tradition." Deirdre Coleman has argued that *Cintra* sees Wordsworth "hold fast to earlier beliefs whilst positioning them within a Burkean framework." Wordsworth's statement of the need for "scions of polity" to be "engrafted on the time-worn trunk" is, Coleman argues, a direct reference to the image in the *Reflections* of the constitution as a "body and stock of inheritance," upon which "we have taken care not to inoculate any cyon alien" (Coleman 1989, 146, 156; Burke 1987, 28). This "pointed" parallel suggests to Coleman that Burke is implicated among those who are, according to Wordsworth, "indiscriminately afraid of new things." Moreover, Wordsworth's constitutional fortress, an "indomitably new structure" is, for Coleman, wholly alien to "the metaphorical 'building'" of the *Reflections*, "which can only be changed according to the principles of preservation and reparation" (Coleman 1989, 156–57).

I think Coleman overstates the conservatism of Burke's "metaphorical building." His advice to the French to recur to *imagined* ancestors, and to rebuild from the *foundations* of the ruined castle of France (1987, 31), implies a mandate for more radical change than the mere stewardship Coleman envisages. However, the apparent spontaneity with which Wordsworth's "fortress" is "reared" upon the rock, like the "Fabrick huge" of Pandemonium rising "out of the earth...like an Exhalation" in *Paradise Lost* (I, 710–711), does indeed seem to imply a building method quite different from Burke's painstaking restoration work. Burke himself used exactly this imagery to differentiate Britain's organic constitutionalism from the abstract procedures of the Revolution. The *Reflections* figured the National Assembly as a spontaneous birth just like Pandemonium: it was "a theoretic, experimental edifice" produced *ex nihilo*—as though the French were "a people of yesterday" (1987, 111, 32, 77). Wordsworth's approval of a similarly new building in Spain thus seems to put him at odds with Burke.

This suggestion that *Cintra*'s overgrown fortress is actually the antithesis of Burke's organic castle is seconded by Wordsworth's later figuration of Burke himself as an overgrown structure. This passage— the apostrophe to the "Genius of Burke" inserted into book seven of *The Prelude* in 1832—likens Burke to an old English oak:

> I see him,—old, but vigorous in age, –
> Stand like an oak whose stag-horn branches start
> Out of its leafy brow, the more to awe
> The younger brethren of the grove.
> (*1850* VII, 519–22)

Jonathan Wordsworth offers an explanatory note for this image. At a certain stage in the life cycle of English oaks, he says, "the top branches...tend to die back, the tree forming a second crown from growth sent out lower down the trunk. Through this new foliage older branches protrude, stag-horn-like, because the wood is so hard that they become seasoned instead of rotting" (1995, 605n). Wordsworth's equation between Burke and such an oak thus appears to image his discourse "Of Institutes and Laws, hallowed by time" and "social ties / Endeared by Custom" as a benignant shelter for "ingenuous...bewildered men" against "upstart Theory" (*1850* VII, 526–28, 514, 529). Like the Lorton tree of Wordsworth's "Yew Trees" poem of 1811, whose epochal growth made it seem coeval with English history, Burke's principles seem here to grow organically out of English history in a way that makes them indestructible: "Produced too slowly ever to decay" (l. 11; *MW* 334–35).

However, the passage subverts Burke's "Genius" in ways that remind the reader that it occurs to Wordsworth among memories of the "specious wonders" (*1850* VII, 513) to be seen in London. The corollary of the fact that the Oak-Burke provides shelter is, evidently enough, that it overshadows and overawes "younger brethren," stunting their growths through a "vigorous" obscurantism. With "stag-horn branches" starting from his "leafy brow," Burke is clearly in his second growth. On one level, this is an extremely economical figure for Burke's "second career" in the period of the French Revolution—following his "first career" as a Rockinghamite opponent of the war in America—and for his political philosophy of the "method of nature." But if his "stag-horn branches" are visible, it can only be because the renascent Burke is diminished. Like the professors at Cambridge described in book three of *The Prelude*, "tricked out like aged trees / Which through the lapse of their infirmity / Give ready place to any random seed / That chooses to be reared upon their trunks" (*1805*, III, 575–79), Burke is a teacher whose second efflorescence is a "lower" growth than that of his prime. This was certainly the young Wordsworth's opinion of his move from opposition to the war in America to—by the time of *Letters on a Regicide Peace* (1796)—advocacy of a war of extermination against the Revolution in France. Intriguingly, Burke had imagined an alternative second career in the *Reflections* that points to the idea of second growth as inferior and unnatural, and that may indeed underlie Wordsworth's decision to figure him as an oak. Speaking of the contempt of experience in the National Assembly, and imagining himself in the place of one of its elder members, Burke had hoped that

> if I could not attain to the wisdom, I would at least preserve something of the stiff and peremptory dignity of age. These gentlemen deal in regeneration; but at any price I should hardly yield my rigid fibres to be regenerated by them, nor begin, in my grand climacteric, to squall in their new accents or to stammer, in my second cradle, the elemental sounds of their barbarous metaphysics. (1987, 190)

The suppressed image—of Burke as an ancient tree-spirit regenerated by Jacobin metaphysics, as Lear in the throes of his madness—is picked up and inverted by Wordsworth. Burke has second birth, and, just as in Wordsworth's nightmare of the September Massacres, of the "earthquake…not satisfied at once" (*1805* X, 74), it is precisely a daemonic rebirth, a "Gothic" repetition rather than a "metaphysical" barbarization. The image of the stag-horned oak carries a disquieting implication of a rank and parasitic growth, a "cyon alien" indeed grafted onto a once sound "body and stock of inheritance." When Burke's "Wisdom" is subsequently described, breaking forth from him like Hesiod's Athene from Jove's brain, "in armour of resplendent words, / Startling the Synod" (*1850* VII, 538–40), there is surely at least a rumor of incipient madness and/or daemonic possession. After all, the image comes to Wordsworth mediated through Milton's adaptation of this very myth in *Paradise Lost*'s account of the birth of Sin from the forehead of Satan (*Paradise Lost*, II, 746–61). Where Burke's "Genius" promises to guide "ingenuous…bewildered" men, misled by "systems built on abstract rights" (*1850* VII, 524), he is in fact himself dangerously close to the Satanic synod "reason[ing] high" on the abstruse laws of government and finding "no end, in wand'ring mazes lost" (*Paradise Lost*, II, 558–61). In making Burke's own "Wisdom" into a fully formed prodigy that recalls Milton's depictions of Sin and Pandemonium, Wordsworth seems to repeat the charge made in the *Letter to the Bishop of Llandaff* that Burke is at least as "infatuated" as those who support "systems built on abstract rights."

The imagery Wordsworth uses to depict the daemonic character of Burke's "Genius" is very close to that used for the "fortress" of *Cintra*. Both passages allude to *Paradise Lost* and to the *Reflections*, and both feature a sound structure overgrown by "ivy and wild plants." It is therefore possible to see the Oak-Burke as a retrospective commentary upon *Cintra*'s fortress—or to see the fortress as a prototype for the Oak-Burke. The ivy overgrowing the new fortress in *Cintra* thus becomes legible as analogous to what the *Letter to the Bishop of Llandaff* saw as the inevitable growth of "an interest distinct from that of the general body" in even the most representative government: the "natural tendency of power to corrupt" generates a network external to the original structure of government that buries it in its own interests (*Prose Works*, I, 37). The ivy of custom makes the "fortress" look ancient "in the day of its youth"—but primarily in the negative sense of Benjamin Franklin's statement on the American Constitution that the new republic would last until the private interests miraculously set aside in the Convention returned to stifle it, and despotism alone could govern the corrupted people.[11]

Wordsworth's imagery in *Cintra* thus suggests a deep ambivalence regarding the Gothic garb proposed for the new edifice of the Spanish constitution. Far from valuing antiquity for its own sake, he retains a philosophically radical sense that the evolutionary operation of custom is a process of corruption, an overgrowth of "natural" private and familial interests upon the disinterested benevolence and impartiality of a republican system of political justice. Custom and habit threaten to obscure beneath layers of "natural" artifice what Tom Paine called "the right-angled character of man" (Paine 1995, 142). It is not sufficient, Wordsworth's figure of the overgrown fortress seems to urge, for the revived Cortes to be clad in the trappings of the Gothic: it must instead be founded securely upon the rock of "Gothic Virtue."

## Miltonic Gothic

In concluding the pamphlet, Wordsworth turns decisively from matters in Spain to matters at home. The guilt for signing the Convention of Cintra is, as yet, "unexpiated," and, he says, "[w]anting light, we want strength" (*Cintra* ll. 4941–42). The necessary "light" on the subject can only be gained, Wordsworth suggests, through a more comprehensive worldview than that afforded by full immersion in its "busy" concerns (l. 4945). His own "humble efforts" and his own seclusion in the Lake District are paralleled with Petrarch's withdrawal "from the too busy world—not out of indifference to its welfare, or to forget its concerns—but . . . for wider compass of eye-sight, that he might comprehend and see in just proportions and relations" (ll. 4943–47). The view adopted at the conclusion of *Cintra* is thus precisely that of the projected modern epic *The Recluse*, the "philosophical Poem" announced in the Preface to *The Excursion* as a panoramic survey of "Man, Nature, and Society . . . having for its principal subject the sensations and opinions of a Poet living in retirement."

To Coleridge, who ought to have known, the similarity between the stance of *Cintra* and that of *The Recluse* was clear. Writing to Daniel Stuart that the pamphlet's sales were likely to be dampened by its detail on an event in which public interest had lapsed, Coleridge echoed closely Wordsworth's early characterization of *The Prelude* as "a sort of portico to the Recluse" (*EY* 594): "the long Porch," he feared, "may prevent Readers from entering the Temple" (Griggs, ed. 1956–71, III, 214). The pamphlet was, Coleridge continued, "almost a self-robbery from some great philosophical poem." And in this light it is particularly striking that the quotation "to the same purpose" (*Cintra* ll. 4961–62) that follows Petrarch is taken from the *History of Britain* of Wordsworth's "great Predecessor" (*MY* II, 146) and epic compeer, John Milton:

> Milton . . . contemplating our ancestors in his day, thus speaks of them and their errors:—"Valiant, indeed, and prosperous to win a field; but

to know the end and reason of winning, injudicious and unwise. Hence did their victories prove as fruitless, as their losses dangerous; and left them still languishing under the same grievances that men suffer conquered. Which was indeed unlikely to go otherwise; unless men more than vulgar bred up in the knowledge of ancient and illustrious deeds, invincible against many and vain titles, impartial to friendships and relations, had conducted their affairs." (ll. 4962–71)[12]

Wordsworth's text here is known as the "Digression," Milton's meditation upon the parallels between the vices of Britain in his day and in the period immediately "after the Romans goeing [*sic*] out" (Patterson, ed. 1931–38, X, 317–18). Wordsworth's quotation of this passage seeks in turn to enforce a further parallel between vicious "Britans" in antiquity, in Milton's day, and in modern times. Inadequate to their own liberty in the past, they are profligate with that of others—in Spain and Portugal—in the present. Since Milton's analogy between Britons ancient and modern relies upon what J. G. A. Pocock calls the common law or "immemorial" view of Britain as a historically continuous entity that knows, like Satan, "no time when we were not as now" (Pocock 1987, 30–55; *Paradise Lost*, V, 859)—Wordsworth's quotation of the *History* at the conclusion of *Cintra* appears to place the pamphlet squarely in the most ecumenical tradition of the "ancient constitution."

But Milton's "immemorial" view of the Britons is, as Samuel Kliger has shown, strangely mixed with ideas about the "Goths" who, in the form of the Anglo-Saxons, brought radical rupture (if not an infusion of "Gothic Virtue") to Britain when they invaded in the fifth century. This is more than straightforward error or anachronism. According to Kliger, "Milton is echoing the racial ideas in the *translatio* thought-complex": an ideology derived from the Reformation that "suggested forcefully an analogy between the breakup of the Roman empire by the Goths and the demands of the humanist-reformers of northern Europe for religious freedom" (Kliger 1952, 33–66, 149–52). The *translatio*, which predated the Renaissance view of Gothic darkness, specifically identified the Goths with enlightenment, and viewed historical progression as the process whereby Rome's world empire was transferred or translated to the Germans. In calling the "Britans" "[v]aliant…and prosperous to win a field," Milton "clearly has in mind the conception of the German humanist-reformers which stressed the distinctive entity of the German folk by virtue of their invincibility, manliness, and so forth." But his "diatribe on old English immorality," "bifurcat[es]…the two elements in the Gothic tradition," with "racial inheritances" of excessive valor ultimately preventing "the English from achieving the political inheritance of democracy." For Milton, martial prowess is nugatory if not sublimated also in moral invincibility. The fault-line that runs right through *Cintra*, celebrating British liberty and martial valor, and decrying British servility and moral cowardice, replicates precisely the "bifurcation" in Milton's view of "Gothic" Britain.

I want to suggest that this meeting of the Gothic and the Miltonic at the conclusion of *Cintra*, with its implicit dubiety regarding Britain as a bringer of "Gothic Virtue" to Spain, anticipates Wordsworth's figuration of *The Recluse* as a "gothic Church" in the Preface to *The Excursion* of 1814. The Preface suggests that *The Prelude* (the "preparatory poem") and the "minor Pieces," will, when properly arranged, "be found by the attentive Reader" to contribute, along with *The Excursion*, to the architecture of *The Recluse*. Or, to employ the terms of *Cintra* and Milton's *History*, readers "more than vulgar," who were able to perceive "just proportions and relations" among the fragments of *The Recluse*, would be able to comprehend its system at a glance and proleptically to construct the poem. As I suggested earlier, such a proleptic "reading" had public significance because, as John Barrell argues in "The Public Prospect and the Private View," political authority in late eighteenth- and early nineteenth-century Britain was predicated upon, and legitimated by reference to, the ability to abstract and to build parts and details into complex wholes (1992, 46, 42, 52). In what Barrell calls the discourse of civic humanism, the political representative, usually a man of independent means, was required to view the world not (as the "vulgar" did) as a set of "concrete particulars," but "in terms of...abstract or formal relations." He was required that is, to imagine the public sphere and to abstract thence the public interest. "It was precisely the ability of the liberal mind of the free citizen to do this which constituted his claim to be a citizen, a free man, or, as he was often described...a 'public man'" (Barrell 1992, 46, 42, 52). This "liberal" mentality, derived from an education and a leisure intimately associated with landed wealth, was conventionally imaged in terms of a panoramic view of landscape taken from an eminent and implicitly proprietorial position. As Burke's *Letters on a Regicide Peace* put it:

> Statesmen are placed on an eminence, that they may have a larger horizon than we can possibly command. They have a whole before them, which we can contemplate only in the parts, and even without the

necessary relations. Ministers are not only our natural rulers but our natural guides. (1796, 132)

Wordsworth had already laid claim to this "liberal" mentality in *The Prelude*: amidst the "undistinguishable" chaos of London, he had "among least things / An under-sense of greatest—see[ing] the parts / As parts, but with a feeling of the whole" (*1805*, VII, 710–12). Like Burke, Wordsworth associates this mentality with panoramic vision. But in this interestingly ambiguous passage of *The Prelude*, he ascribes it not to the experienced statesman but to the visionary child "Fostered alike by beauty and by fear" among the "enduring things" (I, 306, 436) of nature:

> This (*of all acquisitions first*) awaits
> On sundry and most widely different modes
> Of education, nor with least delight
> On that through which I passed. Attention comes,
> And comprehensiveness of memory,
> From early converse with the works of God
> ...
> The mountain's outline and its steady form...
> (VII, 713–22; my emphasis)

This is a challenge to Burke's statesman, for the abstract figure of panoramic sight is here referred directly back to its origin in the natural, as opposed to the artificial and "ministerial," world. Indeed, the potentially radical nature of Wordsworth's claim here is underlined by the revision in the generally more conservative 1850 text: the slight addition of a comma ("This, of all acquisitions, first awaits") resolving the ambiguity as to whether panoramic sight is the property of the child or the man in favor of (Burkean) experience. A similar effect is achieved by the replacement in the 1850 text—as Jonathan Wordsworth notes, one of Wordsworth's final revisions (1995, 608n)—of the simple appeal to "The mountain's outline" with a world survey that encompasses India and Arabia, and all the sea and all the sky (*1850* VII, 745–56). The panorama becomes not the first view but the last.

Midway between these competing ascriptions of panoramic vision to the child and to the aged philosopher, the Preface to *The Excursion* appropriates such vision to the figure of the Poet of *The Recluse*, who takes a survey of "Man, Nature, and Society" from among his "native Mountains." Like Burke's statesman, constructing from "the necessary relations" of "parts" an imagination of the "whole," the Preface suggests that the reader who is able to "extrac[t] the system for himself" and to visualize *The Recluse*, would be able to "see" the public sphere and the public good in a disinterested way, and would hence be fitted for public, representative life. Indeed, Wordsworth's "attentive Reader" far surpasses the actual political representative. For according to *Cintra* the politically active "public man" is (paradoxically) rendered incapable of a truly impartial view of the public good by reason of his personal stake in "public measures"—by, that is, his "vulgar" occlusion within the public sphere (l. 3371). The conduct of the British government in honoring and defending the Convention was a case in point. Fearing that the "odium" for the treaty might fall upon both the generals and "those who have appointed" them—the links between the two being, as the liberal weekly *The Examiner* insinuated (September 25, 1808, 610–11), corruptively close—the government sought by "incorporating its own credit with the transaction" to effect "one sweeping exculpation" of both "servant" and "master" (ll. 2495–96, 2511–16). Government ministers thus manifested a "selfish spirit" that sacrificed public to private interests (l. 2509).

By contrast, Wordsworth says, the man who, "taking no part in public measures, and having no concern in the changes of things but as they affect what is most precious in his country and humanity—will doubtless be more alive to those sensations which are the materials of sound judgment" (ll. 3371–74). The Recluse-figure thus replaces the Statesman as the ideal "public man" and "natural guide." And he is a specifically Gothic replacement, for he possesses precisely those Gothic virtues of invincibility and impartiality to "titles...friendships and relations" that Milton required in public leaders. Indeed, the Recluse-poet promises to fulfill the implicit prophecy of Milton's "Digression" that when public policy is guided by such "men more than vulgar," then the "end and reason of winning" will truly be known. In 1814, in the first (and false) dawn of peace that followed Napoleon's abdication in April, such knowledge was needed more than ever. On such a view, the challenge in the Preface of July 1814 to reconstruct the "gothic Church" of *The Recluse* constitutes a sort of aptitude test for the philosophical national leadership that *Cintra* had shown to be in such short supply.

In fact, the idea of such an "aptitude test" is adumbrated first in the pages of *Cintra*. Wordsworth calls his "retrospect" of events surrounding the Convention

> a composition made out of fragments of...[d]eclarations from various parts of the Peninsula, which, disposed as it were in a tesselated

pavement, shall set forth a story which may be easily understood; which will move and teach, and be consolatory to him who looks upon it. (ll. 255-59)

In clear anticipation of the poetic jigsaw-puzzle offered in the Preface to *The Excursion*, Wordsworth here images the situation in Spain as a picture, a mosaic or "tesselated pavement" to be pieced together. But where in *Cintra* Wordsworth puts the puzzle together for the reader—using what he implicitly claims are his powers of panoramic vision to create a comprehensive "retrospect" on behalf of the "vulgar"—the "aptitude test" set by the 1814 Preface excludes precisely those "vulgar" readers. In other words, the "gothic Church" of the Preface is at one (conservative) remove from the progressive Gothic stance of *Cintra*. And it represents a new—and, for *The Recluse*, a fatal—humility regarding the visionary and didactic powers of the poet. A supreme act of readerly sympathy and imagination may recreate the "gothic Church" that flashes upon Wordsworth's inward eye, but it is clearly not in the power of the poet to "set [it] forth" as "a story which may be easily understood."

It seems likely that this reduced estimation of the Gothic is keyed to the historical failure of the progressive-Gothic Cortes in Spain upon the restoration of the Bourbon monarchy in May 1814. In February 1816, Wordsworth would speak explicitly of the fall of the Cortes in terms of historical failure. The Cortes had, Wordsworth said, "worked nobly" for the cause of national independence, but had been betrayed by its leadership's political affinity with "the most headstrong Jacobins of France" (*MY* II, 281). "Think," he wrote, "of a Republic in Spain— what horror to go through before such a thing could be brought about; and what worse than horrors would have attended its rapid destruction!" In 1814, Wordsworth's reduced expectations of Gothic republicanism are implicit in the strictly virtual nature of his "gothic Church," and in his close circumscription of its congregation. But even if the "Gothic edifice" is now reserved exclusively for "public men," it remains an engine for bodying forth their public spirit, and, by extension, for upholding ancient liberties against the corruptions of government. In both *The Recluse* and *The Convention of Cintra*, a Gothic structure composed of fragments is an image of public presence: a figure not of ruin and decay but of growth and imaginative freedom. What *Cintra* allows us to see, in sum, is that the analogy between *The Recluse* and a "gothic Church" is not simply architectural, but develops from the Gothic politics and the Gothic discourse of the public realm developed in Spain's—and Wordsworth's—war of words against Napoleon.

The next chapter will argue that the Gothic politics that Wordsworth and his fellow Lake Poets developed in response to the Peninsular War and the Convention of Cintra was not limited to that context, but indeed extended to other topics, including, preeminently, education. But before I move to make this argument, I want to offer a brief coda to the account of the Wordsworthian Gothicism given in this chapter.

## Coda: The Voice within *Cintra*

In her essay "Re-imagining Jacobinism," Deidre Coleman has imagined *Cintra* as a sort of political "kaleidoscope," composed of facets of Jacobin and Burkean political thought that, taken together, reveal the ongoing turmoil in Wordsworth's political views in the first decade of the nineteenth century (Coleman 1989, 146). This chapter has looked through that kaleidoscope and explored that political spectrum. But it has also attempted to establish that a distinctive political position does indeed emerge from the pamphlet, and that the tract's apparent incoherencies are properly seen in the context of the revaluation of the Gothic by Wordsworth and his contemporaries. Indeed, a Gothic structure stands at the very heart of *Cintra*'s imagination of the Spanish Revolution. Picking up his earlier statement that the "resolution" of "the people of Great Britain" for war with France in 1798 was prompted by their obedience to an "authentic voice" of "human nature" unheard by even "the wisest of their practical Statesmen" (ll. 113–18), Wordsworth imagines the people's support for the war in Spain in the summer of 1808 as a "voice" with "the unquestionable sound of inspiration;" adding:

> If the gentle passions of pity, love, and gratitude, be porches of the temple; if the sentiments of admiration and rivalry be pillars upon which the structure is sustained; if, lastly, hatred, and anger, and vengeance, be steps which, by a mystery of nature, lead to the House of Sanctity;—then was it manifest to what power the edifice was consecrated; and that the voice within was of Holiness and Truth. (ll. 2776–83)

The sympathy of the British people with the Spanish cause here erects a "temple" of public spirit opposed to the corrupt "Gothic edifice" that the Convention had shown their government yet to be. But this spiritual "temple," constructed in the medieval allegorical manner, with passions disposed about the structure by analogy with their function in the soul, is clearly a prototype of the "gothic Church" of *The Recluse* that was to be built out of poems with functions analogous to those of anti-chapels, "little Cells, Oratories, and sepulchral Recesses" in real churches. Indeed, the Preface to *The Excursion* develops from the Gothic politics of *Cintra* in just the way advised by Edward Young for composing in a manner at once classical and original. Building in the spirit of *Cintra* but not with its materials, Wordsworth now proposes to construct a public-spirited "Gothic edifice" not out of stone or out of political institutions, but out of poetry.

In concluding this chapter, then, I want to offer an alternative image to set beside Coleman's of the political coloring of *Cintra*; an image of fragmentariness *and* emergent harmony, derived from the pamphlet's two dominant metaphors of light and architecture. Like the stained glass windows in a Gothic church, I suggest, *Cintra* composes from patches of vivid political color an ambient light (*The Prelude*'s "visionary dreariness" [1805 XI, 311], perhaps) that is no color, its own color, and every color at once.

The voice that speaks in *Cintra* is the authentic voice of *The Recluse*.

# Chapter 4

# Wordsworth's Gothic Education

> *Our education is in a manner wholly in the hands of ecclesiastics…And after all, with this Gothic and monkish education (for such it is in the groundwork) we may put in our claim to as ample and as early a share in all the improvements in science, in arts, and in literature which have adorned the modern world, as any other nation in Europe.*
>
> —Burke, *Reflections on the Revolution in France (1987, 87–88)*

William Wordsworth was strangely given to speaking of education in the language of Gothic Romance. In *The Prelude*, he imagined swearing fealty to "written lore" as to a "liege lord" among the "Gothic courts" of Cambridge. And he echoed Edmund Burke's account of the "Gothic and monkish education" provided in the Universities with an image of the "glorious time" "of old," when Cambridge's Gothic regulation of "piety and zeal," "Spare diet, patient labour, and plain weeds," had brought youths "errant in the quest" of knowledge (*1850* III, 379, 47, 450–69). Similarly, in *Reply to Mathetes* (1809–10), an essay on education and the sense of history, Wordsworth likened "an aspiring youth, leaving the schools in which he has been disciplined" to "a newly invested Knight appearing with his blank unsignalized Shield, upon some day of solemn tournament, at the Court of the Faery-Queen…[H]e looks round him with a beating heart; dazzled by the gorgeous pageantry, the banners, the impresses, the Ladies of overcoming beauty, the Persons of the knights…"(*Prose Works* II, 20).

The analogy, Wordsworth lamented, could not hold, for "ours is…a degenerate Age" (*Prose Works* II, 20). And as though to confirm

Burke's pronouncement that the age of chivalry had departed and that of economists and calculators arrived, Wordsworth soon moved toward endorsing a new plan of mass-education that was apparently wholly unromantic. This was the so-called Madras system of the Anglican clergyman Dr Andrew Bell, which, in its most massified (and reactionary) formulation, was an "economical plan" to give a rudimentary education to all "those doomed to the drudgery of daily labour," allowing "the generality...to read their Bible and understand the doctrines of our holy religion," but without necessarily teaching them to write, and hence without the "risque of elevating" their minds "above their condition" and "rendering them discontented and unhappy in their lot" (Bell 1805, 62). In the final book of Wordsworth's *Excursion* (1814), the central character, the Wanderer, prays in similar (though somewhat more progressive) terms for "this Imperial Realm" to "*teach* / Them who are born to serve her and obey":

> Binding herself by Statute to secure
> For all the Children whom her soil maintains
> The rudiments of Letters, and to inform
> The mind with moral and religious truth,
> Both understood and practised,—so that none,
> However destitute, be left to droop
> By timely culture unsustained, or run
> Into a wild disorder; or be forced
> To drudge through weary life without the aid
> Of intellectual implements and tools...
> (IX, 294–307)[1]

Although *The Excursion* assumes what its preface calls "something of a dramatic form," there is clearly very little distance here between the "Author" and the "Character speaking" (1814, x). In a footnote to the Wanderer's speech, Wordsworth described Bell's scheme as likely to bring benefits whose importance would be "impossible to overrate" (447).

Wordsworth knew whereof he spoke. By the time he was at work on the final book of *The Excursion* in late 1811, he had "been the means of *introducing*" the Madras system at the village school in Grasmere, had spent time teaching there himself, and had met and become friends with Bell (*MY* I, 514; Reed 1975, 679). In November 1811, Wordsworth had "the great pleasure of seeing Dr Bell here with Southey for half an hour, two thirds of which were spent in the School, he kindly taking upon himself to teach the Boys, and also the Master and myself" (*MY* I, 514–15). The following August, the Wordsworths welcomed Bell to the parsonage at Grasmere, with Dorothy working "constantly" to help the doctor prepare a new book on the system (*MY* II, 41–45). And by the spring of 1815, Wordsworth was echoing Robert Southey's pro-Bell propaganda in the *Quarterly Review*, telling friends such as Thomas Poole that the Madras system was, "[n]ext to the art of Printing," "the noblest invention for the improvement of the human species" (*MY* II, 210). Wordsworth's personal relationship with Bell deteriorated around the beginning of 1816, but his support for the Madras system remained constant until well into the 1820s.[2] When in early 1819 his son John was rejected by the Charterhouse, which had lately adopted Madras, Wordsworth responded with an exposition of the "characteristic excellence" of the system in allowing even "slow Boys…to advance according to their talents" (*MY* II, 513). Implicitly claiming to be a better disciple of Bell than the headmaster of a major public school, Wordsworth had by early 1819 set himself up as a leading figure in the propagation of the Madras system.

What factors drove Wordsworth's embrace of Madras and made it seem worthy of mention at the end of *The Excursion*, his most prestigious and public-minded publication to date? Alison Hickey has argued for an aesthetic explanation, noting the affinity between the system's transformation of the classroom into a "spectacle" of "sweet contention," and Wordsworth and Coleridge's account of the Imagination's reduction of multiplicity "into a unity of effect" (Hickey 1997, 114). R. A. Foakes has pointed the way toward a personal explanation with his argument that Wordsworth was driven "into the arms of the Bell system" by the contradiction between his faith in the teachings of Nature and his "sense of the need for…discipline" in the education of his own children (Foakes 1989, 187–206). Wordsworth and Bell had shared friendships in Coleridge, Southey, and William Johnson (schoolmaster at Grasmere until 1811 and at Bell's metropolitan Central School thereafter), and a further personal connection through Wordsworth's brother Christopher, who in 1811 helped to found the pro-Bell National Society for the Education of the Poor in Accordance with the Principles of the Established Church. However, ideological considerations have generally bulked largest in literary-critical accounts of Wordsworth and Bell. For Philip Connell, as for Carl Woodring, the Lake poets embraced Bell in an attempt to reconcile their reactionary perceptions of secular education as a "political and constitutional threat" and their residual radical commitments to the diffusion of knowledge (Connell 2001, 135–39; Woodring

1970, 136–37). In a recent study of Southey's politics, David Craig has argued that Southey's support for Madras was the logical product of his twofold analysis of the civilizing force of Christianity, and the homology between the "mixed" constitution and the "Eclectic Church" (Craig 2007, 94–100, 158–65, 199). According to Alan Richardson, similarly, Wordsworth and his fellow Lakers saw the monitorial system as a sort of panacea for "England's social ills and political unrest...and (in Bell's version) a prop for that great edifice of stability, the Established Church" (Richardson 1994, 95). Kevin Gilmartin, meanwhile, sees the Lake Poets' support for Madras as the pragmatic expression of their shared program for restoring the literary class (what Coleridge called the "clerisy") to its pre-Reformation role in national education, and thus righting the historical wrong that lay at the root of its contemporary disaffection and attraction to Jacobinism (Gilmartin 2007, 232–52). This chapter seeks to extend the work of Woodring, Connell, Craig, Richardson, and Gilmartin. I will be arguing that the decisive factor in the Lake Poets' support for Madras was indeed the system's political and religious tendency; specifically its congruency with what my last chapter called the "progressive Gothic politics" developed by the Lake Poets in the context of the Peninsular War. It is because Bell's system was both appreciably "Gothic" *and* potentially socially progressive that it was given such prominence in *The Excursion*, a poem that was, according to its preface, addressed to the "existing state of things," and patterned upon a "gothic Church" (Bushell, Butler, and Jaye, eds. 2007, 38).

## The Odin of Education

Andrew Bell's *Experiment in Education* (1797) was the fruit of the best part of a decade spent at the British East India Company's asylum for mixed-race male children in Madras. Beset by difficulties with his subordinates and by the sheer number of pupils requiring tuition, Bell had hit upon the idea of using boys as monitors, and subsequently refined this into a successful system of "tuition by the scholars themselves" (Bell 1808, 2). Continuous ranking by performance allowed each boy to find "his own level," "being promoted or degraded from place to place or class to class, according to his proficiency" (1808, 15). Bell had prospered in India. His various posts allowed him to accrue a fortune estimated at just under £26,000, and to secure a pension from the Company worth an additional £200 per annum (Thompson 1983, 6). But upon the appearance of the *Experiment*, he found that his hopes of a triumphant homecoming as a sort of pedagogical nabob had fallen rather flat. All the cautionary counsels of his friends had not prepared him, Bell recalled in 1808, for "the cool and phlegmatic manner, in which my humble and lowly essay was at first received, and the very small degree of notice, which my experiment attracted" (1808, 131).

The self-imagination of this educational prophet from the east was so far from being "humble and lowly," however, that it is unsurprising that the book's reception failed to live up to his expectations. "[W]ith such an engine in his hands," Bell wrote in the advertisement to the new edition of 1808,

> he fears not now to tell aloud, what eleven years ago he only whispered—when he put the original reports of the Male Asylum into the hands of his bookseller, and what he has never ceased to repeat to his friends,—"You will mark me for an enthusiast; but if you and I live a thousand years, we shall see this System of Tuition spread over the world." (viii–ix)

Echoing Edward Gibbon's description of "the Mohamet of the North," hatching his "immortal revenge" on Rome by building institutions on a millennial scale (Gibbon 1777, I, 294), Bell clearly pictured himself as little less than the Odin—the "Gothic" prophet—of education.

Wordsworth, who read Bell's *Madras School* (1808) between June and October 1808 (Wu 1995, 20–21), and who claimed in *The Prelude* to have once projected a poem on Odin (*1805* I, 185–89), might well have recognized in Bell a kindred spirit. The 1797 *Experiment* had appeared just months before the "experiments" of *Lyrical Ballads* (1798), and both had had clear leveling tendencies. Bell proposed to enforce discipline not, like his rival Joseph Lancaster, through "newly-invented racks or screws, or whips, or cords," but through a trial system that allowed "the inferior orders" to indict their superiors (1808, 3, 29–30). Wordsworth, meanwhile, was writing poetry on the semi-Saxonist hypothesis that "the language of conversation in the middle and lower classes of society" was better "adapted to the purposes of poetic pleasure" than the "gaud[y] and inane" idiom preferred by "Readers of superior judgment" (*Prose Works* I, 116). Bell's "Madras" system would likely have remained attractive to Wordsworth in 1808 for its quiet Whiggish radicalism. Its machinery was geared toward making the school, like Cambridge in *The Prelude*, "something.../ Of a republic" (*1805* IX, 229–30). The "jurisdiction...of themselves and their peers" was, Bell wrote, "an immunity of which [the pupils] are no less jealous than every Englishman is of his invaluable privilege, the trial by jury" (Bell 1808, 34). Moreover, Wordsworth would likely have recognized that the essential principle of the system, "tuition by the scholars themselves," under which "the tutor far more effectually learns his lesson than if he had not to teach it to another" (Bell, 23), was a practical version of William Godwin's claim for his *Political Justice* (1793) as a "scheme...that embraces millions in its grasp, and that educates in one school the preceptor and the pupil" (Godwin 1793, II, 865 and I, 27). In the 1808 edition of his book, Bell claimed just such an extensive reach for Madras. The "parochial clergy" was "an order of men formed, as it were, for the purpose" of education, and by following his scheme each member of this "order" could, "if able and diligent," "conduct ten contiguous schools, each consisting of a thousand scholars" (Bell 1808, 318–20, 2).

But if Wordsworth in 1808 would have seen something kindred in Bell's system, he would also have seen this other Odin far surpassing him in the prosecution of his "revenge." Unlike Wordsworth's, Bell's vindication was now complete. The monitorial system was established in schools in Lambeth, Whitechapel, and Marylebone, and his status as the "beginner" of the system was acknowledged even in periodicals, such as the *Edinburgh Review*, sympathetic to the rival system of the Quaker Joseph Lancaster. Or at least so Bell convinced himself, taking for the monitorial system in general the praise accorded to Lancaster's version by the *Edinburgh*, which called it an improvement in education

> as great...as the introduction of noncommissioned officers would be in an army which had before been governed only by captains, majors, and colonels: they add that constant and minute attention to the operations of the mass, without which, the general and occasional superintendance of superiors is wholly useless. (*Edinburgh Review* 11 [1807], 65; qtd. in Bell 1808, 25)

The *Edinburgh*'s military analogy is indicative of the highly regimented nature of the monitorial method of education in general. But whereas the pacifist Lancaster would have been pained by the analogy, having taken pains "to avoid all commands which are strictly military" (Lancaster 1805, 108), Bell clearly found it highly appropriate to the system he had developed specifically "to fill the various occupations which presented themselves" during the East India Company's war of 1789–92 with Tipu Sultan's kingdom of Mysore (Bell, 7). The system's efficacy in not just meeting but exceeding its remit was neatly captured in Bell's account of one of his pupils, William Smith, going on to become both an emissary and a tutor to the court of the defeated Sultan (Bell, 167, 234–42).

This episode became in turn one of the founding myths of Bell's pedagogical power, noted and fictionalized by Maria Edgeworth, the antisectarian author of the educational treatise *Practical Education* (1798). In *Lame Jervas*, the first story in her collection of *Popular Tales* (1804), Edgeworth transported Bell back to India, and made him one of a series of benevolent patrons who enable the hero to work his way out of poverty, to turn the Sultan's "oriental pomp" to his own advantage, and to rescue a slave who, "as soon as [he] touched the English shore...obtained his freedom" (Edgeworth 1804, I, 86, 131). Edgeworth thus anticipated Coleridge's lecture of 1808 that pictured Bell and the antislavery campaigner Thomas Clarkson "as the two contemporaries 'who had done most for humanity'" (qtd. in Richardson 1994, 91). Bell's potentially leveling "engine" had meshed with the larger moral and military machinery of the British state. A "check sufficiently powerful" to the proliferation of vice and luxury in a civilization "verging to...[its] meridian," the system was, Bell claimed in 1808, an "engine of the most general and extensive utility [that] furnishes means of giving new strength and force to our army and navy" (Bell, 96).

Wordsworth was initially skeptical of the real potential of this "engine." In 1797, he and Coleridge had been sounded out by Thomas Wedgwood as "superintendents of the practical part" of a painstakingly engineered Rousseauvian "nursery of genius," and had not only declined, but indeed proceeded to elaborate a directly antithetical ethos of natural education in poems such as "Frost at Midnight" and "The Tables Turned" (Erdman 1956, 495). In *The Prelude*, Wordsworth sublimated the Wedgwood scheme in a way that recalls the carefully staged natural childhood of Rousseau's *Emile*—and leads James Chandler to see Rousseau rather than Wedgwood, Bell, or Lancaster as the target of Wordsworth's invective against the educational "workmen of our later age" (Chandler 1984, 96–119). In giving artistic shape to his own natural education, Wordsworth acted as in effect his own superintendent, working to "control / All accidents," even as the perspectival shifts within the poem allowed his youthful self to be presented simultaneously as naively immersed in "the unreasoning progress of the world" (*1805* V, 380–384). Wedgwood's prison-like "nursery" with "plain grey walls with one or two vivid objects" (qtd. in Erdman, 495), also returns in uncanny form in the "spots of time," with their fundamentally static experiences of "visionary dreariness" (XI, 310). The function of the "spots," for Wordsworth, is their ability to sustain a sense of mental depth and spiritual extension across time and space, whereby, "unknown to me / The workings of my spirit thence are brought" (XI, 387–88), thus severing the tyranny of preestablished codes of decision, including plans of education, that "would confine us down / Like engines" (V, 382–83). If it was not among the immediate targets of *The Prelude*'s attack on modern methods of education, Bell's "engine" would nevertheless have fallen under collateral suspicion.

Writing in this skeptical vein in a letter of October 2, 1808, Wordsworth told Francis Wrangham that he had found "Dr Bell's Book upon education...a most interesting work" and would "strenuously recommend" adoption of the system wherever possible, but added, "I cannot say [it has made] any material change in my views" (*MY* I, 269–70). This lack of "material change" was evident in Wordsworth's *Reply to Mathetes*, published in two parts in Coleridge's *The Friend* in December 1809 and January 1810 (*Prose Works* II, 6). As in the books of *The Prelude* that dealt specifically with education, showing how the accidents of a provident nature had cooperated to lead out the poet in the child, Wordsworth here retained a fundamentally active notion of education. "There is a life and spirit in knowledge," he wrote, "which we extract from truths scattered for the benefit of all, and which the mind, by its own activity, has appropriated to itself—a life and a spirit, which is seldom found in knowledge communicated by formal and direct precepts" (*Prose Works* II, 8). The monitorial method, also known (especially in Bell's Anglican version) as the "catechistical" method, was nothing if not the communication of "formal and direct precepts." The *Reply*'s *Prelude*-like picture of the progress of knowledge not as "a Roman road in a right line" but as a meandering "River...frequently forced back towards its fountains, by objects which cannot otherwise be eluded or overcome" (*Prose Works* II, 11) is directly at odds with Bell's account of his schoolboys, disciplined like an army, daily making regular, measurable progress (1808, 11, 28).

But by the time of the *Reply*, Wordsworth's position had in fact already begun to change. Only two months after communicating to Wrangham his qualified support for Bell's "interesting work," he wrote again on December 3, 1808 to assert the high importance of the system and the equal importance of recognizing it as the peculiar property of Bell alone. The occasion of this letter (touched on in chapter three) was Wordsworth's reading of a sermon given by Wrangham in July 1808 on the topics of the war in Spain, the "Catholic question," and education. With a striking echo of the "Gothic" cause of the Spanish patriots resisting Napoleon, Wrangham's sermon offered an image of Britons defending "the fabric of their liberties" from the Napoleonic "colossus," and vowing to unborn generations that "they shall exert, and if necessary exhaust, every sinew in it's support, and that they shall not survive it's destruction" (Wrangham 1816, II, 168–69). Wrangham's tone was less stridently "Gothic" when it came to education, however. Under the banner of "Toleration," Wrangham praised Wordsworth's literary hero, Thomas Percy, for contributing funds toward both a Roman Catholic chapel and a dissenting meeting-house within his Irish diocese of Dromore. He also argued that the "questions of priority, or superiority" being debated between the "partisans" of Bell and Lancaster were of "less consequence" than the utility of their respective systems (Wrangham, II, 146–62). Wordsworth's letter of December 1808 rejected such toleration. "I am not prepared," he wrote to Wrangham, "to see the Catholic religion as the Established Church of Ireland," and he went on to assert that "[i]f Dr. Bell's plan of education be of that importance which it appears to be of, it cannot be a matter of indifference whether he, or Lancaster, have a rightful claim to the invention" (*MY* I, 278). If Wordsworth was not prepared to allow Bell priority over his own ideas on education, he was certainly determined to insist on Bell's priority over Lancaster; a priority clearly analogous to that of the Church of England within the British state. But in taking this position he was certainly not original. Rather, as I want to move on now to show, Wordsworth was adding his voice to a growing chorus of conservative support for Bell's "Gothic" system against Lancaster's version, the antisectarian ideology of which looked to the supporters of the Church Establishment worryingly like a revival of English Jacobinism.

## National Remedies, National Evils

On August 19, 1805, Joseph Lancaster had an audience at Weymouth with George III. The charismatic Lancaster, who in the same year lectured at London's Pantheon, treated the king to an exposition of his system of mass education, with its groundbreaking use of pupil-tutors and its cultivation of "public spirit" in school. He then presented George with a freshly printed copy of the third edition of his book *Improvements in Education*—accompanied by a "humble petition" for "Royal Sanction and Benevolent support" for new schools "at Weymouth and elsewhere for *Ten thousand* children."[3]

Apparently impressed, the king subscribed £100 per annum, and so added his name to a catalogue of patrons that already numbered Pitt and Wilberforce among its many notables (Lancaster 1805, 20, 24, 207; Salmon 1932, ix). Lancaster's school, and the related scheme for setting up a national system of education—described in *Improvements* as a "national remedy" for a "national evil" (viii)—thus gained royal backing. George's statement of approval was subsequently writ large as a sort of royal charter in Lancaster's schoolroom in the Borough Road, where "princes, ambassadors, peers, commoners, ladies of distinction, bishops, and archbishops, Jews and Turks" came to watch him orchestrate the instruction of seven hundred children "with 'wonder waiting eyes.'"[4]

"National remedies" like Lancaster's were at the heart of political debate at the turn of the nineteenth century. Political economists such as Thomas Malthus promoted rudimentary education for the "lower classes" in order, as Alan Richardson puts it, to harmonize their "perceived self-interest...with the interests of the middle classes" (Richardson 1994, 89). Political radicals such as William Godwin, however, opposed national education on just these grounds. Godwin may have described his *Political Justice* (1793) as an educational "scheme...that embraces millions in its grasp," but he argued against institutionalized national education because of its invidious tendency to reproduce error and irrational social relations: "[E]ven in the petty institution of Sunday schools, the chief lessons that are taught, are a superstitious veneration for the church of England, and to bow to every man in a handsome coat" (Godwin 1793, I, 27, and II, 668). National education was also opposed by the establishment in its moral panic following the Revolution in France. In 1797 the admiralty blamed the mutinous condition of the navy on the "Sunday Schools" and "opposition papers" providing education and opinion "disproportionate to situation," and in 1800 the Bishop of Rochester interpreted the proliferation of educational institutions as the spread of "schools of Jacobinical rebellion" (Watson 2003, 69; Richardson 1994, 119). The specter of "Jacobinical rebellion" had raised its head even within the feeder-schools of the establishment. As H. C. Barnard notes, miniature Revolutions broke out at major public schools throughout the 1790s: the Winchester rebellion of 1793, for example, "set[ting] up the red cap of liberty" (Barnard 1947, 21). The year 1818 saw another rash of unrest, with Winchester being obliged to call in the army (Barnard 1947, 21), and Wordsworth receiving rumors of a "mutiny" at the Charterhouse (*MY* II, 509). In 1812, with Luddite disturbances in the countryside, riots in support of the radical MP Francis Burdett in the capital, and the assassination of the Prime Minister Spencer Perceval, the growth of literacy among the "lower orders" was again a political issue of the first order. Robert Southey's article on the Poor Laws for the December *Quarterly Review* envisioned a conspiracy of unchecked literacy on foot against the constitution:

> If one political writer vilifies every measure of the existing administration; if another reviles all parties in their turn with equal virulence; if a third systematically holds up the Royal Family to derision and abhorrence; and a fourth labours to bring the whole system of government into contempt and hatred…though these persons should be utterly unconnected, or even hostile to each other, they co-operate as effectually together to one direct end as if they were bound by oaths and sacraments, and…the end is as directly the overthrow of their country as if all four were the salaried instruments of France. (*QR* 8:16 [1812], 340–341)

Lancaster, a Quaker whose schools were organized on what N. J. Hollingsworth pejoratively called "latitudinarian" principles (1812, 33), was, despite his royal blessing, a key operative in Southey's imaginary conspiracy. Southey's pamphlet on *The Origin, Nature, and Object, of the New System of Education*, published in 1812, deployed the full range of "Gothic" hyperbole against Lancaster. Lancaster himself was a superstitious "quack," a "Dragon," and "a snake in the grass" (1812, 97, 186). And his system, characterized by an attempt to inculcate "public spirit" through "emulation" and ritual humiliation ("accusations" of even minor infractions leading to the "pillory," the "shackle," and the "yoke" [Lancaster 1805, 34, 101–3]), was a monstrous hybrid of revolutionary terrorism and Roman Catholic extremism:

> He…contrives to make punishment a matter of diversion and laughter for the spectators; having heard perhaps of the good effects which result from making an auto-da-fe a raree-show for the people, and the beneficial consequences arising to an English mob from regarding an execution as a holiday, which, in their own expressive language, they call hang-fair. (Southey 1812, 89)

For Southey, such humiliating punishments intimated the Jacobinical character of the "public spirit" animating Lancaster's system. "[B]odily pain is nothing," he wrote, "to the sting of shame, nothing to the burning anguish produced by the sense of insult, inhumanity, and injustice"

(1812, 93–94). In this, Southey followed Coleridge's lead. According to Southey's report of Coleridge's lecture on education at the Royal Institution on May 3, 1808:

> When Mr. Coleridge…came to this part of the subject, he read Mr. Lancaster's account of these precious inventions verbatim from his own book, and throwing the book down with a mixture of contempt and indignation, exclaimed, "No boy who has been subject to punishments like these will stand in fear of Newgate, or feel any horror at the thought of a slave ship!" (1812, 95–96)

If Lancaster's system thus threatened to throw even the state's most "Gothic" modes of deterrence into the shade, and to undermine the nation's self-construction as a land of liberty and sensibility, it clearly posed a real ideological threat to the state. In making this equation, Southey and Coleridge followed the example of Sarah Trimmer, an educationalist who, meeting the queen to discuss Sunday Schools in 1786 (Salmon 1932, xxv), had beaten Lancaster to royal approval by nearly twenty years, and who had long seen the growth of nonsectarian schooling as nothing less than a menace to the British Constitution.

Recently described by Mitzi Myers as "a conservative woman doing radical things," and by M. O. Grenby as both a "religious fundamentalist" and a "radical" apostle of children's literature (Ruwe, ed. 2005, 138–39, 155–56), it will not do simply to categorize Trimmer as an arch-conservative critic of new developments in education. Kevin Gilmartin brackets Trimmer with the evangelical moral reformer Hannah More as a proponent of a "paradoxically reactionary progressivism" (2007, 66–67). But whatever the remote effects of her educational campaigns, Trimmer certainly saw herself as the defender of "good *old paths*" in education dating back to the Reformation, and as the enemy of "innovation" in the field (Trimmer 1805, 15). The opening number of her periodical, *The Guardian of Education* (1802–6), drew extensively on the Jacobin conspiracy tracts of John Robison and the Abbé Barruel, and expressly offered itself as a "powerful antidote" to the free-thinking "*conspiracy against* CHRISTIANITY *and all* SOCIAL ORDER" that was (as the *Anti-Jacobin Review* had alleged in 1799 [Vol. 2, 450–451]) attempting "to infect the minds of the rising generation through the medium of *Books of Education* and *Children's Books*" (1802–6, I, 2). With Voltaire as its "chief," Frederick II of Prussia as its "protector," and the Encyclopedists D'Alembert, Diderot, and Rousseau as its "agent[s]," this fundamentally educational "conspiracy" had, according to Trimmer, been exported from France and Germany to Britain first through Rousseau's *Emile*, and then through a "torrent" of "infidel" German literature (Trimmer 1802–6, I, 9–15). The "torrent," she claimed, had its fountainhead in the German pamphlet war over the new plan of education set forth by Johann Bernard Basedow. His "PHILANTHROPINE," a "seminary of practical ethics" founded in the German principality of Anhalt-Dessau in 1774, which aimed at "moderating the differences" between the Lutherans, Calvinists and Catholics of Germany, had ended, Trimmer said, quoting Robison's *Proofs of a Conspiracy*, in the school's "ground-work of Christianity [being] refined and refined till it vanished altogether, leaving *Deism*, or *natural*, or as it was called *philisophical* [*sic*] *religion*, in its place." Preferring "separate schools" for "different religious persuasions," Trimmer lamented that Basedow's ecumenical plan had already made its baleful influence felt in introducing the exclusion of religion into "many schools and academies" in England. But, Trimmer noted with relief, "[w]e do not recollect to have heard of any open attempts to establish seminaries of education" upon Basedow's plan.

That was in June 1802. By March 1803, however, Trimmer identified the arrival of just such an "open attempt" in Lancaster's *Improvements* (1803), with its outline of an unsectarian school and a proposal for a "friendly society" supporting a multidenominational academy of metropolitan schoolmasters. Her review of the book praised its practical parts, but worried that the plan of condensing religious instruction down to "a few *general points*...would in fact lead immediately to DEISM." Thus associating Lancaster with the "*generalizing plans*, which, as we showed at the commencement of our work, began with the *Philanthropine Institutions* in Germany," Trimmer argued that if his plan were "adopted for the great bulk of the people, the cause of Christianity would be materially injured" (1802–6, II, 172–75). In late 1805, following a visit to Lancaster's school in Southwark, an increasingly dismayed Trimmer began soliciting support for a campaign against him from Andrew Bell, whose *Experiment in Education* had just gone into a second edition. In the September 1805 number of the *Guardian*, Trimmer reviewed Bell's new edition, and found clearly delineated there "the Prototype of the popular Institution, conducted at this time upon a more extended scale by Mr. Joseph Lancaster, in the Surry Road" (IV, 371). Then, figuring Lancaster as the "Goliath of Schismatics," "engrossing the instruction of the common people," Trimmer wrote to Bell on September 24, 1805 that not only was Lancaster "building on your foundation," but that his plan was so "formidable" as to threaten "to supplant the Church" (qtd. in Salmon 1932, xxv–xxvi). But Bell's unchivalrous response—"I have cast my gauntlet: let them wield it who may" (qtd. in Salmon 1932, xxvi)—left Trimmer facing the Lancasterian Goliath alone. The result was her *Comparative View of the New Plan of Education Promulgated by Mr. Joseph Lancaster...and of the System of Christian Education Founded by our Pious Forefathers*, published in November 1805.

In the *Comparative View*, Trimmer aimed at nothing less than a wholesale reconstruction of Reformation-era intentions for education. The book attempted counterfactually to construct an absent national education system upon the "ground-work" laid down at the Reformation in the "clause...in the Act of Uniformity, requiring all parochial ministers diligently to hear, instruct, and teach the catechism set forth in the Book of Common Prayer" (1805, 101). Trimmer admitted the historical failure of the Church to build an adequate "edifice" upon the "ground-work," but she insisted that this was "not from any defect in the *system* itself, but from its not having been properly *acted upon*" (1805, 123). Conceding the comparative mechanical efficacy of Lancaster's plan, Trimmer nevertheless zoned in on its antisectarianism as disqualifying it from becoming the basis of a new national system. Responding to Lancaster's "wish...that names may perish, but truth prosper," and subverting the strong-man imagery of his disclaimer of any intention "by more than Herculean labour, to produce...a new establishment" (Lancaster 1805, ix, 195), Trimmer asserted that no loyal subject could "agree to give up the very *name* of that CHURCH which is the *glory of the nation*; that CHURCH, to which, as connected with the STATE, even her very enemies owe the protection of the laws of our excellent government; for, should it fall, it would involve all that is valuable in our Constitution in its ruins!" (Trimmer 1805, 14). The "Goliath of Schismatics" was now, in the flexible imagination of the Bible-minded Trimmer, a sort of dissenting Samson. His push against the Church monopoly in education was a push at "one *of the pillars of the* CONSTITUTION" (1805, 150). And danger lurked even in Lancaster's free-thinking model of evolutionary loyalism, illustrated in the story of "a lad" who, "wholly swallowed up" in writing, worked out his own errant course through "a sermon...an answer to Paine's Rights of Man...a *new* System of Physic, a Democratic Pamphlet, and A Defence of Revealed Religion" (Lancaster 1805, 37–39). Seeing more luck than judgment in the boy coming finally to rest on revealed religion, Trimmer turned the episode into a cautionary tale on the necessity of the Establishment's inhibiting involvement in education:

> *Poor* boys sent out into the world, without fixed principles, may in consequence of having been taught to write and read become very dangerous members of society.—Had this boy for instance retained his *democratical principles*, he would have been a *ready instrument of sedition and rebellion*. (Trimmer 1805, 31)

Trimmer then continued to paint Lancaster's scheme in much the same colors as, back in the 1790s, Burke had painted Price and the Revolution Society. For Burke, the Revolution Society had trespassed upon the prerogatives of the legislature by setting itself up as a "committee" with the "public capacity" to address the French National Assembly (1987, 5–6). And if its advocacy of the "rights of men" was a renewal of the Gunpowder Plot that had "wrought under ground a mine" to "blow up at one grand explosion all examples of antiquity, all precedents, charters, and acts of parliament" (51), then for Trimmer the Lancasterian proposal for a central school and a seminary for nondenominational schoolmasters was equally presumptuous and posed an analogous danger:

> I cannot help thinking that an *organized body of schoolmasters and boys*, under one *principal*, conducted on a *generalizing plan in respect to religion*, is a concern of too much national importance to be hastily approved...[It] would require the disannulling of some acts of parliament, and the making of others; which is the proper business of the legislature only. According to the constitution of this country, therefore, it could not be done by any *society* that could be formed, independent of government. (Trimmer 1805, 96–97)

Trimmer's pamphlet set the tone for the subsequent battle to claim the monitorial system, and indeed for the parliamentary debate on the pro-Lancaster Parochial Schools Bill brought forward by the Whig MP Samuel Whitbread in the summer of 1807. In the Commons debate on 13 July, Davies Giddy, the MP for the rotten borough of Bodmin and a long-standing opponent of electoral reform, argued that by enabling "the labouring classes" to "read seditious pamphlets, vicious books, and publications against Christianity," Whitbread's schools "would render them insolent to their superiors; and in a few years the legislature would find it necessary to direct the strong arm of power towards them" (Barnard 1947, 66). Passing the Commons, the Bill was stopped in the House of Lords, where on 11 August the Archbishop of Canterbury opposed it as an "innovation" that would "subvert the first principles of education in this country," and "shake the foundations of our religion" (qtd. in Murphy 1968, 17). The Archbishop may not have had Burke's analogy between the Gunpowder Plot and the "mine" of the "rights of men" immediately in mind. But this kind of imagery had a high currency at the time. In a print of 4 June, James Gillray figured the fall of Whitbread and the Ministry of all the Talents as the discovery of that ministry in the act of piling powder-kegs of liberal legislation around the Gothic "Pillar of the Constitution."[5]

For the Establishment, the threat posed by the Lancasterian system was effectively a renewal of that posed in Burke's analysis by Jacobinism: the revolt of the nation's talent ("All the Talents," perhaps) against its (Gothic) property (Burke 1796, 98). As Coleridge later put it, Lancasterian education was "a species of Jacobinism, proceeding from the same source, and tending to the same end, the rage of innovation, and the scorn and hatred of all lasting establishments" (Erdman, ed. 1978, II, 396). In a desperate rhetorical move that further recalls the treason trials of 1794, in which the prosecution insisted that the parts of the constitution were so deeply interfused that reform of one was the ruin of all—effectively staking the survival of the whole constitution upon the survival of its most manifest corruptions—the pro-Bell camp sought to overawe arguments for the historic failure of the clergy in the matter of national education by bundling together the clerical role in education and the survival of the Church as a whole. As Bell put it rather nervously in *The Madras School* (1808), given "the purest form of apostolical government in the church, and the most perfect model of a free constitution in the state," the "parochial clergy" was the answer to all the nation's educational needs, being "an order of men formed, as it were, for the purpose" (318–20). "It is obvious to remark," Bell continued, "how the forms and arrangements of the Madras school harmonize and combine with the gradations of orders in the church—the natural consequence of the one being framed in the same spirit, on the same principle, and with the same view, as the other" (321). The displacement of the clergy from education would, Bell implicitly warned his readers, entail the obsolescence of the clerical profession, and, by extension, of the existing constitution in church and state. A similar rhetoric of interdependency sounded in Southey's pro-Bell pamphlet of 1812. "[T]he system of English policy," Southey wrote,

> consists of church and state; they are the two pillars of the temple of our prosperity; they must stand or fall together; and the fall of

either would draw after it the ruin of the finest fabric ever yet reared by human wisdom under divine favour. Now to propose a system of national education, of which it is the avowed and distinguishing principle that the children shall not be instructed in the national religion, is to propose what is palpably absurd. (Southey 1812, 106)

Southey then proceeded to formulate the whole controversy as a question of institutional architecture. Echoing Burke's paradoxical portrait of the "atheistical fathers" of the French Revolution "talk[ing] against monks with the spirit of a monk" (Burke 1987, 97), and applying to the Lancasterians William Warburton's words on the Quakers, Southey claimed that "[T]hese very men, the most averse to every thing that looks like a church, or church policy, have by their use of it under another name, borne, before they were aware, the strongest testimony for its necessity" (1812, 205–6). As E. P. Thompson suggests, a political message is encoded in this sort of distinction between the meeting houses and chapels of dissent and the churches of Anglicanism: "In the agricultural or mining village, the polarization of chapel and Church might facilitate a polarization which took political or industrial forms" (Thompson 1980, 50). For Southey, Coleridge, and Bell, it was the rural Gothic church rather than the metropolitan Pantheon—Lancaster's public forum, and a byword for libertinism in the early 1790s—that provided the proper venue for propagating the "national system" of education.

## "THE DISCIPLINE OF VIRTUE": GOTHIC EDUCATION IN *THE EXCURSION*

Wordsworth's figuration of *The Excursion* as part of "the body of a gothic Church," and of his bildungsroman *The Prelude* as an "Anti-chapel," suggests his full agreement with the pro-Bell party; a "Gothic" stance on education that comes out still more strongly in his correspondence with Francis Wrangham. As I noted above, Wordsworth was concerned in his correspondence with Wrangham to protect the priority of both the Church and of Bell's system, and in a subsequent letter of March 1809 he imagined the position of the Church in physical terms very similar to those that Southey would use. "[W]ith the Methodists on one side and the Catholics on the other," he asked in a letter of late March 1809, "what is to become of the poor Church and people of England, to both of which I am most tenderly attached [?]" (*MY* I, 313). His tender attachment to the Church of England is, Wordsworth says, not least "on account of the pretty little spire of Brompton Parish Church," "under which" he (like Wrangham before him) had been made a "happy man" in marriage.[6] This associational chord was still resonating when *The Excursion* went to press in July 1814: Wordsworth shared a private joke with Wrangham in passing on Sara Hutchinson's "command" to "give my Love to Brompton Spire" (*MY* II, 150). His private correspondence bearing witness to his full appreciation for "every thing that looks like a church, or church policy," in education as well as in the state, Wordsworth appears to be in complete alignment with the Gothic cause of the Church in education.

We are now in a position to see the traces of the highly political monitorial controversy in Wordsworth's apparently innocuous statement of support for Bell. In the footnote appended to the Wanderer's prayer for a new "Statute to secure / For all.../ The rudiments of letters" and of "moral and religious truth," Wordsworth claimed that:

> The discovery of Dr. Bell affords marvellous facilities for carrying this into effect; and it is impossible to overrate the benefit which might accrue to humanity from the universal application of this simple engine under an enlightened and conscientious government. (*The Excursion* [1814], 447)

First, the phrase "[t]he discovery of Dr. Bell," allows Wordsworth to announce his partisanship for Bell while eliding the existence of any controversy at all. Second, the description of how benefits "impossible to overrate...might accrue to humanity" from "this simple engine," actually collates partisan statements by Wordsworth's fellow "Lakers" Coleridge and Southey, who had respectively likened Bell's system to the abolition of slavery and to the invention of printing. Third, the reference to the "universal application" of the system puts the most egalitarian construction possible upon Bell's scheme. Bell had after all proposed in 1805 that it was unnecessary to teach children "doomed to the drudgery of daily labour" how to write, inviting the Lancasterian accusation of "advocating the universal limitation of knowledge" (Salmon 1932, xlvi). Joseph Fox pointed out that the benefits proposed to be withheld from the "children of Britons" had, by Bell's own account, had wonderful effects when imparted to the orphans of Madras: "'...doomed to the drudgery of daily labour.' Strange language indeed to be addressed to the sons of England, when the half-cast children of Madras were qualified to fill the most important offices of society, and one of them to become a lecturer on Experimental Philosophy to Tippoo Sultaun!" (Fox 1808, 39).

Southey had defended Bell by way of a Burkean metaphor of equipoise: "The obstacle in his way was a charge that he entertained Utopian schemes for the universal diffusion of knowledge...Never dreaming that he should be accused of asking too little, he did not weigh his words on that side" (Southey 1812, 163). Bell toned down and explained away this passage in later editions, possibly with help from Dorothy Wordsworth (Connell 2001, 136), and Wordsworth here continues the work. Fourth, and finally, the statement that "an enlightened and conscientious government" is a prerequisite for such benefits to "accrue," seems—given that the whole note relates to the question of new statute law—to constitute a direct reference to Samuel Whitbread's failed pro-Lancaster Parochial Schools Bill of 1807. As we have seen, the "talents" ministry with which Whitbread was associated had fallen over Catholic Emancipation—over, that is, questions of conscience (the Anglican Establishment requiring oaths of allegiance for state positions) and enlightenment (Catholicism being a byword for superstition). Wordsworth's specification of the utility of Bell's system under "an enlightened and conscientious government" is thus effectively a statement that only under a constitutionally conservative ministry, opposed to any compromise with Catholicism, might the system prove a source of "benefit"; and otherwise harm would be the likely result. Four years later, campaigning in the 1818 general election in the interest of *The Excursion*'s dedicatee Lord Lonsdale, Wordsworth made the politics of this position more explicit. Wordsworth told the Freeholders of Westmoreland that when in power the Foxite Whigs had made "so many offensive compromises" that "a Government of Talents...was proved to be the most mischievous sort of government which England had ever been troubled with" (*Prose Works* III, 159, 162). And the "Body" that this offensive and compromised "Opposition" had put up for election in Westmoreland was none other than Henry Brougham, Whitbread's successor in promoting national education in Parliament (Barnard 1947, 77–78).

It is thus clear that by 1814 Wordsworth has adopted the contorted posture of the antidisestablishmentarian. But the more painful contradictions of his stance—the establishment of Bell's system being both analogous to the abolition of slavery ("with the exception of the abolition of the Slave trade, the most happy event of our times" [Moorman II, 179]) and incompatible with a ministry like the one that had (in February 1807) actually carried out that abolition—are in fact generated by pressures not merely domestic. Indeed, they can be seen as largely shaped by the negative example of France. As

James Chandler has argued, Wordsworth is likely to have been well informed about the developments in education in France from the period of his residency in 1792 onward, and to have known of the plan proposed by Joseph Lakanal in late 1794 for a uniformly educated republic stretching "to the Pyrenees and to the Alps," with education and the constitution treated as "correlative parts of the same conception" (Chandler 1984, 99–107, 233–34). *The Excursion* reproves such utopian schemes with a Burkean figuration of them as the breakup of settled realities reaching from the Pillars of Hercules to the Gothic north:

> Look! and behold, from Calpe's sunburnt cliffs
> To the flat margin of the Baltic sea,
> Long-reverenced Titles cast away as weeds;
> Laws overturned,—and Territory split;
> Like fields of ice rent by the polar wind
> And forced to join in less obnoxious shapes,
> Which, ere they gain consistence, by a gust
> Of the same breath are shattered and destroyed.
> (IX, 337–44)

The link between Napoleonic misrule and French miseducation is implicit here in the sickly habits of mind that prevent "consistence" and foster precipitate reform: solid "Titles" are mistaken for "weeds." But the contrast with Britain makes explicit the importance of education in avoiding such error:

> Meantime, the Sovereignty of these fair Isles
> Remains entire and indivisible;
> And, if that ignorance were removed, which acts
> Within the compass of their several shores
> To breed commotion and disquietude,
> Each might preserve the beautiful repose
> Of heavenly Bodies shining in their spheres.
>
> —The discipline of slavery is unknown
> Among us,—hence the more do we require
> The discipline of virtue...
> (IX, 345–54)

The Wanderer's vision of a "Sovereignty...entire and indivisible," to be maintained through education, is, as Chandler argues, clearly formulated as the antithesis of Lakanal's educational nationalism (1984, 232). Wordsworth attacks as unnatural and divisive the "system" of unitary nationalism that posits sovereignty as (in Benedict Anderson's formulation) "fully, flatly, and evenly operative over each square centimetre of a legally demarcated territory," and as "wedged between other sovereignties" (Anderson 2006, 19, 172), but he assumes precisely this fit between government and geography when speaking of Britain's (paradoxically) tripartite but "indivisible" sovereignty. In a perfect example of what Chandler calls Wordsworth's dialectical system against system, the conception of the unitary nation-state, repudiated in theory, is assimilated and transformed into its opposite. His attack upon "Jacobin" nationalism indeed recalls Burke's well-known vision of revolutionary France as "expunged" from political existence, as a missing piece or "chasm" in the interlocking "system of Europe" (Burke 1790, 5; Paine 1995, 188), inasmuch as both writers adopt the revolutionary model of the nation state as a "wedge" of uniform sovereignty in order to envision France as a pure absence on an older "dynastic" view. But I want to add to Chandler's account the point that Wordsworth is able to sustain this contradictory position because he has in mind as he writes Bell's "Gothic" education system, which, being intertwined with the fabric of the Church, not only maintained a degree of institutional separation (what Burke called "independence" [1987, 88]) from government, but was susceptible of representation as a growth of ages rather than a product of the winds of revolution. What else but the "simple engine" described as the bringer of benefits "impossible to overrate" could do what is here formulated as the impersonal work of removing ignorance? Against a Lakanalian national system that only accentuates "French" disorder, Wordsworth posits the Bell system as a framework for bringing security to the existing ancestral order: a "discipline of virtue" that is the antithesis of the Napoleonic "discipline of slavery." Indeed, Bellite education comes to fulfill the Burkean ideal of good government as an "entailed inheritance," for by such "discipline" shall "licentiousness and black resolve / Be rooted out, and virtuous habits take / Their place; and genuine piety descend, / Like an inheritance, from age to age" (IX, 361–64). Madras indeed promises the recovery of what "London, 1802" had called the "ancient dower" (ll. 2–3) of virtue reposed in the nation's Gothic halls:

> [F]rom the pains
> And quiet care of unambitious Schools
> Instructing simple Childhood's ready ear:
> Thence look for these magnificent results!
> Vast the circumference of hope—and Ye

> Are at its centre, British Lawgivers,
> Ah! sleep not there in shame! Shall Wisdom's voice
> From out the bosom of these troubled Times
> Repeat the dictates of her calmer mind,
> And shall the venerable Halls ye fill
> Refuse to echo the sublime decree?
>
> (IX, 397–407)

Wordsworth's position is, as Alan Richardson notes, "at once reformist and reactionary": the "unambitious" concessions of an unreformed Parliament shall bring about controlled social change (1994, 100). In the event, however, the "venerable Halls" signally failed to "echo the sublime decree." The monitorial controversy continued to dominate educational discourse for decades to come, and to keep national education penned in a fen of stagnant waters until the Elementary Education Act of 1870 (Barnard 1947, 66–67). This fact makes Wordsworth's partisanship for Bell look like Gothic politics in a rather negative sense. Indeed, Wordsworth's position on education was one of the targets of the aggressive third installment of Hazlitt's review of *The Excursion*. Hazlitt's October 1814 review went out of its way to mention the monitorial controversy, and to figure it as a theatrical diversion from the real work of education. With an ironic invocation of Aristotle that may also recall Southey's description of Lancaster's punishments as "making an auto-da-fe a raree-show for the people," Hazlitt wrote that if "tragedy purifies the affections by terror and pity," then "a company of tragedians should be established at the public expence [*sic*], in every village or hundred as a better mode of education than either Bell's or Lancaster's" (*The Examiner*, October 2, 1814, 637). Wordsworth's support for Bell's variety of the obscurantist monitorial system was thus for Hazlitt only a further index of his backsliding. In 1817, Hazlitt broadened his attack to include the Lake Poets as a group in his radical broadside, *What Is the People?* Hazlitt now identified the whole monitorial controversy as nothing less than a conspiracy for preventing the spread of literacy. "It is the fear of the progress of knowledge and a *Reading Public*," Hazlitt argued, with the "renegado poets" Southey and Coleridge firmly in mind, "that has produced all the fuss and bustle and cant about Bell and Lancaster's plans" (Wu, ed. 1998, IV, 252–53).

Hazlitt's claims were clear-sighted, inasmuch as the Lake Poets did indeed assimilate Madras to their elaboration of a constitutional conservatism. As Kevin Gilmartin has shown, the Madras system was one of the very few practical tools that Coleridge found to hand for achieving his vision of a self-sufficient "National Church" that would redeem the unreformed Constitution in Church and State, while the legislative implementation of Bell's scheme was central to Southey's periodical campaign for "completing the Reformation in England" by ensuring that the "forms" and "ceremonials" of the Church were "dextrously interwoven" with the education of the people (Gilmartin 2007, 232–52). But if Hazlitt was correct in his diagnosis of the politics behind the Lake Poets' support for Bell, it is less clear that he was correct as to the ultimate tendency of the monitorial system. For, as Frances Ferguson notes, monitorial schools did indeed offer "substantial learning" to the poor, and (especially as further developed by Jeremy Bentham) their ranking mechanisms helped to counteract invidious social relations by manifesting the internal differentiation of Burke's "swinish multitude" (Chandler and Gilmartin, eds. 2005, 141–45). *The Excursion* in fact registers something of this latter function of the system in its vision of the suspension (if not cancellation) of the social divide between the son of the Pastor, and his "Cottage-comrade." Equally the "thriving Prisoners of their Village school," the comradeship of the two boys points toward what the poem calls the "true equality" of nature: "At least, whatever fate the noon of life / Reserves for either, sure it is that both / Have been permitted to enjoy the dawn" (IX, 274, 259, 247, 280–282).

Wordsworth's perception of the socially progressive effects of monitorial education might also help to explain the otherwise shocking and puzzling vision that occurs at the end of *The Excursion*. Rapt "in holy transport," the Pastor tells the assembled party how, "if living eyes / Had visionary faculties to see / The thing that hath been as the thing that is," they might "Aghast...behold" performed amid the Lakes the sacrificial rites of the Celtic deities Andates and Taranis: "human Victims, offered up to appease / Or to propitiate (IX, 613, 694–98). The sacrificial wicker man had been a presence in Wordsworth's poetry since at least *Salisbury Plain* (1794), and it reappears here as though, as Richard Gravil puts it, "Wordsworth felt constrained to publish some version...in his lifetime" of this "primal scene" of his poetic vocation (Gravil 2003, 16, 20). But since it was a time-honored radical symbol for slavery and priestcraft, and since it haunts the Wanderer's harangue on education ("Our Life is turned / Out of her course, wherever Man is made / An offering, or a sacrifice" [IX, 114–16]), the shocking apparition of the wicker man can also be read as a symbolic restatement of the poem's larger progressive argument in favor of national education. Wordsworth appropriates the Lancasterian rhetoric of a "national evil" requiring a "national remedy." If "visionary faculties" allow the past to appear "as" the present, they also implicitly allow some "thing that is" to appear "as" a wicker man—which can be nothing other than the (supposedly "unknown") "discipline of slavery." Already invoked in the poem as the very antithesis of "slavery," Bell's system, filled with "thriving prisoners" rather than sacrificial victims, is thus implicitly posited as the virtuous antitype of the wicker man; as a wholesome new body for the old Gothic state.

## Coda: "Gothic" or "Gradgrind"

The support of the Lake Poets for Bell has often been seen, as by Carl Woodring, as an almost "grotesque" aberration (1970, 136). As David Simpson puts it, there has been no difficulty in seeing why "Wordsworth would be in favour of the 'Romantic' elements in Bell's writings, approving as he did the idea of 'voluntary and self-originating effort' and 'the practice of self-examination,'" but accepting the evidence that he fully "approved of the system in its complete form, Gradgindian principles included," has been quite another matter (Simpson 1987, 198). Simpson's description of Madras as "Gradgrindian" is legitimated by the fact that "Gradgrind" served E. P. Thompson as a sort of "mental shorthand" in his seminal theorization of bourgeois utilitarianism and its dialectical relationship with the creation of the English working class (Collini, Whatmore, and Young, eds. 2000, 251). But at least part of the conceptual difficulty surrounding the Lake Poets and Madras is due to the anachronistic habit of mind that this kind of long view entails: looking at the Lake Poets' support for the monitorial method in retrospect, through the lens of a (historically posterior) Dickensian typology, which, in turn, receives many of its categories of praise and blame from the textual products of a (historically *anterior*) phase of Romanticism. The history of ideas thus places a pair of brackets, as it were, around the ideological formation that sees the Lake Poets supporting the monitorial method. I hope that this chapter has (to change the metaphor) at least contributed to the task of loosening this mental knot, and I would like to conclude by telling the story forward. For if it is misleading to speak of the Lake Poets and Madras in terms of "Gradgrindian principles," it is nevertheless certainly true that the Romantic-era debate over catechistical schooling is indispensable to an adequate understanding of the Victorian discourse of education, as represented in Charles Dickens's *Hard Times* (1854). Thomas Gradgrind's "model school" produces prodigies of fact and calculation whose subsequent histories are readily legible as embodying the life of hollowness and lies that Wordsworth had predicted for the scientific child in book five of *The Prelude*. Dickens also gestures throughout toward an alternative education by accident and by romance that seems patterned upon Wordsworth's high-Romantic account of poetic childhood in poems such as "Tintern Abbey" and the "Intimations" Ode. The drift of Wordsworth's sacrificial vision at the end of *The Excursion*, meanwhile, is turned out of its own course. The novel's antiheroine, Louisa, imagines her "hard-fact" education by her father, Thomas Gradgrind, as a prolonged sacrifice of her imagination to Reason: not one "beneficent god" among many, but "a grim Idol, cruel and cold, with its victims bound hand and foot, and its big dumb shape set up with a sightless stare, never to be moved by anything but so many calculated tons of leverage" (Dickens 1964, 190). Wordsworth's tenuous distinction between "thriving prisoners" and abject slaves here collapses back upon itself.

Wordsworth himself came to revise his view of Bell and Madras. As Alan Richardson has shown, Wordsworth in later years went even further than Bell in advocating the "universal limitation of education," and he also rejected the Madras system on the grounds of the mechanistic qualities—a "simple engine" capable of "universal application"—that had made it attractive in the first place (Richardson 1994, 103–4). In a letter of 1828 to Hugh James Rose, Wordsworth argued that Madras, with its emphasis on "practical understanding" and its denial of the imagination, mistook "the constitution of our nature" and hence threatened (with shades here of Trimmer on Lancaster) the existing balance of society. Directing his comments at the planned Madras school for girls in Ambleside, Wordsworth rejected Bell's system even as he echoed his worries about the "risque of elevating" the minds of the "lower orders" above their lot of "drudgery":

> What are you to do with these girls?...Will they not be indisposed to bend to any kind of hard labour or drudgery?...A hand full of employment, and a head not above it, with such principles as may be acquired without the Madras machinery, are the best security for the chastity of the wives of the lower rank. (*LY*, I, 685–86)

Madras is now rejected for precisely the "massified" qualities that had previously made it attractive, in favor of a *Prelude*-like advocacy of a gradual culture of the mind through a direct engagement with nature—"pictures stuck up against walls," and other such reproducible "mummery" rejected in favor of exceptional and accidental observation "of a red-breast pecking by a winter's hearth" (*LY*, II, 20). In a typical "retrograde" movement, Wordsworth returns to something like the position he had held before Madras made a "material change in [his] views." But he returns with a difference that is conditioned by the politics of the monitorial controversy discussed in this chapter. His final position on education is, indeed, now structured in direct opposition to the "paradoxically reactionary progressivism" of the "Gothic" party he had once sought to lead, inasmuch as it is theoretically liberating in direct proportion as it is practically exclusionary and elitist.

# Conclusion

## The Staring Nation

The chapters of this book have made repeated use of visual metaphors in discussing the Romantic culture of the Gothic: stereoscopes, cartoons, maps, stained glass windows, kaleidoscopes, and theatrical spectacles. In this concluding chapter, I want to give more explicit articulation to this implicit argument for the intimate connection between the Romantic cultures of visuality and of the Gothic. Recent years have seen a major revival of interest in the technologies and the practices of viewing in the Romantic period. Building on the work of William Galperin in theorizing a Romantic "return of the visible," scholars such as Sophie Thomas and Peter Simonsen have explored the intimate relationship between the Romantic cult of the visual and Romantic historicism, and shown the ongoing cultural tug of war between the literary and the plastic arts in the period. As the visual register of much of this book has been designed to suggest, the Lake Poets were fully engaged in the process by which Britain, with its "love for shows," was transformed into what Edward Bulwer-Lytton's *The Siamese Twins* (1831) called "the Staring Nation" (45).

There has, historically, been a tendency to link the supposed artistic decline of the Lake Poets with their political "apostasy" and their development of a more "sculptural" aesthetic. As I noted in chapter one, William Hazlitt figured Wordsworth as having collapsed from radicalism into support for the Gothic restoration after Waterloo, and as having then proceeded to fashion "classical and courtly" poems with "the smoothness and solidity of marble" out of the "dereliction of his first principles" (Cook, ed. 1999, 351–52). But it is also possible to see late Wordsworth as epitomizing the modus vivendi achieved in the early nineteenth century between literature and the plastic arts. His publications after 1814 simultaneously acknowledge the imminent displacement of the word by the image, treat print as a special kind of visual experience, and also progressively aestheticize the absence of pictures and the profusion of text. As Simonsen puts it, "In the meeting of poetic word and the materialities of the medium, Wordsworth and his age came to recognize, new communicative and aesthetic possibilities are released even as this presupposes a more than linguistic understanding of what constitutes 'the poem' or 'poetry'" (2007, 56). Indeed, Simonsen contends that late Wordsworth's "master trope" is the "famous metaphor" of the "gothic Church" in the preface to *The Excursion*; the Gothic analogy with which so much of this book has been concerned. For Simonsen, the way that Wordsworth "maps his oeuvre on to a gothic church" generates "the eminently ekphrastic and inscriptional idea of the poem as a 'speaking monument'" (10). The gothic metaphor is indeed a useful synecdoche for the complex negotiations between the cultures of writing and seeing at this historical moment. But this is primarily because it is a visual image that is left strikingly unvisualized. The oeuvre is not, as Simonsen suggests, really "mapped onto" the building. Rather, as we have seen, Wordsworth makes a somewhat diffident "allusion" to the similar relationship that obtains between *The Recluse* and his "miscellaneous Pieces" and between the "body" of a church and its ante-chapels, "cells," and "oratories"—and then leaves the reader to "extract the system for himself" (1814, ix–x). Wordsworth thus stimulates the reader's visual imagination even as he withholds the detail that might fix and deaden it. One year later, the publication of *Poems* (1815) further heightened the para-visual effect by supplying an exhaustive catalogue of the poet's "miscellaneous Pieces," while the Preface expressed a hope that the collection could be reconciled with the Gothic metaphor to make Wordsworth's *oeuvre* visible "under a two-fold view" (*Prose Works* III, 28). Directing the reader's attention to a pair of overlapping images, and assisting in the cultivation of a binocular view through the mismatch between the "oratories" of 1814 and the "categories" of 1815, Wordsworth's paratextual prose thus worked to flash upon the reader's inward eye a three-dimensional apparition of a Gothic church—fully forty years in advance of David Brewster's exhibition of the Stereoscope. As Wordsworth told George Beaumont, he "should not wish" to make either a realistic or an idealistic art, "but to have in my own mind the power of turning to advantage...every object of Art and Nature as they appear before me" (*MY* I, 506). His was not—to borrow the terms of "Elegiac Stanzas"—the analogue "Painter's hand" (l. 13; *MW* 326–28), but rather a virtual hand, poised between reference and abstraction, and reaching spectrally out of the printed page toward the reader.

This spectral quality of the Gothic church metaphor also perhaps owes something to the tendency of visual technologies of the period—from window transparencies to the Eidophusikon and the Diorama—to take what John Imison's treatise on transparencies called the "admirably adapted...gloomy Gothic ruin" as their theme (1803, II, 332). As Thomas puts it, ruins appeal to the imagination because they "are by definition paradoxical: they represent...the *modern* form of the past...This is a problem illustrated rather effectively by popular scenes of antiquity that situated characters and events amid ruined structures that would have been in perfect condition at the putative time represented" (2008, 80). Still more strikingly, R. W. Westall's 1824 illustrations for Southey's *Roderick* depicted the eighth-century hero surrounded by Gothic ruins—by ruins, that is, in a style not devised until more than four centuries after his death. If ruins represent not so much history as the sense of history, then there is a clear sense in which Westall's anachronistic ruins construct Gothic architecture as the visual sign of historicity. Developing the "latent link" between the "disordered and dynamic" Gothic ruin and the turbid "mental states associated with Gothic fiction," images of ancient ruins thus fused the visual, historiographical, and literary elements in the Gothic Revival, and reconstructed their viewers as "Gothic subjects" (Thomas 2008, 132–33).

This fusion took perhaps its purest technological form in Louis Daguerre's "Diorama," which made its London debut in 1823, and which typically took deserted Gothic ruins for its subjects. The spectacle of the Diorama involved the alternating exhibition of "photogenic" paintings on translucent canvases, viewed from a rotating "saloon" inside a specially adapted theatre. Daguerre's primary innovation here was a painting technique that he called "the decomposition of form" (Daguerre 1839, 69). Colored screens operated behind the scenes to refract natural light onto the canvases, which had been painted on both sides with differential levels and qualities of pigment. At its simplest level, this meant that, as Daguerre put it, "if a green and a red part of the painting are illuminated by red light, the red object will vanish while the green object will appear black, and vice versa" (Daguerre 1968, 34). With these facilities for manipulating light to mimic temporal transitions and to make inanimate objects appear to move in a rudimentary fashion, the Diorama created a sense of the uncanny within the natural, and deranged the viewer's habitual sense of time and place. This effect of the Diorama is clearly visible in reviews such as the one carried in the *Times* on March 24, 1828, of "The Interior of the Cloisters of St. Wandrille." The review begins by commending the picture's attention to detail, reserving particular praise for the "old barrels that stand about midway in the avenue," looking "as if they were left there on purpose to overthrow any wanderer who might stray down it in the dark" (6). But it then proceeds to clog up with anxieties about the "mechanical arrangement," in particular a door that "seems to open...of [its] own device," without any "acting force,—no current of air, for example [...] which should account for such movement." And it concludes by advising its readers to sit in the front row of the "amphitheatre; because, in looking from the background of the building, where the frame-work of the picture and the company are necessarily taken into the prospect, half the illusion is destroyed." The review bears eloquent testimony to the Diorama's uncanny effect, both in its self-conscious praise for the way the barrels make visible a latent intent, but also in its unconscious linkage between perceiving movement without an "acting force" and avoiding seeing the "company," or the real "acting force." The way the hidden "company" reappear in mechanical form within the picture is clearly so powerful (and so powerfully suppressed) that it unsettles the boundary between the natural and the artificial, the real world and the picture, such that the viewer is transformed into an actor in an "amphitheatre," suddenly capable of being in "the back-ground."

If Wordsworth drew on the contemporary vogue for Gothic imagery in his 1814 Preface, *The White Doe of Rylstone* of 1815 saw him preempt the Diorama in combining the literary and the visual to reconstruct the reader as a "Gothic subject." Wordsworth achieved this in part through an innovative deployment of "black letter" or "Gothic" type. As Christine Baatz notes, it was conventional in eighteenth-century print culture to distinguish between the archaic and the modern by way of a transition from black letter to roman type. The title page of Locke's *Two Treatises of Government* (1690), for example, embodies its rational agenda in the typographical modulation from the black letter "False Principles" of "Government" to the roman "True Original" of "Civil Government" (Korte, Schneider, and Lethbridge, eds. 2000, 115). As Nick Groom notes, Gothic type was used with an equal and opposite valuation by the patriotic proponents of "national culture": *The Connoisseur* for March 1754 prophesied "the most certain success" to "any patriot...who should prin[t] his addresses in the Old English Character" (qtd. in Groom 1996, 59). In the 1790s, loyalist publications such as Hannah More's Cheap Repository Tracts adopted precisely this tactic, producing bills and posters with visual features including Old English geometrical figures and the "Gothic" imprimatur, "Entered at Stationers' Hall" (see Gilmartin 2007, 81, 84). The edition of Edward Young's *Night Thoughts* published by Thomas Heptinstall in 1798, meanwhile, contained a frontispiece in which the title and the place of publication appeared darkly visible through an elaborate shroud of Gothic type, while the names of the author and publisher, and the edition's unique selling-point of "NOTES CRITICAL & EXPLANATORY" were all given in bold roman capitals.

*The White Doe* exploits these conventions with a difference, using Gothic typography for inscrutable past utterances that are embedded deep within the volume and surrounded by roman type. The final canto of *The White Doe* depicts the heroine, Emily Norton, surviving the wreck of her family in the Catholic uprising of 1569:

> When the Bells of Rylstone played
> Their Sabbath music—"God us ayde!"
> That was the sound they seemed to speak;
> Inscriptive legend, which I ween
> May on those holy Bells be seen,
> That legend and her grandsire's name;
> And oftentimes the Lady meek
> Had in her childhood read the same,
> Words which she slighted at that day;
> But now, when such sad change was wrought,
> And of that lonely name she thought,
> The Bells of Rylstone seemed to say,
> While she sate listening in the shade,
> With vocal music, "God us ayde!"
> And all the Hills were glad to bear
> Their part in this effectual prayer.
> (ll. 1780–95; *WDR* 142)

Emily's slow deep feeling, the way "she sustains her part" (l. 1803) in the "sad change," transforms the meaning of the cryptic Gothic inscription on the bell. Investing the words with an emotional and historical resonance beyond their original devotional import, Emily translates the sound of the bells into "vocal music," into speech. The Gothic type thus serves to enhance the reader's sympathy with Emily, allowing the reader to visualize the "Inscriptive legend" before Emily's mind's eye. Similarly, in "The Force of Prayer," a ballad first published in *Poems* (1815) and republished as a supplement to *The White Doe*, Wordsworth alternates between Gothic and roman type in such a way as to render visible the poem's exercise in cultural translation. The typographic oscillation sets up a complex equation between the poem's modern narrative and the ultimately irreducible quantum of Gothic culture crystallized in the black letter:

> 𝔚𝔥𝔞𝔱 𝔦𝔰 𝔤𝔬𝔬𝔡 𝔣𝔬𝔯 𝔞 𝔟𝔬𝔬𝔱𝔩𝔢𝔰𝔰 𝔟𝔢𝔫𝔢?
> With these dark words begins my Tale,
> And their meaning is, whence can comfort spring
> When prayer is of no avail?
>
> "𝔚𝔥𝔞𝔱 𝔦𝔰 𝔤𝔬𝔬𝔡 𝔣𝔬𝔯 𝔞 𝔟𝔬𝔬𝔱𝔩𝔢𝔰𝔰 𝔟𝔢𝔫𝔢?"
> The Falconer to the Lady said;
> And she made answer "ENDLESS SORROW!"
> For she knew that her Son was dead.
> (ll. 1–8; *WDR* 147)

Wordsworth here generates a poetic form that is both corporeal and hyper-real. The unfamiliar lettering is both opaque *and* transparent: the words look more like illegible *things* to modern eyes—like Gothic relics standing in need of antiquarian explanation—but that very alienating thing-ness also generates the illusion of momentary access (of literally *seeing through* the words) to an unmediated past. For Elizabeth Fay, the poem's "odd textualism…forces a connection with Gothic narratives" even as it also "forces a rupture through the poet's exception of himself from the poem's medievalism" (2002, 97). The Gothic type thus operates in a manner similar to the Diorama's "decomposition of form" to deconstruct the modern reader and to reconstruct the reader as a haunted "Gothic subject." This effect is only enhanced by the intellectual half-rhyme sustained across the volume between the relics of Gothic type and the frontispiece engraving by Sir George Beaumont of the ruins of Bolton Priory. The visual properties of the 1815 edition of *The White Doe* are, then, intimately tied to what Wordsworth told Walter Scott was the poem's attempt to revive the spirit of feudal times (*MY* I, 264). Wordsworth's late "Gothic" style is thus legible as a mediating stage between high-Romantic anti-visuality and what Simonsen calls the "full-fledged pictorial and Arthurian turn in Victorian verse, fully realized in Tennyson's *Idylls of the King*" (2007, 138).

It is worth pausing over the fact that the historicizing effect of the Gothic type is wholly dependent upon the visual sense—upon the very sense whose "tyranny" (*1805* XI, 180) the "polite" reader was (as I noted in chapter three) supposed to be able to overcome, and the reliance upon which was frequently associated with a vulgar mentality. The striking dependence on the visible in this poem can be gauged from the bathetic effect of the opening phrase of "The Force of Prayer" when spoken rather than read. In a letter of April 25, 1815 discussing his reading of *Poems* (1815), Charles Lamb told Wordsworth that

> [W]hen I first opened upon ["The Force of Prayer"], in a careless tone I said to Mary, as if putting a riddle, "What is good for a bootless bene?" To which, with infinite presence of mind (as the jest-book has it) she answered, "A shoeless pea." It was the first joke she ever made. (Marrs, ed. 1978, III, 147–48)

Without the supplementary effect of the *visible* Gothic type, the opening phrase descends from learned cryptography to the level of a homely "jest." Lamb's comment is clearly designed to pick up on the vital interpretive role of the typographical properties of the poem, for he also comments in the same letter that he looks forward to seeing *The White Doe* "when dressed, i.e., printed. All things read raw to me in MS.; to compare magna parvis, I cannot endure my own writings in that state" (148). Lamb's comment implies that Wordsworth's use of Gothic type had been intended as an appeal to readers of his materialist and bibliophile sensibilities. And Lamb's repetition of Mary's joke seems designed to remind Wordsworth of how far he has moved from his own earlier ideology of oral presence, of the poet as "a man speaking to men" (*Prose Works* I, 159). Entering the world of print, Wordsworth must expect his "authentic" signifiers to escape his control—to take on meanings other than those that they had in their own historical and material context, and other than those that he had reinvested them with by inserting them in his poem.

Indeed, Wordsworth's use of Gothic type is itself unstable. The phrase "God us ayde" in *The White Doe* purports to be a direct transcription from a motto engraved on a bell dating to the mid-sixteenth century. But the speech "What is good for a bootless bene" in "The Force of Prayer" has no such claim to be rendered in Gothic type. Far from being an inscription, it is in fact the very opposite, a traditional oral form (recorded in Thomas Whitaker's *History and Antiquities of the Deanery of Craven* (1805), placed in the mouth of the archetypal figure of a "forester" (*WDR* 147–48). The Gothic type in "The Force of Prayer" is thus superadded, by the conceit that medievals, or Gothic subjects, spoke in the black letter, in "dark words." The Gothic type thus stands not for historical authenticity as such, but rather it stands as the visual sign of historicity, of the historical change that has rendered originally transparent (if riddling) words "dark."

It is surely significant in this context that the reply of the Lady to the Falconer is rendered in roman capitals. Her words, standing in no need of translation, illustrate the claim of the Preface to *Lyrical Ballads* that the "pure" core of the language was unchanged, making "the affecting parts of Chaucer...intelligible even to this day" (*Prose Works* I, 144). The Gothicizing of the Falconer's speech, meanwhile, serves as an implicit reminder of the fundamentally historical processes of survival and obsolescence by which such permanency is achieved. As Wordsworth put in the earliest extant draft of the poem, "*Her* words are plain; but the Falconer's words / Are a path that is dark to travel thorough" (ll. 3–4; *WDR* 384).

Wordsworth's publications after 1814 thus anticipate and in part precipitate the dethronement of the word by the image as the primary currency of cultural exchange. But it is also possible to see them as seeking simultaneously to ensure their own survival in the coming climate by treating print as a special kind of visual experience. Wordsworth's intense desire for his work to survive in a visually oriented posterity meant, in turn, that his own historical consciousness crystallized around the visual aspects of his publications—where it remains encrypted and amenable to reconstruction. This can be seen nowhere more clearly than in relation to the paradigmatic visual technology of the period, the wrap-around painting of real scenes in the Panorama.

With what Richard Altick calls "the forthright appeal of topicality realistically and dramatically presented" (1978, 136), the Panorama was a visual technology of enormous social and historical significance; regularly transporting metropolitan spectators, as Peter Otto notes, "into the thick of historical events: the battles of Nile, Copenhagen, Salamanca, Vittoria, and Waterloo" (2007, § 22). For Altick, such Panoramas were "the newsreels of the Napoleonic era" (1978, 136). But the London Panorama began life as something much more complicated and much more revealing about the link between visual technologies and the sense of history. When Robert Barker opened his "New Panorama" in Leicester Square on May 25, 1793, the placid spectacle he offered Londoners of the Russian Fleet riding at anchor off Spithead in 1791 was in a very strange counterpoint with the invasion scares dominating the newspapers and the daily hazard to Britain's real "walls of oak." The Panorama was, of course, founded upon a contradiction. Requiring a specially designed rotunda, hidden skylights, and a viewing platform capable of mimicking hilltops and frigate-decks, and with 10,000 square-foot's-worth of canvas crammed with visual detail, it was intended to be wholly engrossing, to "mimic.../ The absolute presence of reality," as Wordsworth put it in *The Prelude* (*1805*, VII, 248–49). But it was also intended as an artistically respectable refinement in painting—as Barker's assiduous courting and eventual winning of Sir Joshua Reynolds's approval suggests (Galperin 1993, 41). In line with what Reynolds called the "fullness of effect" achievable in oils but not in fresco (1783, 12), Barker had dropped the viscous tempera paint used in the early Panoramas of Edinburgh and London, and had painted the "Fleet at Spithead" in oils that conferred upon the unnatural stasis of the Panorama a certain consecrating gleam. The sensational effect of the show in fact consisted in the suspense thus generated between enchantment and disillusionment; the ideal viewer continually experiencing what Sophie Thomas describes as the perceptive lurch between seeing "the represented distance of the painted scene" and apprehending "the relative proximity...of the painted wall" (2008, 16).

We get a glimpse of this effect in the experience of the very first visitor to the New Panorama, King George III, given a sneak preview on May 24, 1793. Barker's son recorded the event in his diary. The king, attended by Lord Harcourt, "asked many questions; and when answered, turned around" and "gave the answer verbatim," and frequently had recourse to "a large gold-headed cane" to point out objects of curiosity "so small that I could not otherwise understand him" (qtd. in Otto 2007, § 28). Here is a perfect negative testimony of the Panorama's intended effect. As Otto puts it, the king is "unable, without the help of the artist, to mediate between first order and second order realities, still less between second order realities and the ideal," becoming instead "an imitator, repeating verbatim what he has been told" (§ 28). Obsessed with local details, the king gets (vulgarly) trapped "between realities" instead of oscillating between them. Queen Charlotte's credentials as an ideal (oscillating) viewer, by contrast, may be gauged by young Barker's report that she "said that the sight of the picture made her feel sea-sick" (Ellis 2008, 142). The king's failure to appreciate the Panorama is doubtless primarily an effect of his general distractedness, while the queen's apparent pass with flying colors is doubtless partly owed to Barker's reading of her reactions in line with the cult of sensibility. But the contradictory responses of the king and queen might also owe something to the fact that to view the "Fleet at Spithead" in May 1793 was to enter a sort of historical contradiction. The fleet had been mobilized in 1791, as Markman Ellis notes, in order to influence Russia's dealings with the Ottoman Empire, and had been disbanded without firing a shot (2008, 140). Barker's Panorama thus represented the world-beating potency of the mere rumor of a British fleet as recently as 1791—and threw into sharp relief the changed geopolitical realities of 1793, when the British fleet was again at Spithead, but now in urgent defense of Britain herself. Geopolitical changes that had occurred, as it were, behind the scenes, meant that the picture's delicate aesthetic balance was wholly deranged. Any paper-reading viewer would be well aware that the real fleet was now mustering precisely where the picture placed the scarecrow "Russian Armament," and would therefore see right through the illusion. The Panorama's effect of timeless verisimilitude was thus ruined and converted at a stroke into an effect of historical dislocation (Queen Charlotte) and cognitive faulture (King George).

But the aesthetic catastrophe was a resounding commercial success. It is easy to see why. If *The Times* for April 24, 1789, had recommended Barker's Edinburgh Panorama to the sedentary royal family for the way it rendered a scene "perfectly in idea, the same as nature could impress" (qtd. in Otto 2007, § 19), then there is a clear sense in which the royal visit to the "Fleet at Spithead" signaled that the Panorama offered an unparalleled opportunity to make a virtual troop inspection and to imagine oneself in the cockpit of national destiny—all for the price of a shilling. If newspaper-reading viewers inevitably saw through the illusion, they could *see through* it in a strong sense too. Like *The Times* for May 25, 1793 whose front page jumbled together reports on the royal preview of the Panorama, the spectacle of the "MIRACULOUS FISH" at the Eidophusikon, military intelligence from all over Europe, and a "desperate" seven-hour battle between two British ships and a French East Indiaman, Barker's Panorama blurred the boundaries between viewing and volunteering, and between the cosmopolitan and the tar. The blur was infectious. In his *Picture of the Isle of Wight* of 1794, Henry Wyndham segued from an "enraptured" description of the "commanding" view of Spithead from the town of Ryde, into a note on the proprietorship of this view by a "gentleman" whose house was "fortunately and conspicuously introduced in the justly celebrated *Panorama* of Spithead" (Wyndham 1794, 42–44). If the gentry could behold both the nation and the real fleet at Spithead from their holiday homes on the Isle of Wight, the Panorama allowed the urbanite to look back at them in imagination—triangulating the country and the city on the shared spectacle of a fleet stilled in the middle distance. The Panorama was thus to some extent a physical realization of the "virtual representation" in Edmund Burke's ideal Constitution.

For Wordsworth, as is well known, the Panorama was too straightforwardly dedicated to topicality and far too transparently *technological* to qualify as art. In the catalogue of the sights of London in *The Prelude*, the Panorama appears with its "circumambient scenery" and its power to "Plant us…/…in a ship on waters," as a "plain / Confession of man's weakness, and his loves;" something to be acknowledged rather than boasted of as a "means refined attaining purest ends" (*1805* VII, 253–62). But as James Chandler and Kevin Gilmartin have recently suggested, what is usually taken as a quintessentially Wordsworthian economy of preternatural stillness and uncanny depth might in fact be an effect of his frequently writing not about nature as such, but about nature as mediated through works of plastic art. "Composed Upon Westminster Bridge," for example, with its evocation of London as a "mighty heart…lying still" (l. 14; *MW* 285) can be read as an ekphrasis of Thomas Girtin's 1802 London panorama, or Eidometropolis (Chandler and Gilmartin, eds. 2005, 11–12). Once one starts to see the brush-strokes in Wordsworthian nature, they are everywhere. Take, for example, the *Prelude* lines describing how the poet has

>                              stood,
> Even while mine eye has moved o'er three long leagues
> Of shining water, gathering as it seemed,
> Through every hair-breadth in that field of light,
> New pleasure like a bee among the flowers.
>                              (*1805* I, 604–8)

This "field" of vision has length ("three long leagues") and breadth ("every hair-breadth"), but where one might expect a corresponding depth, there is instead the close foreground of "a bee among the flowers." The eye is uncertain whether it moves "through" or moves "o'er" the scene. And now one looks more closely, doesn't "hair-breadth" contain the lurking possibility of a brush-mark or a brush-hair, whose unintentional "breadth" (concretely "in" rather than abstractly "of" the "field of light") might shock the viewer out of the illusion of the Panorama?

If Wordsworth had still not fully assimilated the new visual technology by the time of the 1805 *Prelude*, its immediate impact can be felt in a fragment-poem composed in summer 1793 on the Isle of Wight, "How sweet the walk." Like Wyndham's "gentleman," the poem's speaker looks across at the fleet at Spithead from the vicinity of Ryde, and then proceeds to recompose the scene as a panorama.

Even as "summer seas are charmed to sleep," and tranquility oozes through earth, air and sea, the poet hears how

> ...from yon proud fleet in peal profound
> Thunders the sunset cannon; at the sound
> The star of life appears to set in blood
> Old ocean shudders in offended mood
> Deepening with moral gloom his angry flood.
> (Landon and Curtis, eds. 1997, 744)

The poem seems to rigidify at the "sound" of cannon—and, as though reversing Barker's progression from tempera to oil paint, the language congeals around the wrenching wound of the caesura (the semicolon being an appropriately *artificial* punctuation mark), passing in quick succession through the somatic stages of bleeding, mortifying, and dying, and through the artistic modes of music ("peal"), sculpture ("set"), theatre ("shudders"), and prose ("moral gloom"). Flux gives way to stasis, life to form, and this transition is figured in terms of an uncanny pictorial representation—"The star of life appears to set." There is a juddering sense in the lines of nature turned into a machine—the same sense of betrayal that would soon produce *Salisbury Plain*'s vision of liberticidal Britain as a sacrificial wicker man, and that would later inform *The Prelude*'s figure of Napoleon's coronation as a sun setting like an opera phantom (*1805*, X, 936–41). "Nature never did betray / The heart that loved her," Wordsworth affirmed in "Tintern Abbey," explicitly rejecting the panoramic paradigm with his refusal to "paint / What then I was" (ll. 123–24, 76–77; *MW* 131–35). It is, however, only through this negation that the affirmation is achieved. And we might begin to suspect that Wordsworth's subsequent repudiation of the Panorama as a childish cleaving to the visual conceals a recognition of his deep poetic debt to its congealing and coagulatory effects.

Much of the imaginative interest of *The Excursion*, as well as of parts of *The Prelude*, consists in the Panorama-like perceptive lurch between seeing through the poem's surface to its represented depths and apprehending the flat, matter-of-fact, contours of the words used to evoke those depths; a "lurch" that in practice takes the form of rapid transitions between the vocabularies of spatial description and of pictorial representation. In book two of *The Excursion*, for example, the poet sees the "Cloudscape New Jerusalem" at one moment as "A wilderness of building, sinking far / And selfwithdrawn into a boundless depth," and the next as a spatially indistinct mass of clouds, rocks, and sky. It is both an extensive city, "In avenues disposed," and an "appearance," an "effect," composed from nature's palette of "dark materials" (II, 871–82).

The *Guide to the Lakes* (1835) sees a further stage in Wordsworth's renegotiation of the relationship between words and pictures. The *Guide* was originally written for money as a textual supplement to Joseph Wilkinson's *Select Views in Cumberland, Westmoreland, and Lancashire* (1810). It was separated from the pictures in *The River Duddon* (1820), and was then revised over time with an increasing confidence in the ability of words to excel actual images. Wordsworth's writing becomes more pictorial in proportion as he purges the visual image from his text. This simultaneous turn to and from the image makes the *Guide* an epitome of the late-Romantic ambivalence toward the visible world. Indeed, Wordsworth claims that the ideal lacustrine scene is something "not easily managed in picture," but "how pregnant with imagination for the poet," and then goes on to prove his point with a sublime word-painting:

> The happiest time is when the equinoxial gales are departed; all […] speaks tranquillity; not a breath of air, no restlessness of insects, and not a moving object perceptible—except the clouds gliding in the depth of the lake, or the traveller passing along, an inverted image, whose motion seems governed by the quiet of a time, to which its archetype, the living person, is, perhaps, insensible: or it may happen, that the figure of one of the larger birds, a raven or heron, is crossing silently among the reflected clouds, while the voice of the real bird, from the element aloft, gently awakens in the spectator the recollection of appetites and instincts, pursuits and occupations, that deform and agitate the world...(*Prose Works* II, 192)

The strangeness of what Wordsworth is saying is easily missed if we read with a view to an actual *picture*, but the passage is all about something that cannot (by definition) be "managed in picture": the difference between seeing objects disposed in space and seeing objects disposed on a flat surface. This traumatizing difference (which is indeed the enabling problematic of painting) is registered in the mutually incompatible and equally impossible images of "clouds gliding in the depth of the lake" (that is, *in the actual depth*, not just figuratively "in the depths"), and the "raven or heron...crossing silently among the reflected clouds" (that is, on a single level with them). What Wordsworth makes us do is to see the surface and the depth at the same time, or rather, to make the depth the surface, and vice versa—an effect that the paratactic mode of his prose, with its shifts of register and of perspective, serves to generate. Paul de Man calls Wordsworth the poet of the "double vision," seeing "landscapes as objects, as well as entrance gates to a world lying beyond visible nature" (1984, 132). And in the vision here of an inhuman "image" traversing an inaccessible region with a "motion...governed by the quiet" of an unknown time, Wordsworth seems to gain access not only to another world of perception but to another order of time and history.

The visual-historical portal that opens in the *Guide* also opens in "After-Thought," the sonnet that concludes the *River Duddon* sequence. The poem is peculiarly susceptible to interpretation as a literary-visual encryption of the sense of history, since it was printed all in italics from the collected works of 1827 onward, and since the tension embodied in the typeface between fixity and movement recurs in the poem's argument and imagery, with its retrospective optimism and its vision of a *still gliding* stream (*MW* 351). For Peter Simonsen, the visual impact of the poem's italics, which encourage the reader to stare at the poem rather than to read it, further intimates the paradoxical nature of Wordsworth's printbound bid for immortality: "It is a poem not only about what comes after speech, for example listening and the silence of thought, but about what comes after we have finished listening and, more disturbing, *after* the silence of thinking, what comes *after* thought even as it also comes after speech...where thought and consciousness, personality and self, are absent and have been vacated" (2007, 124). This eerie evocation of the aesthetic gaze represents in miniature the uncanny connection between visuality and the sense of history. Casting its eyes back beyond its own beginning and forward beyond its own posterity, "After-Thought" hallucinates the Gothic subject within the abstracted present—and suggests the unique form of historical insight that Wordsworth's poetry worked to inculcate in the British "staring nation":

> *Enough, if something from our hands have power*
> *To live, and act, and serve the future hour;*
> *And if, as tow'rd the silent tomb we go,*
> *Thro' love, thro' hope, and faith's transcendent dower,*
> *We feel that we are greater than we know.*

## Afterword: The Gothic Enterprise

In 1791–92, Wordsworth opposed himself to Britain's "Gothic regulation" in politics and education. In 1793–94, he worked out agonized fantasies of the disappearance of "Gothic England." In the late 1790s, he collaborated with Coleridge on generating a purer Gothic poetry. In the first decade of the nineteenth century, he rallied to the defense of Britain's "Gothick halls," exhorting Britain and Europe to recover their "Gothic Virtue." And in the years around 1815, he supported the "Gothic" side in arguments over education, and participated in the cultural transformation of the citizen into a visually oriented Gothic subject. Put like this, Wordsworth's career up to 1815 is clearly visible as the working-through of a "Gothic cultural enterprise."

In 1819, just as an alternative, less defensively nativist Romanticism was taking shape in the writings of Keats, Shelley, Byron, and others, Wordsworth published *Peter Bell*, under a dedication to Southey that expressed a wish for "filling *permanently* a station, however humble, in the Literature of the Country" (qtd. in Garrett 2008, 114)—a "Literature" that Southey himself had defined as essentially Gothic in October 1814. Since dedication has the effect of incorporating the dedicator and the dedicatee, Wordsworth's address to Southey can be interpreted as the public announcement of a new cultural corporation—or, perhaps, a Gothic enterprise. 1819 is the moment of the public floatation of Gothic culture. As recently as January 1815, however, Wordsworth had been much less confident of the public's preparedness for their Gothic venture, writing to Southey that the "benighted age" that had crushed *The Excursion* in its birth ought to be left "to love its own darkness and to cherish it" (*MY* II, 187). Accumulating "Gothic" resonances in his language— the word "benighted" punningly suggesting the mismatch between the degraded public and the "knightly" ethos of the Lake school— Wordsworth thus indicated the inhospitable nature of British culture as currently constituted to a great Gothic revival. But in a postscript, Wordsworth thanked Southey for the "very acceptable" copy of his epic bestseller allegorizing Britain's heroic war effort in Spain and Portugal, *Roderick, the Last of the Goths* (*MY* II, 187). If the "gothic Church" had few worshippers, there was yet some Gothic virtue to oppose to Gothic vice. And the Gothic cultural enterprise was still struggling to be born.

# Notes

## Preface

1. Notable reviews include: Nick Groom's invited publicity review for the first edition of *Gothic Romanticism* (see back jacket); Gregory Leadbetter in *The Wordsworth Circle* 41, no. 4 (2010), 215–217; Sue Zlosnik in *BARS Bulletin and Review* 39 (Dec 2011), 40–41; Elizabeth Massa Hoiem in *Journal of the Fantastic in the Arts* 23, no. 1 (2012), 119–122; David Punter in *European Romantic Review* 23, no. 4 (2012), 479–85; and Jeffrey C. Johnson in *Romanticism* (forthcoming). David Punter's piece is a wide-ranging review essay also featuring Diane Long Hoeveler's *Gothic Riffs* (2010) and Carol Margaret Davison's *History of the Gothic* (2009). My quotations of Groom, Leadbetter, Hoiem, and Johnson, are taken from the sources listed above, and extracts from the reviews can be found on the book's website, http://gothicromanticism.weebly.com. The MLA Prize citation is available at: http://library.constantcontact.com/download/get/file/1102018840316–125/IND-Duggett.pdf. The prize selection committee included Crystal Bartolovich, Daylanne English, Barbara Harlow, Anthony Purdy, and Alan Rosen. I offer this preface to them, in thanks.

## 1 Romantic Poets and Gothic Culture

1. The description of Jeffrey's review as "crushing" was widespread. Wordsworth reported to Catherine Clarkson on December 31, 1814 that it was called "a crushing review" by Jeffrey's—"the Coxcomb's"—"Idolators" (*MY* II, 182). The *Athenaeum* for April 27, 1850 noted that Jeffrey "boasted wherever he went that he had *crushed* [*The Excursion*] in its birth" (447).
2. For the equation between the Jesuits (founded in 1540 and suppressed in 1773) and casuistry, see, for example, John Poynter's *Brief Account of the Jesuits* (1815, 10–11); and the new English edition of Blaise Pascal's anti-Jesuit satire, *Provincial Letters* (1816). See also Chandler 1998, 205–6, 228–29, 315. For the papal bull of August 7, 1814 reconstituting the Jesuit order, see *The Annual Register for the Year 1814* (1815, 81, 438–41). For knowledge in Britain of the rehabilitation of the Jesuits by the time of Hazlitt's review, see the report

in *The Times* for August 23, 1814 on the Pope's celebration on July 31 of "[t]he feast of St. Ignatius of Loyola, founder of the Order of the Jesuits" (3). And for a corroborating instance of the equation made by Hazlitt and *The Examiner* between "casuistical" or sophistical argument and the Gothic restoration, see *The Examiner* for September 11, 1814, where a report on the restoration of the Jesuits leads onto a satire on the Spanish Inquisition (the restoration of which the paper had reported on August 7 [500]), which is followed in turn by a note on "Syllogistic Reasoning": "Epimenides has said that all the Cretans are liars: now he was himself a Cretan; therefore he has lied; therefore the Cretans are not liars; therefore Epimenides has not lied; and therefore the Cretans are liars!" (586).
3. For a detailed discussion of the anti-Saxonist politics of Warton's *History*, and its relationship to the Gothic writings of Percy and Hurd, see Connell 2006, 182–89.
4. For relevant discussions of Tooke's linguistic politics, see Fulford 1996, 161–62, Olivia Smith 1984, 119–40, and Manly 2007, 5–59.
5. See Richard Verstegan's *Restitution of Decayed Intelligence* (1605, 57), Michael Drayton's *Poly-Olbion* (1613 and 1622; Hebel, ed. 1931–41, IV, 381), and John Thelwall's *Rights of Nature* (1796; Claeys, ed. 1995, 496). David Erdman notes that this "inaccurate legend" was "not corrected until after Wordsworth's time" (Erdman 1988, 3).
6. See "Ground-plan of the two Houses of Parliament and adjoining Edifices," published after the 1834 fire alongside the elegy for the "giant of the Gothic age," in the *Gentleman's Magazine*, 2 (new series, 1834), 481.

## 2 Radical Gothic: Politics and Antiquarianism in *Salisbury Plain* (1794)

1. The print, number D13016 in the Reference Collection of the National Portrait Gallery, London, is reproduced in Gatrell 2006 and in Colley 1996, and can also be viewed online at: http://www.npg.org.uk/collections/search/portrait.php?firstRun=true&sText=the+french+invasion&search=sp&rNo=0/.
2. For a detailed and fully illustrated account of how the "contrast" format (e.g., Thomas Rowlandson's *The Contrast 1792*) was used and subverted in loyalist commissions by both Gillray and Newton in the mid-1790s, see Barrell 2006, 228–42.
3. The image, number 071937 in the British Library's Images Online gallery, can be viewed online at: http://www.imagesonline.bl.uk/results.asp?image=071937

    The image is also reproduced in high resolution, and at full-page size in my article, "Celtic Night and Gothic Grandeur: Politics and Antiquarianism in Wordsworth's *Salisbury Plain*," *Romanticism*,

13:2 (July 2007), 164–176; 166; available online at: http://muse.jhu. edu/login?uri=/journals/romanticism/v013/13.2duggett.html/.
4. Richard Price's *Discourse on the Love of our Country* (1789) hailed the French Revolution as "the dominion of priests giving way to the dominion of reason and conscience" (Price 1789, 50). Paine, tracing the origins of all "old governments," saw them as founded ultimately upon the "government of priestcraft," a "fraud" which, subsequently "united...to force" under conquerors, "set up an idol...called *Divine Right*, and which, in imitation of the Pope...twisted itself afterwards into an idol of another shape, called *Church and State*" (Paine 1995, 121).
5. Other notable prints on the same themes of druidism and dismemberment include *Un Petit Souper, a la Parisienne* (September 1792), showing sans-culottes as cannibals, and *Presages of the Millenium* (June 1795), showing a wraith-like Pitt as a horseman of the apocalypse. The Gillrays mentioned here are usefully grouped together in Gatrell 2006, 263, 280–283. The theme of the wicker man also appears in the satires of Thomas Rowlandson: his 1813 print, *Napoleon*, for example, shows the emperor with a head composed of a multitude of contorted corpses (McCalman, ed. 1999, 617).
6. Stephen Gill and Richard Gravil both suggest that Wordsworth had seen this illustration (Gravil 2003, 12; Gill, ed. 1975, 35n).
7. For Wordsworth and the "outrages" around Orléans, see Liu 1989, 151; Roe 1988, 70; and Roe's "Politics, History, and Wordsworth's Poems," in Gill, ed.2003, 205–9.
8. Except where otherwise stated, all quotations of the poem are taken from the reading text provided in *The Salisbury Plain Poems of William Wordsworth*, ed. Stephen Gill (Ithaca, NY: Cornell University Press, 1975).
9. For *Salisbury Plain* as an exercise in literary Gothic, see, for example, Karen Swann's essay, "Public Transport: Adventuring on Wordsworth's Salisbury Plain," *English Literary History*, 55:4 (1988), 811–34.
10. See Michael Drayton, *Poly-Olbion*, IX, 425–434, in Hebel, ed. 1931–41, IV; Thomas Chatterton, "Battle of Hastings (No. 1)," ll. 301–306, in Chatterton 1799, 237; and Erasmus Darwin, "The Loves of the Plants," III, 101–108, in Darwin 1789–91, II, 97. Drayton's scene of Druid sacrifice features in Wordsworth's list of authorities for "Druids" in DC MS. 12 (*SPP* 35).
11. According to Blair it is "past all doubt" that "the ancient Scots were of Celtic original," and the Celts are, he says, "altogether distinct from the Goths and Teutones"—the poetry of whom "nearly resembles" that of the Anglo-Saxons (Blair 1763, 11, 5).
12. Duncan Wu notes that Wordsworth probably did not own Percy and Mallet's book until 1797, but he also notes that Wordsworth was introduced to Percy's earlier *Reliques of Ancient English Poetry* (1765)

by his school master Thomas Bowman (Wu 1993, 93, 163). *Northern Antiquities* expanded upon the argument of the *Reliques* that the origins of English poetry were to be found in "the ancient historical songs of the Gothic Bards and Scalds" (Percy 1775, III, vii–viii). And Bowman, an avid reader himself (Wu 1993, 163), might well have pointed his pupil to further reading of a book recently described by Peter Mortensen as the key text for all things Gothic in the late eighteenth century (Mortensen 2000, 213).

13. See Verstegan 1605, 57, 187; Bacon 1689, I, 9; Bolingbroke 1743, 52–3; Hurd 1811, IV, 231–350; and Tacitus, *Germania*, Chapter xi, in Clery and Miles, eds. 2000, 51.
14. Blair and Percy's ancestral schism would not have been news to Wordsworth in the early 1790s. He almost certainly studied the relevant writings of both Tacitus and Caesar—the *Germania* and the *Gallic Wars* respectively—in preparation for the classics tripos at Cambridge; and on the relative merits of the ancient Celts and Goths he could easily have drawn a conclusion similar to Percy's for himself. See Wu 1993, 166–67; Wu 1995, 258; and Schneider 1957, 15. The *Gallic Wars* stated quite explicitly that the customs of the Gauls and the Germans were wholly distinct. The Gauls engaged in human sacrifice and other rites, but, Caesar said, "[f]rom these customs…the Germans differ greatly, having neither druids to preside in sacred rites nor troubling themselves with sacrifices" (Bladen, ed. 1750, 116).
15. The image is reproduced in my article, "Celtic Night and Gothic Grandeur," 170.
16. William Sharp McKechnie notes that Blackstone was unaware of the existence of a fourth surviving copy at Lincoln cathedral (McKechnie 1914, 169). The Lincoln charter lay undiscovered until the early nineteenth century (Turner 2003, 65).
17. McKechnie notes that Gilbert Burnet, bishop at the period of the manuscript's disappearance, was "accused…of appropriating it" by his "political adversaries": an "undoubted calumny" (1914, 168).
18. For the possibility that Wordsworth, recently returned from France, was present to hear Tweddell's oration in Trinity Chapel on November 4, 1790, see Roe 1988, 15–16.
19. Grégoire proposed the motion for the abolition of the monarchy on September 21, 1792.

## 3 "By Gothic Virtue Won": Romantic Poets Fighting the Peninsular War

1. All quotations of *The Convention of Cintra* are taken from the text presented in *Prose Works* I, 221–343. References are to line numbers in this edition.

2. The "chief" of these divisions was that of the two kingdoms of Castile and Aragón, a "distinction as ancient as the period [of]…the marriage of Isabella with Ferdinand" in 1469. The two kingdoms differed "with respect to their interior administration" and taxation, and they were subdivided into provinces, twenty-two for Castile and four for Aragón, with three of Castile's provinces "form[ing] separate states" with "scarcely any thing connected with the collection of taxes." The provinces of the kingdoms nominated members of the "shadow" Cortes, but this reasonably transparent and "public" system was complicated by the existence within and across the provinces of parallel and incommensurate systems, including the thirteen "military governments" (most of which did, however, correspond to a single province), and the ecclesiastical system of dioceses with "different limits from the provinces." Even the functions of "public welfare" and justice in the state were divided between three systems—tribunals, audiences and chanceries—all of which were "equally absolute" and disputed jurisdiction amongst themselves. See Bourgoing 1808, I, 167–72, 318–19.
3. For more on the mythology of *reconquista*, see O'Callaghan 2003, 4–7. For Coleridge on Napoleon's "mercenary trick" of conversion to Islam, see "Buonaparte and the Emperor Julian," *The Courier*, December 26, 1812, in Erdman, ed. *The Collected Works of Samuel Taylor Coleridge, No. 3*, 1978, II, 350. See also "Analysis or Skeleton of the Debate in the House of Commons, Monday, February 3, 1800," *The Morning Post*, February 6, 1800, in Erdman, ed., *Collected Works, No. 3*, I, 164.
4. The image, number 11061 in the British Museum's Catalogue of Personal and Political Satires, can be viewed online at: http://www.britishmuseum.org/collectionimages/AN00211/AN00211632_001_l.jpg. It is reproduced on the cover of the hardback first edition (2010) of *Gothic Romanticism*, and can be accessed via this book's website, at: http://www.gothicromanticism.weebly.com/images. See also the description given in George, ed. *Catalogue of Political and Personal Satires*, 1870–1954, VIII, 697. The print's title refers to James Gillray's *The Spanish Bullfight* of July 11, 1808. Its imagery appears to be indebted to the German artist Hans Sebald Beham's 1545 engraving, "Hercules Slaying the Hydra." A copy of this print is held by Japan's National Museum of Western Art, and it can be viewed online at: http://collection.nmwa.go.jp/en/G.2003-0094.html/.

  Beham's print can also be viewed through Wikipedia, at: http://en.wikipedia.org/wiki/File:Hercules_slaying_the_Hydra.jpg#file/.
5. The image, first employed by the sixth-century historian Jordanes, for whom the Goths "burst forth like a swarm of bees…into the land of Europe," was echoed in English writings as diverse as John Milton's *Paradise Lost* (I, 351–55), James Thomson's *Liberty* (IV,

802–5), Richard Hurd's *Letters on Chivalry and Romance*, Mallet and Percy's *Northern Antiquities*, and John Thelwall's *Rights of Nature*. See Kliger 1952, 11–12; Hurd 1811, IV, 284–85; Mallet 1770, I, 226; and Thelwall 1995, 494.
6. Gillray's cartoon is image no. D12911 in the holdings of the National Portrait Gallery, London, and can be viewed online at: http://www.npg.org.uk/collections/search/largerimage.php?sText=spanish+patriots+attacking+the+french+banditti+&OConly=true&search=sp&firstRun=true&rNo=0/.
The print is also reproduced in Bainbridge 1995, 104.
7. Cruikshank's print is no. 11003 in the British Museum's *Catalogue of Political and Personal Satires*, and can be viewed online at: http://www.britishmuseum.org/research/search_the_collection_database/search_object_image.aspx?objectId=1509102&partId=1&asset_id=112648/.
The print is described thus by Mary Dorothy George: "In the background (l.) two monks armed with muskets lead a band with a cross and spears; they have a banner inscribed *F. VII*" (George, ed. 1870–1954, VIII, 657–8). George further notes the accuracy of this depiction: "The clergy took a leading part in the insurrection; bands of peasants were led by monks."
8. As Owen and Smyser note, *The Courier* printed *Cintra*, ll. 1–209 and ll. 210–564 on December 27, 1808 and January 13, 1809 respectively. See *Prose Works*, I, 199–200.
9. For Mallet as Wordsworth's source, see Wu 1993, 93. The plan may also derive from Mallet through the mediation of Coleridge—whose "Historical Sketch of the Manners and Religion of the ancient Germans" in the third number of *The Watchman* (March 17, 1796) summarized Mallet on ancient German religion and politics and on Odin. See Lewis Patton, ed. *The Collected Works of Samuel Taylor Coleridge*, No. 2, 1970, 89–92.
10. For the dating of the list of epic subjects to the period around January 1804, see Jonathan Wordsworth, ed. *The Prelude: The Four Texts*, 1995, 556; and Mark Reed, ed. *The Thirteen-Book Prelude*, 1991, I, 10–11, 5.
11. Franklin's speech of September 17, 1787 urging the state legislatures to sign the new Constitution contained an oddly pessimistic prophecy: "I agree to this Constitution, with all its Faults—if they are such; because I think a General Government necessary for us, and there is no *Form* of Government but what may be a Blessing to the People if well administered; and I believe farther that this is likely to be well administered for a Course of Years, and can only End in Despotism as other Forms have done before it, when the people shall become so corrupted as to need Despotic Government, being incapable of any other." See Alan Houston, ed. *Franklin: The Autobiography, and Other Writings on Politics, Economics, and Virtue*, 2004, 362.

12. See also Milton's *History of Britain* (1670) in Frank Allen Patterson, ed. *The Works of John Milton*, 1931–38, X, 325. Wordsworth amends the Miltonic original to remove the notions that the Britons are "in good or bad success alike unteachable," and that civic virtues must be imported from abroad. He also removes the statement that "few of them were" men "more than vulgar," presumably in order to shift the passage from a retrospective to a prospective view.

## 4 Wordsworth's Gothic Education

1. All quotations of *The Excursion* are taken from the reading texts in the Cornell edition (Bushell, Butler, and Jaye, eds. 2007).
2. For Wordsworth's withdrawal of his support for Bell's system in the late 1820s, see *LY* I, 685–6, and II, 20; and Richardson 1994, 103–104. In January 1816 Wordsworth asked his brother Christopher to help William Johnson, the former master of Grasmere school and now (with Wordsworth's recommendation) headmaster of Bell's Central School in London, in a dispute with Bell. Wordsworth's language is distinctly unflattering: he calls Bell a "jealous opponent" of Johnson, and the leader of a "Cabal" against him (*MY* I, 661–62, and II, 270–271).
3. For Lancaster's audience with George III, see Salmon 1932, viii–ix. For Lancaster on public spirit, see Lancaster 1805, 34, 94–96, 162. For Lancaster's lectures, see a handbill for a lecture, "combining a practical representation of the ROYAL BRITISH SYSTEM OF EDUCATION with the details of its Theory," to be given at 2 pm on Friday, June 1, 1805, "at the PANTHEON, Oxford Street" [British Library, shelf-mark 1879.c.11 (36)]. For Lancaster's "humble petition," see the manuscript pasted into the copy of *Improvements* (1805) held at the British Library, shelfmark 231.g.17.
4. See Salmon 1932, ix; *Oxford Dictionary of National Biography* (2004), XXXII, 361; Corston 1840, 11; and Lancaster 1805, 23.
5. The print, number 10738 in the British Museum's *Catalogue of Political and Personal Satires*, can be viewed online at:http://www.britishmuseum.org/research/search_the_collection_database/search_object_image.aspx?objectId=1640400&partId=2&asset_id=144701/.
   See also the description provided in George, ed. 1870–1954, VIII, 539.
6. Wordsworth and Mary Hutchinson were married at Brompton in October 1802. For Wrangham's marriage at Brompton, see Moorman 1957–1965, II, 88.

# Bibliography

## Primary Sources

Bacon, Nathaniel. *Historical and Political Discourse of the Laws and Government of England*. 2 vols. London: John Starkey, 1689.

Barbauld, Anna Laetitia. *The Works of Anna Laetitia Barbauld*. 2 vols. London: Richard Taylor, 1825.

Bell, Andrew. *An Experiment in Education, Made at the Male Asylum of Madras. Suggesting a System by Which a School or Family May Teach Itself under the Superintendence of the Master or Parent*. London: Cadell & Davies, 1805.

———. *The Madras School, or Elements of Tuition: Comprising the Analysis of an Experiment in Education, Made at the Male Asylum, Madras; With Its Facts, Proofs, and Illustrations*. London: John Murray, 1808.

Bentham, Jeremy. *A Fragment on Government; Being an Examination of What Is Delivered, on the Subject of Government in General, in the Introduction to Sir William Blackstone's Commentaries*. London: T. Payne, 1776.

Blackstone, William. *The Great Charter and Charter of the Forest*. Oxford: Clarendon Press, 1759.

———. *Commentaries on the Laws of England*. 4 vols. Oxford: Clarendon Press, 1765-9.

———. *Commentaries on the Laws of England*. 11th edition. 4 vols. London: T. Cadell, 1791.

Blair, Hugh. *A Critical Dissertation on the Poems of Ossian, the Son of Fingal*. London: T. Becket and P. A. De Hondt, 1763.

Blake, William. *Blake Records*. Ed. G. E. Bentley. Oxford: Clarendon Press, 1969.

Bolingbroke, Henry Saint John. *Remarks on the History of England*. London: R. Francklin, 1743.

Bonaparte, Napoleon. *The Confidential Correspondence of Napoleon Bonaparte with his Brother Joseph, Sometime King of Spain*. 2 vols. London: John Murray, 1855.

———. *In the Words of Napoleon, The Emperor Day by Day*. Ed. R. M. Johnston. Rev. Philip Haythornthwaite. London: Greenhill Books, 2002.

Bourgoing, Jean François. *Modern State of Spain*. 4 vols. London: John Stockdale, 1808.

Browne [afterward Hemans], Felicia Dorothea. *England and Spain; or, Valour and Patriotism.* London: T. Cadell and W. Davies, 1808.

Bulwer, Edward. *The Siamese Twins: A Satirical Tale of the Times.* New York: J. & J. Harper, 1831.

Burke, Edmund. *A Philosophical Enquiry into the Origin of Our Ideas of the Sublime and Beautiful.* London: R. & J. Dodsley, 1757.

——— *Substance of the Speech of the Right Honourable Edmund Burke, in the Debate on the Army Estimates, in the House of Commons, on Tuesday, the 9th Day of February, 1790.* London: J. Debrett, 1790.

———. *A Letter to Sir Hercules Langrishe on the Subject of Roman Catholics of Ireland, and the Propriety of Admitting Them to the Elective Franchise.* London: J. Debrett, 1792.

———. *Two Letters Addressed to a Member of the Present Parliament, on the Proposals for Peace with the Regicide Directory of France.* 4th edition. London: F. and C. Rivington, 1796.

———. *Three Memorials on French Affairs.* London: F. and C. Rivington, 1797.

———. *Reflections on the Revolution in France.* Ed. J. G. A. Pocock. Indianapolis and Cambridge: Hackett Publishing Company, 1987.

Byron, George Gordon Noel. *Childe Harold's Pilgrimage, a Romaunt.* 2nd edition. London: John Murray, 1812.

———. *Byron's Don Juan.* Ed. Truman Guy Steffan and Willis W. Pratt. 4 vols. Austin: University of Texas Press, 1957

C., D. J. M. R. del, Capitan. *Manifiesto Político que a Todos los Verdaderos Españoles, Fieles y Amantes Vasallos de Nuestro Catolico Monarca El S.r D. Fernando Septimo.* Sevilla, 1808; in *Papeles Varios* Vol. I, British Library shelfmark 8042. bb. 6 (1.)

Caesar, Julius. *C. Julius Cæsar's Commentaries of his Wars in Gaul, and Civil War with Pompey.* Ed. Martin Bladen. 7th edition. London: J. & P. Knapton, 1750.

Chambers, Ephraim. *Cyclopædia: Or, an Universal Dictionary of the Arts and Sciences.* 2 vols. London: J. and J. Knapton, 1728.

Chatterton, Thomas. *Poems, Supposed to Have Been Written at Bristol, in the Fifteenth Century, by Thomas Rowley, and Others.* Cambridge: Lancelot Sharpe, 1799.

Coleridge, Samuel Taylor. *Christabel; Kubla Khan: A Vision; The Pains of Sleep.* 3rd edition. London: John Murray, 1816.

———. *Coleridge's Miscellaneous Criticism.* Ed. Thomas Middleton Raysor. London: Constable & Co., 1936.

———. *Collected Letters of Samuel Taylor Coleridge.* Ed. E. L. Griggs. 6 vols. Oxford: Clarendon Press, 1956–71.

———. *The Collected Works of Samuel Taylor Coleridge, No. 2.* Ed. Lewis Patton. Princeton, NJ: Princeton University Press, 1970.

———. *The Collected Works of Samuel Taylor Coleridge, No. 3.* Ed. David V. Erdman. 3 vols. London: Routledge & Kegan Paul, Princeton University Press, 1978.

———. *Biographia Literaria*. Ed. James Engell and W. Jackson Bate. 2 vols. London: Princeton University Press, 1983.

———. *Samuel Taylor Coleridge: The Major Works*. Ed. H. J. Jackson. Oxford: Oxford University Press, 1985.

Daguerre, Louis Jacques M. *History and Practice of Photogenic Drawing, on the True Principles of the Daguerreotype, with the New Method of Dioramic Painting*. 3rd edition. London: Smith, Elder and Co., 1839.

———. *The History of the Diorama and the Daguerreotype*. Ed. Helmut Gernsheim and Alison Gernsheim. 2nd edition. Mineola, NY: Dover Publications, 1968.

Darwin, Erasmus. *The Botanic Garden*. 2 vols. London: J. Johnson, 1789–91.

Dickens, Charles. *Hard Times*. Ed. Robert Donald Spector. New York: Bantham Books, 1964.

Drayton, Michael. *The Works of Michael Drayton*. Ed. J. William Hebel. 5 vols. Oxford: Oxford University Press, 1931–41.

Dugdale, William. *The History of St. Paul's Cathedral in London*. 2nd edition. London: Edward Maynard, George James, and Jonah Bowyer, 1716.

Edgeworth, Maria. *Popular Tales*. 3 vols. London: J. Johnson, 1804.

Fox, Joseph. *A Comparative View of the Plans of Education, as Detailed in the Publications of Dr. Bell and Mr. Lancaster*. London: Darton and Harvey, 1808.

Franklin, Benjamin. *Franklin: The Autobiography, and Other Writings on Politics, Economics, and Virtue*. Ed. Alan Houston. Cambridge: Cambridge University Press, 2004.

Gibbon, Edward. *The History of the Decline and Fall of the Roman Empire*. 2nd edition. 6 vols. London: W. Strahan and T. Cadell, 1777.

Gillray, James. *The Works of James Gillray, from the Original Plates with the Addition of Many Subjects Not Before Collected*. 2 vols. London: Henry G. Bohn, 1851.

Godwin, William. *Political Justice*. 2 vols. London: G. G. J. and J. Robinson, 1793.

———. *Life of Geoffrey Chaucer, the Early English Poet*. 2nd edition. 4 vols. London: Richard Phillips, 1804.

Hayden, John O. Ed. *Walter Scott: The Critical Heritage*. London: Routledge, 1996.

Hazlitt, William. *The Selected Writings of William Hazlitt*. Ed. Duncan Wu. 9 vols. London: Pickering & Chatto, 1998.

———. *Selected Writings*. Ed. John Cook. Oxford: Oxford University Press, 1999.

Heath, Charles. *Descriptive Account of Tintern Abbey, Monmouthshire*. Monmouth: Charles Heath, 1793.

Hollingsworth, N. J. *An Address to the Public, in Recommendation of the Madras System of Education*. London: Rivingtons and Hatchard, 1812.

Hunt, Leigh. *The Town*. 2 vols. London: Smith, Elder, & Co., 1848.

# Bibliography

Hurd, Richard. *The Works of Richard Hurd*. 8 vols. London: T. Cadell and W. Davies, 1811.
Imison, John. *Elements of Science and Art*. 2 vols. London: Harding, 1803.
Johnson, Samuel. *The Second Part of the Confutation of the Ballancing Letter, Containing an Occasional Discourse in Vindication of Magna Charta*. London: A. Baldwin, 1700.
Johnson, Samuel and Boswell, James. *A Journey to the Western Islands of Scotland, and The Journal of a Tour to the Hebrides*. Ed. Peter Levi. London: Penguin Books, 1984.
Jones, Inigo. *The Most Notable Antiquity of Great Britain, Vulgarly called Stone-Heng, on Salisbury Plain, Restored*. 2nd edition. London: D. Browne, 1725.
Jovellanos, Gaspar Melchor. *Memoria en defensa de la Junta Central* (1810), in *Obras publicadas e inéditas, Biblioteca de Autores Españoles, Vols. 46 & 50*. 2 vols. Madrid: M. Rivadeneyra, 1858–59.
Knight, Richard Payne. *An Analytical Inquiry into the Principles of Taste*. 4th edition. London: T. Payne and J. White, 1808.
Lamb, Charles and Mary Anne. *The Letters of Charles and Mary Anne Lamb*. Ed. E. W. Marrs, Jr. 3 vols. Ithaca, NY: Cornell University Press, 1975–78.
Lancaster, Joseph. *Improvements in Education*. 3rd edition. London: Darton and Harvey, 1805.
Langley, Batty. *Ancient Architecture, Restored, and Improved, by a Great Variety of Grand and Usefull Designs, Entirely New in the Gothick Mode for the Ornamenting of Buildings and Gardens*. London: [no publisher], 1742.
Lemprière, John. *Bibliotheca Classica; or, a Classical Dictionary*. 2nd edition. London: T. Cadell, 1792.
Lovell, Robert and Southey, Robert. *Poems: Containing "The Retrospect," Odes, Elegies, Sonnets, etc*. London: Dilly, 1795.
Lucchesini, Marquis. *History of the Causes and Effects of the Confederation of the Rhine*. Trans. John D. Dwyer. London: [no publisher], 1821.
Malcolm, James Peller. *Londinium Redivivum; or, an Ancient History and Modern Description of London*. 4 vols. London: Nichols & Son, 1802.
Maldonado, D. José Muñoz. *Historia Política y Militar de la Guerra de la Independencia de España contra Napoleón Bonaparte desde 1808 á 1814*. 3 vols. Madrid: Palacios, 1833.
Mallet, Paul Henri. *Northern Antiquities: Or, a Description of the Manners, Customs, Religion and Laws of the Ancient Danes, and Other Northern Nations; Including Those of Our Saxon Ancestors*. Trans. Thomas Percy. 2 vols. London, T. Carnan and Co., 1770.
Marx, Karl. *The Eighteenth Brumaire of Louis Bonaparte*. New York: International Publishers, 1977.
Mathias, Thomas James. *The Pursuits of Literature*. 8th edition. London: T. Becket, 1798.
Milton, John. *Poems Upon Several Occasions*. Ed. Thomas Warton. London: James Dodsley, 1785.

———. *The Works of John Milton*, Ed. Frank Allen Patterson. 18 vols. New York: Columbia University Press, 1931–38.

———. *The Complete Poems*, ed. John Leonard. London: Penguin Books, 1998.

Montesquieu, Charles-Louis. *The Spirit of Laws*. 2 vols. London: J. Nourse and P. Vaillant, 1750.

Morgan, Michael L. Ed. *Classics of Moral and Political Theory*. 2nd edition. Indianapolis and Cambridge: Hackett Publishing Company, 1996.

Muir, Thomas. *The Trial of Thomas Muir, Esq., Younger, of Huntershill*. Edinburgh: Alezander Scott, [1793].

Paine, Thomas. *Rights of Man; Common Sense; and Other writings*. Ed. Mark Philp. Oxford: Oxford University Press, 1995.

———. *Thomas Paine Reader*. Ed. Michael Foot and Isaac Kramnick. London: Penguin Books, 1987.

Pascal, Blaise. *Provincial Letters*. London: Gale and Fenner, 1816.

Percy, Thomas. *Reliques of Ancient English Poetry*. 3rd edition. 3 vols. London: J. Dodsley, 1775.

———. *Reliques of Ancient English Poetry*. Ed. Nick Groom. 3 vols. London and Bristol: Routledge/Thoemmes Press, 1996.

Pope, Alexander. Ed. *The Works of Mr. William Shakespear*. 10 vols. London: J. & J. Knapton, 1728.

Poynter, John. *A Brief Account of the Jesuits*. London: F. C. and J. Rivington, 1815.

Pradt, M. *Memoires Historiques sur la Revolution D'Espagne*. Paris: Rosa, 1816.

Price, Richard. *A Discourse on the Love of Our Country, Delivered on Nov. 4, 1789, at the Meeting-House in the Old Jewry, to the Society for Commemorating the Revolution in Great Britain*. London: T. Cadell, 1789.

Pugin, Augustus Welby. *True Principles of Pointed or Christian Architecture and An Apology for the Revival of Christian Architecture*. Ed. Roderick O'Donnell. Leominster: Gracewing, 2003.

Reynolds, Joshua. *Eighth Discourse, and His Discourse, Delivered to the Students of the Royal Academy on the Distribution of the Prizes, December 10, 1782*. London: T. Cadell, 1783.

Ritson, Joseph. *Observations on the Three First Volumes of the History of English Poetry*. London: J. Stockdale and R. Faulder, 1782.

———. *A Select Collection of English Songs*. 3 vols. London: J. Johnson, 1783.

Robinson, Henry Crabb. *Henry Crabb Robinson on Books and Their Writers*. Ed. Edith J. Morley. 3 vols. London: Dent, 1938.

Rowe, Nicholas. *Jane Shore, a Tragedy*. London: John Bell, 1791.

Ruiz, Dr. *Retrato Político del Emperador de los Franceses, su conducta y la de sus generales en España, y la lealtad y valor de los Españoles por su Soberano Fernando VII*. Cádiz: D. Manuel Bosch y compañía, 1808; in "Latin American Pamphlets," British Library shelfmark CUP. 405. b. 6.

Sammes, Aylett. *Britannia Antiqua Illustrata*. London: T. Roycroft, 1676.
Scott, Walter. *Glenfinlas, and Other Ballads, etc.: With The Vision of Don Roderick; a Poem: Illustrated with Engravings from the Designs of Richard Westall*. London: John Sharpe, 1812.
——. *The Antiquary*. Ed. Nicola Watson. Oxford: Oxford University Press, 2002.
Shakespeare, William. *The works of Shakespear*. Eds. Alexander Pope and William Warburton. 8 vols. London: J. and P. Knapton, 1747.
Sheridan, Richard B. *Speeches of the Late Right Honourable Richard Brinsley Sheridan (Several Corrected by Himself)*. 5 vols. London: Patrick Martin, 1816.
Society for Constitutional Information. *Report of the Sub-Committee; Appointed April 12, 1780, to Take into Consideration All Such Matters, Relative to the Election of Members of Parliament, as May Promote the Purposes of the Present Association*. London, 1780; rpt. London: London Corresponding Society, 1794.
Southey, Robert. *Specimens of the Later English Poets*. 3 vols. London: Longman, Hurst, Rees and Orme, 1807.
——. *The Origin, Nature, and Object, of the New System of Education*. London: John Murray, 1812.
——. *The Life and Correspondence of Robert Southey*. Ed. Charles Cuthbert Southey. New York: Harper & Brothers, 1855.
——. *Poems of Robert Southey*. Ed. Maurice H. Fitzgerald. London: Henry Frowde, Oxford University Press, 1909.
Southey, Robert and Westall, Richard. *Roderick the Last of the Goths*. London: Longman, Hurst, Rees, Orme, and Brown, 1824.
Spenser, Edmund. *The Faerie Queene*. Ed. Thomas P. Roche Jr. London: Penguin, 1987.
Stukeley, William. *Stonehenge a Temple Restor'd to the British Druids*. London: W. Innys and R. Manby, 1740.
Temple, William. *An Introduction to the History of England*. 3rd edition. London: Richard and Ralph Simpson, 1708.
Thelwall, John. *The Politics of English Jacobinism: Writings of John Thelwall*. Ed. Gregory Claeys. Pennsylvania: Pennsylvania State University Press, 1995.
Thomson, James. *The Seasons*. London: M. Millar, 1772.
——. *The Complete Poetical Works of James Thomson*. Ed. J. Logie Robertson. London: Oxford University Press, 1908.
Toland, John. *A Collection of Several Pieces of Mr. John Toland*. 2 vols. London: J. Peele, 1726.
Tooke, John Horne. *The Diversions of Purley*. 2nd edition. 2 vols. London: J. Johnson, 1786–1805.
Trimmer, Sarah. *The Guardian of Education*. London: J. Hatchard and F. C. and J. Rivington, 1802–1806.
——. *A Comparative View of the New Plan of Education Promulgated by Mr. Joseph Lancaster…and of the System of Christian Education Founded by Our Pious Forefathers*. London: F. C. and J. Rivington, 1805.

Tweddell, John. *Remains of the Late John Tweddell.* Ed. Rev. Robert Tweddell. London: J. Mawman, 1815.

Verstegan, Richard. *A Restitution of Decayed Intelligence: In Antiquities. Concerning the Most Noble and Renowned English Nation.* Antwerp: R. Bruney, 1605.

Walpole, Horace. *Anecdotes of Painting.* 4 vols. Thomas Kirgate: Strawberry Hill, 1765–71.

Warner, Richard. *A Walk through Wales, in August 1797.* Bath: R. Cruttwell and C. Dilly, 1798.

Warton, Thomas. *The History of English Poetry, from the Close of the Eleventh to the Commencement of the Eighteenth Century.* Ed. Richard Price. 2nd edition. 4 vols. London: Thomas Tegg, 1824.

Warton, Thomas, Bentham, James, Grose, Francis, and Milner, John. *Essays on Gothic Architecture.* London: J. Taylor, 1800.

Williams, David. *Lectures on Education.* 4 vols. London: John Bell, 1789.

———. *Lessons to a Young Prince, by an Old Statesman.* 3rd edition. London, 1790.

Williams, Edward. *Poems, Lyric and Pastoral, in Two Volumes.* 2 vols. London: J. Johnson, 1794.

Wordsworth, Dorothy. *The Grasmere Journals.* Ed. Pamela Woof. Oxford: Oxford University Press, 1991.

Wordsworth, William. *Lyrical Ballads, with Other Poems.* 2 vols. London: T. N. Longman and O. Rees, 1800.

———. *Poems, in Two Volumes.* 2 vols. London: Longman, Hurst, Rees, and Orme, 1807.

———. *The Excursion, Being a Portion of "The Recluse," a Poem.* London: Longman, Hurst, Rees, Orme, and Brown, 1814.

———. *Poems.* 2 vols. London: Longman, Hurst, Rees, Orme, and Brown, 1815.

———. *The River Duddon, a Series of Sonnets.* London: Longman, 1820.

———. *The Prelude, or, Growth of a Poet's Mind; An Autobiographical Poem.* London: Moxon, 1850.

———. *The Prose Works of William Wordsworth.* Ed. W. J. B. Owen and Jane Worthington Smyser. 3 vols. Oxford: Clarendon Press, 1974.

———. *The Salisbury Plain Poems of William Wordsworth.* Ed. Stephen Gill. Ithaca, NY: Cornell University Press, 1975.

———. *Home at Grasmere, Part First, Book First, of "The Recluse."* Ed. Beth Darlington. Ithaca, NY: Cornell University Press, 1977.

———. *The Borderers.* Ed. Robert Osborn. Ithaca, NY and London: Cornell University Press, 1981.

———. *"Poems, in Two Volumes," and Other Poems, 1800–1807.* Ed. Jared Curtis. Ithaca, NY and London: Cornell University Press, 1983.

———. *The Fourteen-Book Prelude.* Ed. W. J. B. Owen. Ithaca, NY and London: Cornell University Press, 1985.

———. *"The Tuft of Primroses" with Other Late Poems for "The Recluse."* Ed. Joseph F. Kishel. Ithaca, NY and London: Cornell University Press, 1986.

Wordsworth, William. *Poems (1815)*. Ed. Jonathan Wordsworth. 2 vols. Oxford: Woodstock Books, 1989.
———. *Shorter Poems, 1807–1820*. Ed. Carl H. Ketcham. Ithaca, NY and London: Cornell University Press, 1989.
———. *The Thirteen-Book Prelude*. Ed. Mark Reed. 2 vols. Ithaca, NY and London: Cornell University Press, 1991.
———. *"Lyrical Ballads," and Other Poems, 1797–1800*. Ed. James Butler and Karen Green. Ithaca, NY and London: Cornell University Press, 1992.
———. *The Fenwick Notes of William Wordsworth*. Ed. Jared Curtis. London: Bristol Classical Press, 1993.
———. *The Prelude: The Four Texts*. Ed. Jonathan Wordsworth. London: Penguin Books, 1995.
———. *Early Poems and Fragments, 1785–1797*. Ed. Carol Landon and Jared R. Curtis. Ithaca, NY: Cornell University Press, 1997.
———. *Sonnet Series and Itinerary Poems, 1820–1845*. Ed. Geoffrey Jackson. Ithaca, NY and London: Cornell University Press, 2004.
———. *The Excursion*. Ed. Sally Bushell, James A. Butler, and Michael C. Jaye, assisted by David Garcia. Ithaca, NY and London: Cornell University Press, 2007.
Wordsworth, William, and Wordsworth, Dorothy. *The Letters of William and Dorothy Wordsworth: The Early Years, 1787–1805*. Ed. Ernest De Selincourt. 2nd edition. Rev. Chester L. Shaver. Oxford: Clarendon Press, 1967.
———. *The Letters of William and Dorothy Wordsworth: The Middle Years*. Ed. Ernest De Selincourt. 2nd edition. Rev. Mary Moorman and Alan G. Hill. 2 vols. Oxford: Clarendon Press, 1969–70.
———. *The Letters of William and Dorothy Wordsworth: The Later Years*. Ed. Ernest De Selincourt. 2nd edition. Rev. Alan G. Hill. 4 vols. Oxford: Clarendon Press, 1978–88.
Wrangham, Francis. *Sermons, Practical and Occasional; Dissertations, Translations, Including New Versions of Virgil's Bucolica, and of Milton's Defensio Secunda, Seaton Poems, &c. &c.* 3 vols. London: Baldwin, Craddock, and Joy, 1816.
Wyndham, Henry. *Picture of the Isle of Wight*. London: J. Egerton, 1794.
Young, Edward. *Conjectures on Original Composition*. London: A. Millar and J. Dodsley, 1759.
———. *Night Thoughts*. London: Thomas Heptinstall, 1798.

## Newspapers and Journals

*Analytical Review*
*Annual Register*
*Anti-Jacobin Review*
*Athenaeum*
*Augustan Review*

*Eclectic Review*
*Edinburgh Review*
*Examiner*
*Gentleman's Magazine*
*Quarterly Review*
*Tait's Magazine*
*The Times*

## Secondary Sources

Altick, Richard D. *The Shows of London*. Cambridge, MA: Harvard University Press, 1978.

Anderson, Benedict. *Imagined Communities: Reflections on the Origin and Spread of Nationalism*. 3rd edition. London and New York: Verso, 2006.

Bailey, Harry. *Salisbury Cathedral Library, a Brief Account of Its History and Contents*. Salisbury: Friends of Salisbury Cathedral, 1978.

Bainbridge, Simon. *Napoleon and English Romanticism*. Cambridge: Cambridge University Press, 1995.

———. *British Poetry and the Revolutionary and Napoleonic Wars: Visions of Conflict*. Oxford: Oxford University Press, 2003.

Barnard, H. C. *A Short History of English Education, 1760–1944*. London: University of London Press, 1947.

Barrell, John. *The Birth of Pandora and the Division of Knowledge*. London: Macmillan, 1992.

———. *Imagining the King's Death: Figurative Treason, Fantasies of Regicide, 1793–1796*. Oxford: Oxford University Press, 2000.

———. *The Spirit of Despotism: Invasions of Privacy in the 1790s*. Oxford: Oxford University Press, 2006.

Brooks, Chris. *The Gothic Revival*. London: Phaidon Press, 1999.

Carretta, Vincent. *George III and the Satirists from Hogarth to Byron*. Athens, Ca. & London: University of Georgia Press, 1990.

Chandler, James K. *Wordsworth's Second Nature: A Study of the Poetry and Politics*. Chicago and London: University of Chicago Press, 1984.

———. *England in 1819: The Politics of Literary Culture and the Case of Romantic Historicism*. Chicago and London: University of Chicago Press, 1998.

Chandler, James K. and Gilmartin, Kevin. Eds. *Romantic Metropolis: The Urban Scene of British Culture, 1780–1840*. Cambridge: Cambridge University Press, 2005.

Chaplin, Sue. *The Gothic and the Rule of Law, 1764–1820*. Basingstoke and New York: Palgrave Macmillan, 2005.

Clark, Kenneth. *The Gothic Revival*. 3rd edition. London: John Murray, 1962.

Clery, E. J. and Miles, Robert. Eds. *Gothic Documents, a Sourcebook 1700–1820*. Manchester: Manchester University Press, 2000.

Coleman, Deirdre. "Re-living Jacobinism: Wordsworth and the Convention of Cintra." *The Yearbook of English Studies*, 19 (1989), 144–61.
Colley, Linda. *Britons: Forging the Nation, 1797–1837.* London: Vintage, 1996.
Collini, Stefan, Whatmore, Richard, and Young, Brian. Eds. *Economy, Polity, and Society: British Intellectual History, 1750–1950.* Cambridge: Cambridge University Press, 2000.
Connell, Philip. *Romanticism, Economics and the Question of "Culture."* Oxford: Oxford University Press, 2001.
———. "British Identities and the Politics of Ancient Poetry in Later Eighteenth-Century England." *The Historical Journal*, 49:1 (2006), 182–89.
Corston, William. *A Brief Sketch of the Life of Joseph Lancaster.* London: Harvey, Darton, & Co., 1840.
Craig, David M. *Robert Southey and Romantic Apostasy: Political Argument in Britain, 1780–1840.* Woodbridge: Boydell Press, 2007.
Crook, J. Mordaunt. *John Carter and the Mind of the Gothic Revival.* London: Maney & Son Ltd. and the Society of Antiquaries of London, 1995.
Danziger, Danny and Gillingham, John. *1215: The Year of Magna Carta.* London: Hodder & Stoughton, 2003.
Davies, Damian Walford. *Presences that Disturb: Models of Romantic Identity in the Literature and Culture of the 1790s.* Cardiff: University of Wales Press, 2002.
Davis, Alex. *Chivalry and Romance in the English Renaissance.* Cambridge: D. S. Brewer, 2003.
DeLillo, Don. "In the Ruins of the Future: Reflections on Terror and Loss in the Shadow of September." *Harper's Magazine* (December 2001), 33–40.
De Man, Paul. *The Rhetoric of Romanticism.* New York: Columbia University Press, 1984.
Duley, Anthony J. *The Medieval Clock at Salisbury Cathedral.* Much Wenlock, Shropshire: RJL Smith & Associates, 1997.
Duncan, Ian. *Scott's Shadow: The Novel in Romantic Edinburgh.* Princeton, NJ: Princeton University Press, 2007.
Ellis, Markman. "'Spectacles within Doors': Panoramas of London in the 1790s." *Romanticism*, 14:2 (2008), 133–148.
Erdman, David V., "Milton! Thou Shouldst Be Living." *The Wordsworth Circle*, 19:1 (1988), 2–8.
———. "Coleridge, Wordsworth, and the Wedgwood Fund." *Bulletin of the New York Public Library* 60 (1956), 425–43, 487–507.
Eward, Suzanne. *Salisbury Cathedral Library.* 1983. National Library of Scotland shelfmark HP4.84.1069.
Farina, Jonathan. Review Article. *The Wordsworth Circle*, 38:4 (2007), 177–79.
Fay, Elizabeth. *Romantic Medievalism: History and the Romantic Literary Ideal.* Basingstoke and New York: Palgrave Macmillan, 2002.

Ferris, Ina. "Antiquarian Authorship: D'Israeli's Miscellany of Literary Curiosity and the Question of Secondary Genres." *Studies in Romanticism*, 45.4 (2006), 523–42.

Finch, John Alban. "Wordsworth, Coleridge, and the Recluse, 1798–1814." Unpublished Cornell University thesis. 1964.

Fisher, Herbert A. L. *Studies in Napoleonic Statesmanship, Germany.* Oxford: Clarendon Press, 1903.

Foakes, R. A. "'Thriving Prisoners': Coleridge, Wordsworth and the Child at School." *Studies in Romanticism*, 28.2 (1989), 187–206.

Fulford, Tim. *Landscape, Liberty and Authority: Poetry, Criticism and Politics from Thomson to Wordsworth.* Cambridge: Cambridge University Press, 1996.

Fulford, Tim and Hutchings, Kevin. Eds. *Native Americans and Anglo-American Culture, 1750–1850: The Indian Atlantic.* Cambridge: Cambridge University Press, 2009.

Galperin, William H. *The Return of the Visible in British Romanticism.* Baltimore, MD and London: Johns Hopkins University Press, 1993.

Gamer, Michael. *Romanticism and the Gothic: Genre, Reception, and Canon Formation.* Cambridge: Cambridge University Press, 2000.

Garrett, James M. *Wordsworth and the Writing of the Nation.* Aldershot, UK: Ashgate, 2008.

Garrioch, David. "Regeneration." Review Article. *London Review of Books*, 27:21 (November 3, 2005).

Gatrell, Vic. *City of Laughter: Sex and Satire in Eighteenth-Century London.* London: Atlantic Books, 2006.

George, Mary Dorothy. *Catalogue of Political and Personal Satires Preserved in the Department of Prints and Drawings in the British Museum.* 11 vols. London: British Museum Publications Limited, 1870–1954.

Gibbons, Luke. *Edmund Burke and Ireland: Aesthetics, Politics, and the Colonial Sublime.* Cambridge: Cambridge University Press, 2003.

Gill, Stephen. *Wordsworth and the Victorians.* Oxford: Clarendon Press, 1998.

———. Ed. *The Cambridge Companion to Wordsworth.* Cambridge: Cambridge University Press, 2003.

Gilmartin, Kevin. *Writing against Revolution: Literary Conservatism in Britain, 1790–1832.* Cambridge: Cambridge University Press, 2007.

Godfrey, Richard and Hallett, Mark. *James Gillray, The Art of Caricature.* London: Tate Gallery Publishing, 2001.

Gravil, Richard. *Wordsworth's Bardic Vocation, 1787–1842.* Basingstoke and New York: Palgrave Macmillan, 2003.

Greenblatt, Stephen. *Learning to Curse.* London: Routledge, 1990.

———. *Hamlet in Purgatory.* Princeton, NJ: Princeton University Press, 2002.

Grenby, M. O. "'A Conservative Woman Doing Radical Things': Sarah Trimmer and *The Guardian of Education*." Essay in *Culturing the Child, 1690–1914, Essays in Memory of Mitzi Myers.* Ed. Donelle Ruwe. Oxford: Scarecrow Press, 2005.

Groom, Nick. *The Making of Percy's Reliques*. Oxford: Clarendon Press, 1999.

———. "'The Purest English': Ballads and the English Literary Dialect." *The Eighteenth Century: Theory and Interpretation*, 47:2–3 (2006), 179–202.

Hartman, Geoffrey. *Wordsworth's Poetry, 1787–1814*. New Haven: Yale University Press, 1975.

Hearn, Fil. *Ideas That Shaped Buildings*. Cambridge, MA: MIT Press, 2003.

Herr, Richard. *The Eighteenth-Century Revolution in Spain*. Princeton, NJ: Princeton University Press, 1969.

Hickey, Alison. *Impure Conceits: Rhetoric and Ideology in Wordsworth's "Excursion."* Stanford, CA: Stanford University Press, 1997.

Hill, Christopher. *Puritanism and Revolution*. London: Panther Books, 1968.

Hobsbawm, E. J. and Ranger, Terence. Eds. *The Invention of Tradition*. Cambridge: Cambridge University Press, 1983.

Holt, J. C. *Magna Carta*. Cambridge: Cambridge University Press, 1965.

Horne, Alistair. *The Age of Napoleon*. London: Phoenix, 2004.

Janowitz, Anne. *England's Ruins: Poetic Purpose and the National Landscape*. Oxford: Basil Blackwood, 1990.

Johnston, Kenneth R. *Wordsworth and The Recluse*. New Haven and London: Yale University Press, 1984.

———. *The Hidden Wordsworth: Poet, Lover, Rebel, Spy*. New York and London: W. W. Norton & Company, 1998.

Keen, Paul. "Foolish Knowledge: The Commercial Modernity of the Periodical Press." *European Romantic Review*, 19:3 (2008), 199–218.

Kliger, Samuel. *The Goths in England, a Study in Seventeenth and Eighteenth Century Thought*. Cambridge, MA: Harvard University Press, 1952.

Korte, Barbara, Schneider, Ralf, and Lethbridge, Stefanie. Eds. *Anthologies of British Poetry: Critical Perspectives from Literary and Cultural Studies*. Amsterdam: Rodopi, 2000.

Kuist, James M. *The Nicholas File of "The Gentleman's Magazine."* Wisconsin and London: University of Wisconsin Press, 1982.

Levinson, Marjorie. *Wordsworth's Great Period Poems: Four Essays*. Cambridge: Cambridge University Press, 1986.

Linebaugh, Peter. *The London Hanged: Crime and Civil Society in the Eighteenth Century*. 2nd edition. London: Verso, 2003.

Liu, Alan. *Wordsworth: The Sense of History*. Stanford: Stanford University Press, 1989.

Lovett, Gabriel H. *Napoleon and the Birth of Modern Spain*. 2 vols. New York: New York University Press, 1965.

Manly, Susan. *Language, Custom and Nation in the 1790s: Locke, Tooke, Wordsworth, Edgeworth*. Aldershot, UK: Ashgate, 2007.

Matthew, H. C. G. and Harrison, Brian. Eds. *Oxford Dictionary of National Biography*. 60 vols. Oxford: Oxford University Press, 2004.

McCalman, Iain. Ed. *Oxford Companion to the Romantic Age*. Oxford and New York: Oxford University Press, 1999.

———. "The Virtual Infernal: Philippe de Loutherbourg, William Beckford and the Spectacle of the Sublime." *Romanticism on the Net*, 46 (May 2007).

McKechnie, William Sharp. *Magna Carta, A Commentary on the Great Charter of King John*. 2nd edition. Glasgow: James Maclehose and Sons, 1914.

Moorman, Mary. *William Wordsworth, a Biography*. 2 vols. Oxford: Clarendon Press, 1957–65.

Mortensen, Peter. " 'The Descent of Odin': Wordsworth, Scott and Southey among the Norsemen." *Romanticism*, 6:2 (2000), 211–33.

Murphy, James. "Religion, the State, and Education in England." *History of Education Quarterly*, 8:1 (1968), 3–34.

O'Callaghan, Joseph F. *Reconquest and Crusade in Medieval Spain*. Philadelphia: University of Pennsylvania Press, 2003.

Oman, Charles. *A History of the Peninsular War*. 7 vols. Oxford: Clarendon Press, 1902–30.

Otto, Peter. "Between the Virtual and the Actual: Robert Barker's Panorama of London and the Multiplication of the Real in Late Eighteenth-Century London." *Romanticism on the Net*, 46 (May 2007)

Pallister, Anne. *Magna Carta: The Heritage of Liberty*. Oxford: Clarendon Press, 1971.

Petre, F. Loraine. *Napoleon's Conquest of Prussia, 1806*. London: Greenhill Books, 1993.

Pfau, Thomas. *Romantic Moods: Paranoia, Trauma, and Melancholy, 1790–1840*. Baltimore, MD: Johns Hopkins University Press, 2005.

Pocock, J. G. A. *The Ancient Constitution and the Feudal Law*. 2nd edition. Cambridge: Cambridge University Press, 1987.

Postema, Gerald J. *Bentham and the Common Law Tradition*. Oxford: Oxford University Press, 1986.

Pratt, Lynda. Ed., *Robert Southey and the Contexts of English Romanticism*. Aldershot, UK: Ashgate, 2006.

Punter, David. *The Literature of Terror: A History of Gothic Fictions from 1765 to the Present Day*. 2nd edition. London: Longman, 1996.

Read, Jan. *War in the Peninsula*. London: Faber and Faber, 1977.

Reed, Mark L. *Wordsworth: The Chronology of the Middle Years, 1800–1815*. Cambridge, MA: Harvard University Press, 1975.

Richardson, Alan. *Literature, Education, and Romanticism: Reading as Social Practice, 1780–1832*. Cambridge: Cambridge University Press, 1994.

Roe, Nicholas. *Wordsworth and Coleridge: The Radical Years*. Oxford: Clarendon Press, 1988.

———. *The Politics of Nature: William Wordsworth and Some Contemporaries*. 2nd edition. Basingstoke and New York: Palgrave Macmillan, 2002.

Rovee, Christopher. *Imagining the Gallery: The Social Body of British Romanticism*. Palo Alto, CA: Stanford University Press, 2006.
Saglia, Diego. *Poetic Castles in Spain: British Romanticism and Figurations of Iberia*. Amsterdam-Atlanta: Rodopi, 2000.
St Clair, William. *Lord Elgin and the Marbles*. London: Oxford University Press, 1967.
———. *The Reading Nation in the Romantic Period*. Cambridge: Cambridge University Press, 2004.
Salmon, David. Ed. *The Practical Parts of Lancaster's "Improvements" and Bell's "Experiment."* London: Cambridge University Press, 1932.
Schneider, Ben Ross. *Wordsworth's Cambridge Education*. Cambridge: Cambridge University Press, 1957.
Schoenfield, Mark. *The Professional Wordsworth: Law, Labor & the Poet's Contract*. Athens and London: University of Georgia Press, 1996.
Scott, Robert A. *The Gothic Enterprise: A Guide to Understanding the Medieval Cathedral*. Berkley, Los Angeles, and London: University of California Press, 2003.
Simonsen, Peter. *Wordsworth and Word-Preserving Arts: Typographic Inscription, Ekphrasis and Posterity in the Later Work*. Basingstoke and New York: Palgrave Macmillan, 2007.
Simpson, David. *Wordsworth's Historical Imagination*. New York and London: Methuen, 1987.
———. *9/11: The Culture of Commemoration*. Chicago: University Of Chicago Press, 2006.
Smith, Allan Lloyd and Sage, Victor. Eds. *Gothick Origins and Innovations*. Amsterdam-Atlanta, GA: Rodopi, 1994.
Smith, Olivia. *The Politics of Language, 1791–1819*. Oxford: Clarendon Press, 1984.
Smith, R. J. *The Gothic Bequest, Medieval Institutions in British Thought, 1688–1863*. Cambridge: Cambridge University Press, 1987.
Spooner, Catherine and McEvoy, Emma. Eds. *The Routledge Companion to Gothic*. London: Routledge, 2007.
Stroud, Daphne. *Richard Poore and the Building of Salisbury Cathedral*. Salisbury: the Dean and Chapter of Salisbury, 1996.
Swann, Karen. "Public Transport: Adventuring on Wordsworth's Salisbury Plain." *English Literary History*, 55:4 (1988), 811–34.
Thomas, Sophie. *Romanticism and Visuality: Fragments, History, and Spectacle*. New York and London: Routledge, 2008.
Thompson, E. P. *The Making of the English Working Class*. London: Gollancz, 1980.
Thompson, John. *The Madras College 1833–1983*. Fife Educational Resources Centre, 1983.
Turner, Ralph V. *Magna Carta through the Ages*. Harlow: Pearson, 2003.
Watson, J. R. *Romanticism and War: A Study of British Romantic Period Writers and the Napoleonic Wars*. Basingstoke and New York: Palgrave Macmillan, 2003.

Watt, James. *Contesting the Gothic: Fiction, Genre and Cultural Conflict, 1764–1832.* Cambridge: Cambridge University Press, 1999.

Watts, Michael. *The Dissenters: From the Reformation to the French Revolution.* Oxford: Clarendon Press, 1985.

Weston, Rowland. "Politics, Passion, and the 'Puritan Temper': Godwin's Critique of Enlightened Modernity." *Studies in Romanticism*, 41.3 (2002), 445–70.

Wiley, Michael. *Romantic Geography: Wordsworth and Anglo-European Spaces.* London: Macmillan Press, 1998.

Woodcock, Thomas and Robinson, John Martin. Eds. *The Oxford Guide to Heraldry.* Oxford: Oxford University Press, 1988.

Woodring, Carl. *Politics in English Romantic Poetry.* Cambridge, MA: Harvard University Press, 1970.

Woof, Robert. Ed. *William Wordsworth: The Critical Heritage, Volume I, 1793–1820.* London and New York: Routledge, 2001.

Wordsworth, Jonathan. *The Borders of Vision.* Oxford: Clarendon Press, 1982.

Wright, Paul. "Vile Saxons and Ancient Britons: Wordsworth, the Ambivalent Welsh Tourist." In *Dangerous Diversity: The Changing Faces of Wales, Essays in Honour of Tudor Bevan.* Ed. Katie Gramich and Andrew Hiscock. Cardiff: University of Wales Press, 1998.

Wu, Duncan. *Wordsworth's Reading, 1770–1799.* Cambridge: Cambridge University Press, 1993.

———. *Wordsworth's Reading, 1800–1815.* Cambridge: Cambridge University Press, 1995.

Yates, Frances A. *The Art of Memory.* 2nd edition. London, Melbourne and Henley: Ark Paperbacks, 1984.

# Index

Relatively substantial discussions of persons, topics, and texts are indicated by bold type. Except where otherwise indicated, texts are collated under authors. Titles are given in short form. The Preface is not indexed; *see also* ix–xii, for 9/11; gothicism, architecture; historicism.

9/11, **1–2**, 3, 23

Abbé Barruel, 154
Abramson, Daniel, 34
Alfred the Great, 75, 86, 87, 113
Altick, Richard, 176
American War of Independence, 84, 133
*Analytical Review*, 73
Anderson, Benedict, 53, 163
Anglicanism, 32, 40, 119–20
   and education, 144–6, 150–61, 163–6
*Annual Register*, 40, 100, 131, 185n
*Anti-Jacobin*, 43
*Anti-Jacobin Review*, 154
antiquarianism, 3–6, **10–14**, 20–21, 26, 32–3, 34–6, **41–7**, 51–2, 55–7, 59–60, 61, **69–88**, 92, 94–5, 101, 106–7, 109, 111–16, 122–6, 127, 130, 132, 136–7, 143–4, 156, 165–6, 171, 173–4, 175, 185–6n, 187–8n, 189–90n
   *see also* gothicism, Saxon/s/ism, *and compare* historicism
apostasy (political), **21–2**, **39–41**, 71, 102, 110–11, 164–5, 166–8, 169
architecture, *see under* gothicism
   *see also named buildings*

Arnold, Matthew, 14
*Athenaeum*, 62, 185n
*Augustan Review*, 15, 28–9, 59

Baatz, Christine, 4, 172
Bacon, Nathaniel, 75, 187n
Bainbridge, Simon, 11, 113, 114, 120, 189n
ballads, **4–5**, 11–13, 20, 43–4, 54–5, 173–4
Barbauld, Anna, **29–30**, 31
Barker, Robert, **176–78**, 180
Barnard, H. C., 152, 157, 161, 164
Barrell, John, 20, 83, 101, 137, 186n
Basedow, Johann Bernard, 155
Beaumont, Sir George, 17, 26, 41, 170, 174
Beaumont, Lady Margaret Willes, 15, 31
Beham, Hans Sebald, 189n
Bell, Andrew, 22, 51, **144–51**, 155–6, 158, 159, 160–61, 163–7, 190n
Bentham, Jeremy, 34, 165
Blackstone, William, 33–4, 81, 82, 83–4, 90, 129–30, 188n
Blair, Hugh, 75, 187n
Blake, William, 29
Bolingbroke, Henry Saint John, 75, 187n
Bonaparte, Joseph, 99, 103, 119

Bonaparte, Napoleon, 9, 22, 25, 34, 36, 40, 56, 68, **97–100**, 101–4, 106–9, 111–21, 126–8, 130, 139, 140, 151, 162, 163, 180, 186n, 188–9n
Bourgoing, Jean François, 98, 103, 123, 188n
Bowman, Thomas, 75, 187n
Brand, John, 5, 20
Brewster, David, 170
Brissot, Jacques Pierre, 86
Brompton parish church, 160, 191n
Brooks, Chris, 32, 62, 63
Brougham, Henry, 161
Bulwer-Lytton, Edward, 169
Burdett, Francis, 37, 153
Burke, Edmund: 2, 3, 7, 8, 9, 25, 34, 42, **46–9**, 50, 51, 55, 56, 64–5, 66, 68, 69, 70, 80, 84, 86, 91, 92, 97–8, 105–6, 108–9, 116, 122, 124, 126, 128, 129, **131–4**, 137–8, 141, 143, 144, 157, 158, 159, 161, 162, 163, 165, 178
WORKS:
*Reflections*, 8, 34, **46–8**, 49, 50, 64, 68, 69, 84, 91, 108–9, 122, 126, **131–3**, 134, 143, 157, 158, 159, 163
*Regicide Peace*, 25, **48–9**, 50, **105–6**, 128, 133, 137–8, 158
*Sublime and Beautiful*, 9, 56
Burnet, Gilbert, 188n
Byron, George Gordon, Lord, 14, 15, 29, 41, 114, 183

Cádiz Constitution (1812), 107, 130, 140
*see also* Cortes
Caesar, Julius, 106, 187–8n
Calvert, William, 70
Carretta, Vincent, 68
Carruthers, Mary, 58
Carter, John, **34–6**, 37, 66
Cartwright, Major John, 45

Catholic/s/ism, 2, 5, 12, 17–18, 32, 40, 47, 49, 50–51, **119–22**, 130–31, 150–51, 153, 155, 159, 161, 173, 185n
Celts, 71, 74, **75–7**, 84, 90, 92, 93, 94, 125, 165, 186n, 187–8n
Druids, 69–71, **72–3**, 74, 75, **76–7**, 84, 85, 86, 88, 89, 91, 92, 94, 165–6, 186n, 187n, 188n
*compare* Goths
Chandler, James, 5, 12, 20, 29, 31, 52–3, 59, 149, 162–3, 165, 179, 185n
Chaplin, Sue, 5
Charlotte, Queen of Great Britain, 154, 177–8
Charterhouse, 145, 152
Chatterton, Thomas, 73, 187n
chivalry, 3–4, 5, 8–9, 11, 31, 33, 44, 46–7, 50, 55, 105, 109, **112–14**, 116, 120, 121, 143–4
*The Christian Observer*, 130–31
El Cid, 22, 112, 123
Clark, Kenneth, 35, 62, 78
Clarkson, Catherine, 185n
Clarkson, Thomas, 149
classicism, 3, 4, 5, 10–11, 17, 18, 19, 34, **40–41**, 55, 56–7, 59–60, 61, 108, 124, 142, 169
Clery, Emma, 47, 187n
Coke, Edward, 20
Coleman, Deirdre, 109, 131, 141, 142
Coleridge, Samuel Taylor, 6, 7, 8, 11–12, **14–16**, 22, 25, 59, 60–61, 65, 70–71, 101, 107, 112, **114–15**, 116, 135, 145, 146, 149, 150, 154, 158, 159, 160, 164, 183, 188–9n, 189–90n
WORKS:
"The Ancient Germans," 189–90n

*Biographia Literaria*, 15, 16
"Buonaparte and the Emperor
    Julian," 107, 188–9n
"Christabel," 14–15
*Church and State*, 146, 164–5
*The Friend*, 115, 150
"Frost at Midnight," 149
"The Gothic Mind" [lectures
    1818], 7, 59, 60–61
*Letters on the Spaniards*, 22,
    **114–15**
"Religious Musings," 70
"The Rime of the Ancient
    Mariner," 14
Letters, 15–16, 25, 60–61, 101,
    112, 135
Colley, Linda, 68, 90, 186
Cologne, Cathedral of, 63
common law, *see* Constitution,
    Gothic
*Common Sense*, 32, 33, 55
Connell, Philip, 145, 146, 161, 185n
*The Connoisseur*, 172
Constitution, "Gothic," 2, 7, 10,
    20, 21, 25–6, **32–4**, 35,
    **36–9**, 44–6, **47–52**, 64–6,
    73, 75, 78, 81–3, 84, **86–9**,
    91, 92, 97–8, **102–9**, 113,
    115, 118–20, 122, 125–7,
    128, 129–35, 136, 140,
    146, 154, 156, 158–9,
    162–3, 165, 178, 186n,
    187–8n, 191n
Convention of Cintra, 101, 102,
    **116–17**, 127–8, 135,
    139, 141
Cortes, **103–4**, 106, 107, 108, 112,
    **124–6**, 130–31, 135,
    140, 188n
    *see also* Cádiz Constitution (1812)
Cotton, Sir Robert, 81
*The Courier*, 102, 114, 119, 121,
    188n, 189n
Craig, David, 21, 146
Crook, J. Mordaunt, 35
Croker, John Wilson, 29, 30, 189n

Cruikshank, George, 120, 189n
Cuesta, Gregorio García de la, 97
custom, *see* tradition; *see also*
    antiquarianism

Darwin, Erasmus, 73, 187n
David, Jacques Louis, 69
Davies, Damien Walford, 45, 71,
    83, 86, 87
Davis, Alex, 4
Daguerre, Louis, 171
DeLillo, Don, 1
De Man, Paul, 182
De Quincey, Thomas, 102, 111, 114
De Selincourt, Ernest, 80
Dickens, Charles, 166–7
Digby, Kenelm, 6, 66
Diorama, **171–2**, 174
D'Israeli, Isaac, 26
dissenters, 8, 148, 151, 153, 155,
    156, 159
Drayton, Michael, 55, 73, 185n,
    187n
Druids, *see under* Celts
Duncan, Ian, 92

East India Company, 46, 146, 148
*Eclectic Review*, 11, 25
Edgeworth, Maria, 149
*Edinburgh Review*, 5, 27, 28, 35,
    109–110, 111, 148
Edkins, Jenny, 1
education, 22, 23, 26, 47, 50–51,
    57–9, 66, 77, 137–8, 141,
    **143–68**, 183
Eidophusikon, 171, 178
ekphrasis, 179–182
Ellis, Markman, 177
Engl/and/ish-ness, 2, 4–5, 7–8,
    9–10, 12, 13, 25–6, **30–37**,
    39, 44–6, 48, 52–6, 59–61,
    65, 67, 68, 71, 72–3, **74–84**,
    86–93, 106, 112–16,
    119–22, 132, 136–7, 141–2,
    148, 149, 159, 182–3
    *see also* nationalism

Erdman, David, 115, 149, 158, 186n, 189n
*European Magazine*, 14
*The Examiner*, 2, 21, 28, 39, 40, 63, 99, 104, 117, 139, 164, 185n
Eyre, Sir James, 38

Fairer, David, 7
Fairfax, Lord Thomas, 91
Farina, Jonathan, 12
Fay, Elizabeth, 6, 9, 174
Feinaigle, Gregor von, 59
Fenwick, Isabella, 13, 61
Ferdinand VII, King of Spain, 97, 98, 103, 107, 123, 130
Ferguson, Frances, 165
Ferris, Ina, 26
Foakes, R. A., 51, 145
Fox, Charles James, 37, 65, 161
Fox, Joseph, 160
fragment/ation, 9, 17–18, 21, **26–30**, 41, 61, 62, 63, 66, 80, **93**, 94, 100–101, 106, 111–12, 137–40, 142, 179–80
*compare* ruin/ation
Franklin, Benjamin, 134, 190n
French Revolution, 2–3, 8, 21, 30, 34, 35, 40, 45, 46–8, 55, 64, 65, 67–70, 72, 84, 86–7, 89–90, 92, 97, 105, 106, 108, 109, 110, 116, 117–19, 122, 126, 128, 131–3, 140, 152, 154, 157, 159, 161–3, 186n, 188n
Fulford, Timothy, 39, 95, 185n

Galperin, William, 169, 177
Gamer, Michael, 6–7, 34
Garrett, James, 21, 27, 30, 37–8, 183
Garrioch, David, 97
Gatrell, Vic, 67, 68, 186n
*Gentleman's Magazine*, 26, **32–3**, **35–6**, 37, 39, 65, 123, 186n

George, Mary, 68, 120–21, 189n, 191n
George III, King of Great Britain, 2, 39, 67–8, 69, 151–2, 177–8, 190n
Gibbon, Edward, 125, 147
Gibbons, Luke, 47
Giddy, Davies, 157
Gifford, William, 28
Gill, Stephen, 25, 62, 71–2, 91, 187n
Gillray, James, **67–70**, 89, **113**, 114, **120**, **158**, 186n, 189n, 191n
Gilmartin, Kevin, 2, 35, 42, 43, 65, 146, 154, 164–5, 173, 179
Girtin, Thomas, 179
Glorious Revolution (1688–9), 32, 44, 84
Godoy, Manuel de, 107
Godwin, William, 43, 49–50, 52, 59, 60, 83, 148, 152
gothicism, 6–8, 22–3, 141
  architecture, 1–2, 3, 11, 17–19, 26, 32–3, **34–6**, **56–7**, 59, 61–2, 63, 77–8, 94–5, 129, 171
  literary form, **3–9**, 10–21, 25–31, 33–4, **36–45**, 47–9, **51–66**, 70–71, 75–7, 85, **90–95**, 100–102, 109–16, 124, 135, 137–42, 143–6, 147, 165–7, 169–71, 172–6, 182–3
  politics, 3, 8, 9–10, 20, 25–6, **29–56**, 64–6, **78–91**, 92–4, 101, **102–42**, 145–6, 150–51, **153–68**, 169, 172–3, 182–3
  *see also* antiquarianism, Saxon/s/ism, *and* historicism
Gothic Revival, 6, 26, 36, 61–2, 63, 66, 171
Gothic type, 172–6
Goths, 4, 10–11, 19, **44–7**, 48–9, 55–6, 59–60, 75–8, 105–7, 109, 111–13, 114, 115–16, 123–4, 125–6, 136–7, 187n, 189n

*see also* Saxon/s/ism, *and compare* Celts
"Gradgrind," 166–7
"La Gratitud al Inventor Ingles del Toro Español," front cover, 107–8, 113, 189n
Gravil, Richard, 46, 69, 70, 76, 165, 187n
Gray, Thomas, 57
Greenblatt, Stephen, 23, 30, 92
Grégoire, Henri, 86, 188n
Grenby, M. O., 154
Groom, Nick, 5, 7, 59–60, 76, 172
Gunpowder Plot, 2, 157, 158

Habeas corpus, 82, 83, 90
Hamlet, 1, 23, 109, 110, 116
*see also* Shakespeare, William
Hare, John, 48
Hartman, Geoffrey, 39
Hastings, Warren, 46
Hawkins, J. S., 35–6
Hazlitt, William, vi, 2, 12, 21–22, 25, 28, 29, 35, **39–41**, 62–3, **164–5**, 169, 185n
Hearn, Fil, 34
Hemans, Felicia, 113–14
Hercules, 69, 89, 99, **107–8**, 156, 162, 189n
*see also* Samson
Herr, Richard, 106, 107
Hickey, Alison, 145
Hill, Christopher, 44, 48
historicism, **1–6**, **7–8**, 10, 11, 17–18, 23, **29–31**, **52–6**, **66**, 91–3, 130, 166, **171–6**
*see also* gothicism, *and compare* antiquarianism
Hobbes, Thomas, 68–9, 87
Hobhouse, John, 41
Hobsbawm, Eric, 130
Hollingsworth, N. J., 153
Hone, William, 20
Horne, 40

Hunt, Leigh, 18, 99
Hurd, Richard, 3–4, 6, 10, 16, 34, 44, 47, 60, 75, 185n, 187n, 189n

Imison, John, 171

Jacobinism, 45, 49, 55, 87, 100, 105, 109, 110–11, 126, 133, 140, 141, 146, 151–4, 158, 163
*see also* republicanism
Janowitz, Anne, 74–5
Jeffrey, Francis, 27, 28, 29, 185n
Jesuits, 2, 40, 131, 185n
Johnson, Joseph, 18
Johnson, Samuel, 82
Johnson, Samuel, Dr., 101
Johnson, William, 145, 190n
Johnston, Kenneth, 16, 18, 36, 40, 63, 65, 79, 80
Jones, Inigo, 17, 72
Jones, Robert, 71
Jordanes, 189n
Jovellanos, Gaspar Melchor de, **106**, 109
Juries, 38, 75, 83, 90, 148

Keats, John, 62, 183
Keen, Paul, 26, 42
Kelly, Theresa, 15
Ketcham, Carl H., 111, 113
Kliger, Samuel, 32, 33, 46, 136, 189n
Knight, Richard Payne, 56

Lakanal, Joseph, 162, 163
"Lake School," 6, 7, 11, 12, 14, 15, 20, 21, 22, 27, 66, 114, 141, 145, 146, 160, 164–5, 166, 169, 183
Lamb, Charles, 12, 28, 29, 62, 175
Lancaster, Joseph, 51, 147, 148, 149, **151–2**, 153, 154, 155, 156, 157, 158, 159, 160, 161, 164, 165, 167, 190–91n

Landon, Carol, 80, 180
Landor, Walter Savage, 113, 114
Langley, Batty, 11
LCS (London Corresponding Society), 38, 42, **82–3**
Lemprière, John, 82, 99
Levinson, Marjorie, 58
Levy, Maurice, 8
Linebaugh, Peter, 54
Liu, Alan, 69, 70, 187n
Locke, John, 172
Longman, Thomas, 18, 25
Louis XVI, King of the French, 68, 89
Lovell, Robert, 76
Lovett, Gabriel H., 98, 99, 100, 106, 107, 108, 130
Lowther, William, Earl of Lonsdale, 161

Mackintosh, James, 5, 17
Macpherson, James, 76
Madras system, *see* education
Magna Carta, 33, 77, **81–2, 83–4**, 188n
Malcolm, James P., 18
Maldonado, José Muñoz, 123
Mallet, Paul-Henri, 70, 125, 126, 187n, 189–90n
Malmesbury Abbey, 35
Malthus, Thomas, 152
Manly, Susan, 3, 5, 20, 42, 43–4, 52, 185n
Marx, Karl, 91
Mathews, William, 50, 51, 83, 91
Mathias, Thomas James, 51
McCalman, Iain, 34, 186n
Mckechnie, William Sharp, 84, 188n
medievalism, *see* gothicism
memory, art of, 57–9
Methodists, 8, 159
Miles, Robert, 5–6, 47, 187n
Milton, John, 9, 18–19, 31, 52, 55, 60–61, 84, 99, 108, 112, 132, 134, **135–7**, 139, 189n, 190n

"Ministry of All the Talents," 158, 161, 191n
monks, 47, 50, 51, 58, 98, 120, 143, 159, 182, 189n
Montesquieu, Charles de, Baron, 32, 45, 49, 75, 78
Moorman, Mary, 65, 102, 161, 191n
More, Hannah, 2, 154, 172–3
Mortensen, Peter, 51–2, 125, 187n
Muir, Thomas, 73
Myers, Mitzi, 154

nationalism, 7–9, 12, 20–21, 22, 29–30, **34–9**, 43–6, 52–6, 65, 68, 74–7, 91–2, 97–8, 100, **103–7**, 109, 113–16, 119–21, 124, 127, 128, 130, 140, 151–2, **161–4**, 172–3, 178, 182–3, 186n, 187–8n
*see also* Engl/and/ish-ness
Newton, Richard, 67, 186n
Newton, Sir Isaac, 63
Norman Conquest, 9, **44–5, 48**, 55–6, 74, 77, 81, 82

O'Callaghan, Joseph F., 123, 188n
Odin, 76, 125, 146, 147, 148, 190n
Oman, Charles, 98, 99
Otto, Peter, 176, 177, 178

Paine, Tom, 2, 46, 47, 48, 50, 52, 64, 68, 69, 70, 73–4, 82, 91, 128, 135, 156, 163, 186n
Palafox, José de, 103, 104, 108, 113
Pallister, Anne, 81, 82
Panofsky, Erwin, 58
Panorama, 176–181
Parliament, *see* Constitution, Gothic, *and* Saxon/s/ism
Parochial Schools Bill (1807), 157–8, 161
Pascal, Blaise, 185n
Pasley, C. W., 20
Pelayo, 111, 114, 115–6, 123, 126

Peninsular War, 22, **97–100**, **101–6**, **107–17**, 118–25, 126–31, 134–5, 136, 139, 140, 141–2, 146, 189n
Perceval, Spencer, 153
Percy, Thomas, **4–5**, 8, 34, 44, 46–7, 70, **75–6**, **125–6**, 151, 185n, 187n, 189n
periodicals, culture of, 26–7, **41–3**
  *see also individual titles*
Peter, Hugh, 48, 91
Petrarch, Francesco, 135
Pfau, Thomas, 38
Pitt, William, 2, 47, 65, 70, 74, 83, 92, 152, 186n
Pocock, J. G. A., 35, 136
Pope, Alexander, 9, 60
Postema, Gerald J., 34
Poynter, John, 185n
Price, Richard, 48, 70, 157, 186n
Pugin, Augustus Welby, 6, 36
Punter, David, 9

*Quarterly Review*, 7–8, 28, 29–30, 37, 62, 78, 145, 153
Quintilian, 57–8

Radcliffe, Ann, 7, 113
Read, Jan, 103, 108
reconquista, 107, 111, 115, 123, 188n
Reed, Mark, 18, 144, 190
Reeve, Clara, 113
Reeve, John, 43
Reform Act (1832), 65–6
Reformation, 5, 94, 136, 146, 154, 156, 165
republicanism, 22, 32, 34, 38, 42–3, 45, 46, 49–50, 64–5, 68, 70, 71, 73–4, 81, **86–9**, 91, 92, 97, 109, 110, 118, 130, 134–5, 140, 147, 162
  *see also* Saxon/s/ism *and* Jacobinism
Reynolds, Sir Joshua, 177

Richardson, Alan, 146, 149, 152, 164, 167, 190n
Ritson, Joseph, 5, 44–5
Robespierre, Maximilian, 87
Robinson, Henry Crabb, 13, 29
Robison, John, 154, 155
Roderick, 22, 107, 111, 114, 115–6, 120, 123, 171, 183
Roe, Nicholas, 45, 49–50, 64, 70, 87, 118, 187n, 188n
Rousseau, Jean-Jacques, 42, 61, 69, 149, 154–5
Rovee, Christopher, 41, 89
Rowe, Nicholas, 4–5
Rowlandson, Thomas, 186n
Rozas, Calvo de, 107, 109
ruin/ation, 1–2, 5, 7, **28–30**, 35, 37, 38–9, 41, 47, 61, 63, 66, 94–5, **97–101**, 104, 106, 107, 108, 118, 121, 128, 132, 140, 156–9, **171–2**, 174, 188n, 191n
  *compare* fragment/ation
Ruiz, Dr, 105
Russett, Margaret, 109

Saglia, Diego, 113, 114, 115, 120, 121
St Clair, William, 25, 41
St. Gall, Riechenau, 58
St. Oswald's church, Grasmere, 10, 56–7, 78
St. Paul's Cathedral, 17–19
St. Stephen's Chapel, 65
  *see also* Westminster, Palace of
Salisbury Cathedral, 75, 77–81, 82, 83–4, 90–91, 94
Salisbury Plain, 70, 71, 72–4, 78–80, 81, 83–4, 86–8, 90, 91, 93, 188n
Salmon, David, 152, 154, 156, 160, 190n, 191n
Sammes, Aylett, 69, 70, 71, 73, 85–6, 88, 186n, 187n
Samson, 99, 108, 114, 156
  *see also* Hercules

Saxon/s/ism: 8, 32–3, 35, **44–6**, 48, **52–6**, 72–3, 74, 75–7, 81, **86–9**, 136, 147, 185n, 187n
  *see also* antiquarianism, gothicism, *and* republicanism
Schoenfield, Mark, 17–18
Scott, John, 37
Scott, Robert A., 58, 81
Scott, Sir Walter, 3, **11–15**, 43, 66, 76, 92, 114, 116, 174
SCI (Society for Constitutional Information), 45, 82, 83
Shakespeare, William, 4–5, 6, 9, 52, 55, 59–60
  *see also* Hamlet
Shelley, Percy Bysshe, 62, 183
Sheridan, Richard Brinsley, 109
Simonsen, Peter, 169, 170, 174, 182
Simpson, David, 1, 166
Smith, Olivia, 185n
Smith, R. J., 45
Society of Antiquaries, 34, 77
Southey, Robert, 6, **7–8**, 21–2, 29, 51, 76, 101, 102, 111, 112–3, 114, **115–16**, 120, 144, 145, 146, **153–4**, 158–9, 160, 161, 164, 165, 171, 183
  WORKS:
  *Amadis of Gaul*, 112
  *Chronicle of the Cid*, 22, 112
  "The Death of Odin," 76
  *Letter to William Smith*, 21–2
  *New System of Education*, 51, **153–4**, 158–9, 161, 164
  *Palmerin of England*, 112
  journalism for *Quarterly Review*, 7–8, 37, 145, 153
  *Roderick*, 22, 111, **115–16**, 120, 171, 183
Southey, Tom, 112
Spanish Revolution, *see* Peninsular War
Spenser, Edmund, 3–4, 44, 91
Sterne, Laurence, 28

Stonehenge, **72–3**, 74–5, 78, 79, 90, **91–2**, 93
Stuart, Daniel, 110, 111, 135
Stukeley, William, 72, 75, 79, 90
Supreme Junta of Seville, 103, 104–5, 106, 119, 124–5, 126
Swann, Karen, 187n

Tacitus, 75, 106, 187n
*Tait's Magazine*, 62
Talleyrand, Charles Maurice de, 98
Temple, Richard, 32
Temple, William, 32
Tennyson, Lord Alfred, 66, 174
Thelwall, John, 45–6, **49–50**, 52, 55, 83, 118, 128, 185n, 189n
Thomas, Sophie, 41, 61, 169, 171, 177
Thompson, E. P., 159, 166
Thomson, James, 10, 17, 19, 60, 61, 63, 77, 90, 189n
*The Times*, 69, 103, 104, 108, 117, 172, 178, 185n
Tintern Abbey, 30, 58, 61, 71, **94–5**
Tipu Sultan, 148
Toland, John, 70
Tooke, John Horne, 2–3, 45, 83, 185n
tradition, 4–5, **12–13**, 21, 33–4, 42–4, 72–3, 86, 92, 104–5, 130, 175
  invented, **130**, 131
  *see also* antiquarianism
treason trials (1794), 2, **38–9**, 45, **83**, 158
Trimmer, Sarah, **154–7**, 167
Trinity College Chapel, 63–4, 65, 188n
Turner, Sharon, 46
Tweddell, John, 64, 84, 188n

Urquijo, Mariano Luis de, 97, 100, 101, 103, 108, 118

# Index    217

Verdier, Jean Antoine, 108
Verstegan, Richard, 44, 55–6, 75, 185n, 187n
virtuality, 21, 30, 37–9, 42, 64, 73–4, **79–82**, 92, 95, 105, 140, 170–71, 178
visuality, 23, 39, 57–9, 138–40, 158–9, **169–83**
Vortigern, 72–3

Walpole, Horace, 33, 51, 56, 60, 67
Warburton, William, 60, 78, 159
Warner, Richard, 94
Warton, Thomas, 18–19, 34, 35, 44–5, 77, 112, 185n
Waterloo, battle of, 84, 169, 176
Watson, J. R., 102, 109, 114, 152
Watt, James, 34, 113, 130
Watts, Michael, 91
Wedgwood, Thomas, 149
Wellesley, Arthur (Duke of Wellington), 37, 130
Westall, R. W., 171
Westminster, Palace of, 32, 37, 39, 65, 158, 164, 186n
Weston, Rowland, 59
Whitaker, Thomas, 12–13, 175
Whitbread, Samuel, 157, 158, 161
Wilberforce, William, 152
Wiley, Michael, 77, 79
Wilkes, John, 74, 82, 90
Williams, David, 45, 51, **86–8**, 89
Williams, Edward (Iolo Morganwg), 76, 83
Woodring, Carl, 145, 146, 166
Woof, Pamela, 37
Woof, Robert, 28, 29
Wordsworth, Christopher, 25–6, 29, 31–2, 145, 190n
Wordsworth, Dora, 65
Wordsworth, Dorothy, 37, 58, 145, 161
Wordsworth, Jonathan, 62, 63, 132, 138, 190n
Wordsworth, Richard, 83

Wordsworth, William, vi, 2, 3, 6, 7, 8–10, 11, 12–14, 15, **16–20**, 21, 22, 23, 25–32, 34, 36–41, 45, 46, **50–58**, 60–66, **70–81**, 82–7, 88–91, 92–5, 97, 100–102, 104, 110–12, 113, 114, 116, **117–30**, 131–36, 137–42, 143–6, 147–8, 149–51, 152, **159–68**, 169–71, 172, 173–6, 177, 179–83
Works:
"Adventures on Salisbury Plain" (1795–99), 93
"After-Thought," 182
*The Borderers*, 104
"Composed Upon Westminster Bridge," 179
*The Convention of Cintra*, 9, 22, 71, 94, 101–2, 104, 110–11, 114, 116, **117–120**, **121–25**, **126–30**, 131–32, 134–36, 137, **139–42**, 188n, 189n
*Descriptive Sketches*, 18
"Elegiac Stanzas," 170
*An Evening Walk*, 18
*The Excursion*, 9, 14, 15–16, 21, 22, 25–6, 27, 28–9, 30, 32, 39, 41, 58, 61, 62, 63, 65–6, 137, 144, 145, 159, 160, 161, 164, 180, 183, 185n, 190n; Book I, 25; Book II, 180–81; Book V, 9–10, 19, 40, 56–7, 78; Book IX, 39, 144, 162–4, 165–6, 167; "Preface," vi, 2, 7, 9, 13, 15–19, 21, 22, **25–29**, 30, 31–2, 36, 37, 39–40, 58–9, 60, 61–6, 94, **100–101**, 135, 137, **138–40**, 142, 144, 146, 159, **170**, 172, 183
"The Female Vagrant," 93
"The Force of Prayer," **173–5**
*Guide to the Lakes*, 39, 181–82
*Guilt and Sorrow*, 72, 80

Wordsworth, William
WORKS:—*Continued*
"Home at Grasmere," 16, 28, 90
"How Sweet the Walk," 179–80
"Is there a power that can sustain and cheer," 113
"Laodamia," 41
*Letter to the Bishop of Llandaff*, 50, 70, **88–9**, 118, 119, 128, 134
*Lyrical Ballads*, 7, 9, 13, 14, 16, 27, **51–5**, 93, 100, 147, 175, 176
  "Advertisement," 147
  "Preface," 7, 9, 13, 16, **51–4**, 175, 176
"Malham Cove," 61
"Ode, Intimations of Immortality," 110, 167
"Pelayo," 9, **111–12**, 126
*Peter Bell*, 183
*Poems* (1815), 19, 21, 27, 31, 170, 173, 175; "Preface," 21, 27, 170; "Essay, Supplementary to the Preface," 14, 19, 60
*Poems, in Two Volumes* (1807), 31, 100, 110
*The Prelude* (1799), 19–20
*The Prelude* (1805), 15, 16, 17, 19, 25, 27, 46, 62, 100, 117, 125, 135, 137, 149, 150, 159, 167, 179, 180; Book I, 16, 66, 74, 125, 138, 147, 179; Book II, 27; Book III, 50–51, 63, 133; Book V, 149, 150, 167; Book VI, 62; Book VII, 138, 177, 179; Book IX, 64, 86, 147; Book X, 3, 9, 34, 40, 56, 70, 74, 87, 116, 117, 125, 128, 133, 180; Book XI, 142, 149–50, 174; Book XII, 27; Book XIII, 27, 94

*The Prelude* (1850), 25, 62–4, 65, 66, 138; Book III, 64, 143; Book VII, 65, 132–4, 138
"Prospectus" to *The Recluse*, 15, 16, 28, 29
*Reply to Mathetes*, 143, 150
*The River Duddon*, 39, 181, 182
"St. Paul's," 18
*Salisbury Plain* (1794), 22, 66, 71–2, 73, **74–5**, **76–7**, **78–81**, 82, 83, **84–6**, 88, **89–95**, 165, 180, 186n, 187n, 188n
"Sonnets Dedicated to Liberty," 9, **31**, 55–6: "Anticipation. October, 1803," 31; "It is not to be thought of that the Flood," 55; "London, September, 1802," 31; "London, 1802," 9, **31**, 163; "To the Men of Kent," 9, 31, **55–6**, 127, 185–6n
"The Tables Turned," 149
"Tintern Abbey," 30, 58, 66, 94–5, 167, 180
*Two Addresses to the Freeholders of Westmoreland*, 161
"We are Seven," 54–5
*The White Doe of Rylstone*, 12–15, 18, 23, 37, 66, 172, 173–6
"Yew Trees," 132
Letters: *EY*, 17, 50, 51, 83, 91, 110, 135; *MY*, 12, 13, 14, 18, 20, 25–6, 29, 31, 37, 101, 110–11, 121, 135, 140, 144–5, 150, 151, 152, 159–60, 170, 174, 183, 185n, 190n; *LY*, 76, 167–8, 190n
*The World*, 42
Wrangham, Francis, 110, 121, 150–51, 159–60, 191n
Wren, Sir Christopher, 18, 19
Wright, Paul, 71

Wu, Duncan, 28, 29, 37, 50, 56, 78, 83, 125, 147, 164, 187n, 189n
Wyatt, James, 78, 80
Wyndham, Henry, 94, 178, 179

Yates, Frances, 57–8
Young, Edward, 124, 126, 130, 142, 173

Zaragoza, siege of, 99, 108, 114, 115

Printed and bound in Great Britain by
CPI Antony Rowe, Chippenham and Eastbourne